PRAISE FOR

Terry Pluto and *The Vie...*

Sports fans—particularly the long-suffering variety, can identify with the perspective of *Akron Beacon Journal* columnist Pluto, who presents [his] best in this volume. Not that you want to relive The Drive, The Shot and the ninth inning of the 1997 World Series, but if you must, do it with Pluto. The columnist has remained tickled with his job over the years and his straight-shooting style keeps sports fans equally enamored of him.

– *Northern Ohio Live*

There's probably no better sportswriter than Terry Pluto. His writing is so textured; there's a lot in his head that comes to bear. He writes not just about sports, but about people what's important in their lives. . . . His writing is not superficial. Terry Pluto deserves to win a Pulitzer Prize.

– Fred Griffith, WKYC TV3

Sports writing is often done by the numbers. Too many stats can drain the passion from the writing. But Terry Pluto rarely breaks out his calculator. In fact, the longtime *Akron Beacon Journal* columnist is one of the finest sports scribes in the country.

– *Scene Magazine*

Terry Pluto doesn't pretend to be a know-it-all. You can really put yourself into his stories. He writes for all of us.

– Jim Mantel, WGAR AM Radio

Reader be warned, the[se] stories will remind you why it can be so heart-breaking to be a Cleveland fan. But there are a lot of memories to be mined—and there is no better tour guide for the roller coaster ride that was the past decade in Cleveland sports than Pluto . . . A book that doesn't demand one long continuous reading. You can put it down and come back to it if you need to—if only you can put it down.

– *Hudson Hub Times*

Terry Pluto probably has more insight into local sports than anyone [writing] today.

– Wayne Dawson, Fox8 TV

A great history lesson for anyone new to Cleveland sports. Terry Pluto really knows how to connect with the people of Cleveland.

– Jeff Gravley, WEWS TV5 Sports

THE VIEW
FROM PLUTO

Collected Sportswriting
about Northeast Ohio

Terry Pluto

GRAY & COMPANY, PUBLISHERS
CLEVELAND

Gray & Company, Publishers
1588 E. 40th St.
Cleveland, OH 44103

ISBN 1-886228-78-7

Printed in the United States of America

10 9 8 7 6 5 4 3 2 1

To Irwin Smallwood and Bill Tanton,
who hired me when it wasn't easy.
And to Bill Eichenberger and Dale Allen,
who made me a columnist.

Contents

YOUTH

IT'S PERSONAL

Introduction

I GET PAID TO GO TO BALLGAMES.

I remember my father saying that with both amazement and a little envy.

Yes, I get paid to go to ballgames. Actually, I get paid to write about ballgames, but I'm not going to debate the difference. Not with men like my father, who spent their lives in factories and warehouses where it seemed the world was hard and gray, where it was always surprising to walk outside and see the sun.

I worked several summers and Christmas vacations at the same food warehouse where my father worked. I remember two breaks, 15-minutes each, when guys sat on the cold cement floor of the men's room—the only place they were allowed to smoke. Someone usually had a sports section, and they talked about the Indians, the Browns, the Cavs and what someone had written about them.

I became friends with a heavy, middle-aged guy named Cadillac Joe. He said he played basketball at Kentucky, Tennessee or one of those major Southern schools. He also claimed to have fixed college basketball games back then, and had stories of bookies, gangsters and being on the lam from the authorities, soaking up the sun on the beaches of Costa Rica and Mexico. I had no idea if they were true. Cadillac Joe weighed more than 300 pounds. He drove a forklift. He said he had gone straight, married and raised a family. He was a friendly, upbeat guy. He loved sports. Just about all the guys loved sports.

I'd sit on the men's room floor with them, trying not to gag on the smoke. I didn't smoke, but I liked hanging out with the guys who did. I thought if I could one day have a job writing in the newspaper, and have guys like these men read my stories and talk about them—for me, it was the ultimate calling.

I mentioned this to Cadillac Joe, and he liked the idea.

"You don't want to spend your life in a place like this," he said. "It makes you tired."

He sighed, the air seemingly being sucked out of his huge belly.

"Real tired," he said. "You go out and do something else."

My father said the same thing. Get a job where you don't have to drag yourself out of bed every morning, where you don't work with one eye on the clock, counting down the hours until you can go home.

I have that job.

I write about ballgames and ballplayers. I write about the good guys and the duds. I write about families and fathers and mothers and death and birth and dreams and nightmares.

I write about sports.

I write for the guys at the warehouse. I ask myself what are they talking about, and I write about it. I write it so they can understand, not to show off, or as my father would say, "use some million dollar words not worth five cents."

I started writing sports in 1977 at the Greensboro *News-Record*, and 25 years later, I'm still at it. I've been at the *Akron Beacon Journal* since 1985. I'm blessed by the paper, even more blessed by the people who read the paper. I'm blessed because I grew up in the Cleveland area and I can write about the teams that were a big part of my youth.

I once heard a writer born elsewhere who now works here saying he was sick of hearing about people who walked down the West Third Street Bridge to the old Stadium for Indians and Browns games. I'm not. I was one of those people, led down that bridge by my father to watch the Indians play in front of more pigeons than fans. He took me by the hand. Sometimes, he put me on one of his shoulders and I felt like I was on top of the world. I love those memories.

I'm blessed because I can think of players such as Rocky Colavito, Leon Wagner, Steve Hargan, Mike Paul, Duke Sims and Joe Azcue like an extended family because they were mentioned so often in my house. I remember one day being at the Stadium, staring up at the press box where Russ Schneider, Bob Sudyk, Bob August and Hal Lebovitz wrote about the Indians, telling my father that one day I'd be up there. And I remember the first time I sat in that old press box. It was in 1979, when I came to town to cover a Tribe–Baltimore Orioles game. I was a 24-year-old baseball writer with the Baltimore Evening Sun. The next year, I'd be a regular in that press box as the baseball writer for the *Plain Dealer*.

I was in the press box for the most memorable game of my lifetime, when Dennis Martinez beat Randy Johnson in Seattle's Kingdome, sending the Indians into the 1995 World Series. There were countless nights when I sat in the Jacobs Field press box staring at that sea of red, white and blue wahoo shirts, jackets and caps. I couldn't believe all these people were coming to watch the Indians, or that the Tribe actually played in a ballpark that didn't smell like a backed-up toilet. I couldn't believe it when the Indians beat the Yankees in the 1997 play-offs. Unfortunately, I *could* believe it when Jose Mesa couldn't hold the lead in the Seventh Game of the 1997 World Series.

I started to write that I couldn't believe it when Michael Jordan made The Shot in 1989, but I could. I was sitting next to the Cavs bench, next to coach Lenny Wilkens, who was no more than three feet away. He stared at the court like someone who just drove up to his house only to discover it had burned to nothing but ashes.

I couldn't believe it when Bernie Kosar was cut, or when the Browns moved. I was shocked when Al Lerner ended up as the new Browns' owner, and even more stunned when he turned out to be a very good owner.

There is still so much in sports that I can't believe, so much that surprises me.

Which is why I love to write about it.

Yes, I write about ballgames, and get paid for it.

I've never taken that for granted.

Those who knew me at Cleveland Benedictine High School are astounded by this. I'm the "expert," talking about how Jim Thome needs to cut down on his strikeouts, or the Cavs play dismal defense or Tim Couch has to make better decisions as he throws downfield.

The guys from high school know the truth about me. I can say that I played basketball and baseball, but the truth was that I *sat* basketball and *sat* baseball. I was cut from freshman football for my own physical welfare. The most points I ever scored in basketball was eight—and that was for my entire junior season! In baseball, I never had an extra base hit, and left with a .230 batting average in what I can kindly call limited duty.

I write about games that I could never play, and people read it.

And that just may be the greatest miracle of all.

THE VIEW
FROM PLUTO

Glory Days

Head says yes; heart says no

MY EYES TELL ME that the Indians have their best team since 1954.

My head tells me that they will win the Central Division, that they will be playing baseball at Jacobs Field in mid-October.

My sense of history tells me that if any team is due for a great year, it is our beloved featherheads.

Then my heart says no.

My heart says don't fall for it. It says that being an Indians fan means expecting the worst, and don't forget Frank Lane's Law: The team may not be broken, but some lunkhead in the dugout or front office will try to fix it anyway.

It says Rocky Colavito for Harvey Kuenn. It says Pedro Guerrero for Bruce Ellingsen. It says Chris Chambliss for four New York stiffs.

My heart remembers Super Joe Charboneau, circa 1981—the year after he was Rookie of the Year. My heart remembers Herb Score being hit in the eye, and Pete Rose running over Ray Fosse at home plate.

My heart makes my head remember so many rotten things about the Tribe, it's enough to make me become a Crunch fan.

Then I remember something once said by that great philosopher Bill Belichick: "I can only go by what I see."

What do we see in the 1995 Tribe?

Let's start at the top. When was the last time the Indians had a heavyweight owner such as Dick Jacobs? He can strong-arm the city and the county . . . and taxpayers are just now learning how many pounds of flesh he extracted from the Gateway Corporation.

But he did help to get the stadium built, and Jacobs Field changed everything for this franchise. It was built, and they came—the fans and the big-name free agents.

No Dick Jacobs and there would be no Jacobs Field . . . and the Indians still would be in exile on the lakefront, conducting a fire sale of
their best young players—like we see in Montreal.

While he's not a wild spender, Jacobs has the kind of checkbook
that can produce a player just when the team needs him most. That
should be reassuring.

Then there is General Manager John Hart.

He gave us Kenny Lofton for Eddie Taubensee and Omar Vizquel
for Felix Fermin. He brought us free agents Dennis Martinez, Eddie
Murray, Orel Hershiser and Dave Winfield. He even turned Mark
Whiten into Mark Clark.

It's hard to imagine that Hart will wake up one morning and say,
"Wouldn't it be fun to see how many old Willie Kirkland baseball cards
I can get for Albert Belle?"

Hart has proven to be a sharp operator, and so has his manager.

Fans will second-guess Mike Hargrove, especially if Hart fails to
give him an established stopper.

Hargrove will vow not to listen to the talk shows, but he'll tune in
and boil up. He may even call to try to explain himself, as he did last
year. Aside from his thin skin, Hargrove is the ideal manager to win a
pennant here. He knows what he's doing and what he's up against. He
paid dues with the Indians as a player, minor-league manager and big-
league coach.

We have watched him mature as a major-league manager since the
middle of 1991. While he was raised in the dust of the Texas panhandle, Hargrove has been a part of the Cleveland landscape for so long
that he is one of us.

His goal isn't to be "the world's greatest third-base coach and fungo
hitter," as was the case with poor Dave Garcia. And he isn't on his last
job like John McNamara, or just breaking in as a manager, as Frank
Robinson did here in 1975.

He sure isn't Kerby Farrell, Mel McGaha or Oscar Vitt.

Hargrove is 45. By the end of this season, the only man to manage
the Indians longer will be Al Lopez. Given the talent here, Hargrove
could become the next Lopez—a man who has the team in contention
for most of a decade.

And the team?

"We have perhaps the most potent lineup in baseball," Hart said.
"We have experienced starting pitching. Our defense should be ade-
quate. We have been carefully building a contender."

What can go wrong?

If you are in Indians fan, you know better than to ask.

This has been Team Tragedy. The Indians had the only player ever to die on the field in Ray Chapman. They had a boating accident in the spring of 1993 in which pitchers Tim Crews and Steve Olin were killed. They even had a second baseman, Jack Brohamer, come down with the gout.

I know . . . That was then, but what about now? Well, if you want reason to worry, I don't like how Charlie Nagy came into camp looking as if he just spent three months in an Iranian prison.

I don't like how Mark Clark has been throwing, but it is still early and he is coming off a broken wrist.

I hate the bullpen. I look down there and have terrible flashbacks to Victor Cruz.

I don't like Manny Ramirez in right field, but I love him at the plate. So I'll live with him in the outfield and hope he doesn't knock himself out trying to catch a fly ball.

I also don't like a strike-shortened season followed by a hurry-up spring training—that combination can lead to injuries.

But to be honest, there isn't much wrong with this team. And given that baseball is more diluted than ever, it seems logical to ask: Why shouldn't the Indians win their division? Why wouldn't they play in the World Series?

No reason other than being born in 1955 . . . being from a lost generation of Cleveland baseball fans born after the last pennant.

We want to believe that this is the year—but it's awfully hard.

Why? Well, if you're an Indians fan, you keep having this thought:

It is September 1.

The Indians are in first place by five games.

And guess what?

The jokers go on strike . . . again.

4/25/1995

A new generation of memories

EARLY YESTERDAY MORNING and fighting the World Series blues, I found myself staring out of a jet window as it circled Cleveland.

I saw Jacobs Field and the old stadium. I saw Cleveland State and the Galleria. I saw the city where I grew up and I thought, "It's better now than I ever remember."

How often can we say that about anything?

The Cleveland of my youth was a great place to get a tattoo. It was a dirty lake and an inflammable river. It was the worst ballpark in the major leagues, and it was streets you wouldn't walk down at night without a Pit Bull and an Uzi.

The reason the old Cleveland jokes of the 1960s and 1970s hurt so much is that so many of them were true. I will not hear any argument on this.

I went to Benedictine High on the East side and to Cleveland State. I've lived on both sides of town. Now that the future is bright, I will not allow any revisionist history of the bleak past.

I grew up with the Indians. I loved them, but they fit right in with the town—another Cleveland embarrassment.

They were the Indians of Frank Lane—who traded Rocky Colavito and Roger Maris.

They were the Indians of Jack Kralick and Gary Bell, who once had a fist fight over what to watch on TV—and that was back before cable when there were only three channels.

These Indians had the Beer Night riot, and they passed out deodorant to all women on Mother's Day. These Indians saw Tony Horton's mental breakdown, Herb Score's eye injury and Sam McDowell.

Ah yes, Sudden Sam—who broke two ribs on his first pitch with the Tribe, then broke everyone's heart with his promise lost at the bottom of the bottle.

Perhaps you know all these horror stories already and don't want to hear them again. But it is worth remembering what the Indians were . . . what Cleveland was . . . and how the team and city have changed today.

That most of us waited 20, 30, even 40 years for a World Series . . . that so much time passed with so little to show for it, yet we still cared about this baseball team . . . that should make you treasure this 1995 model even more.

Maybe you need to do an autopsy to get the World Series out of your system. Fine, second-guess Manager Mike Hargrove for a week or so, however long it takes to feel better. Did Hargrove make all the right moves against Atlanta?

In the name of Jim Poole, you know better than that.

But you also should know that even though he is from Perryton, Texas, Hargrove is one of us.

Hargrove and his wife Sharon and their five children invested 14 years of their lives in this team. Hargrove played for the Indians, he managed at every level of their farm system and then became the first manager in 41 years to deliver a pennant.

Never forget that.

Despite his sometimes questionable moves, the only way Hargrove could have won this Series would have been if he could have grabbed a bat and done what Albert Belle & the boys could not—hit the best pitching in baseball.

Don't forget that, either.

The Indians are a talented team. But Manny Ramirez can't remember the count. Kenny Lofton can be hyper-sensitive and withdrawn. Jim Thome is baseball's Forrest Gump. Paul Sorrento grumbles about not playing against left-handed pitchers when he often can't hit righties.

There is more.

Sandy Alomar is constantly fighting injuries and Dennis Martinez is battling Father Time. Charles Nagy can be riddled with self-doubt.

Alvaro Espinoza has to be reminded to leave the tacos and beans alone, because he has a habit of growing bloated while sitting on the bench.

Then there is Albert Belle. Hargrove is the first manager who has not had to suspend the volcano in left field—and Belle has become a superstar while on Hargrove's watch.

Managing these Indians requires a steady hand, a thick hide and a quick head.

Hargrove is 46, still a relatively young manager in terms of age and experience. During his next postseason run, he will handle some things differently—as will the Indians.

As the plane was landing at Hopkins Airport yesterday morning, something else occurred to me.

Suppose you were a kid today—a baseball fan.

Then suppose you grew up with the 1995 Indians as your boys of summer.

Imagine the stories you'll have to tell your children.

Belle-Baerga-Lofton.

Those three names will become one word, rolling off the lips of fans just as Wynn-Lemon-Feller-Garcia came from the mouths of our parents and grandparents.

You could talk about how 40-year-old Dennis Martinez threw the game of his life, beating Randy Johnson in Seattle's Kingdome to put the Tribe in the World Series.

"I never, ever will forget that game," Martinez said late Saturday night. "I just hope that the Cleveland fans will remember it, too."

Don't worry, Dennis, the fans will remember you made history.

Today's kids can tell tomorrow's children about Orel Hershiser's grit, Albert Belle's fire, Omar Vizquel's grace and Kenny Lofton's speed.

They'll have stories about a wonderful park where even all the restrooms work.

This Indians team did more than win the American League pennant, it made a new generation of Cleveland baseball fans—whose memories will be much better than ours.

10/30/1995

At last, that pennant feeling

FINALLY, IT FEELS LIKE A PENNANT.

A big rally. Fans on their feet. High-fives in the Tribe dugout.

Down 9-2, and winning 10-9. Doing it to the Yankees, no less.

Three in a row.

That's three Central Division titles in a row.

Let's not forget that.

Let's not take it for granted.

Let's take a break from carping about Albie Lopez, and worrying about what the Indians must do to win the World Series.

Just enjoy this team.

Three in a row.

They did it the hard way. They lost and/or traded Carlos Baerga, Kenny Lofton and Albert Belle . . . they went through 14 different starting pitchers . . . they had a pitcher break his arm while warming up, a hitter go down with an appendix attack and that was just in the last three weeks.

Yet, the Tribe still had enough to win the Central Division. We should remember that.

We can talk about watered-down baseball, wild-card playoffs and a weak division—and we'd be right.

But think about the Indians for a minute, the Indians of our youth. Do you think any of those teams could win even a single Central Division title, much less three in a row?

If someone had said, "We'll give you three division champions, will you take it and promise not to gripe?"

Wouldn't you have taken it?

Think back for a moment.

We grew up with the old Cleveland Stadium, not Jacobs Field.

We grew up with a team whose motto was "Good Seats Available," a team that played in a ballpark that smelled as if an animal had crawled into a corner and died about a week ago.

Running water was a luxury, so were functioning toilets.

The only time you mention three in a row was when George Hendrick struck out three times in a row—without swinging at even one pitch. Just stood there, like a statue.

But we don't talk about those things anymore. Who wants to dig around the family closet looking for skeletons?

Does the name Tony Horton mean anything to you?

Or Joe Charboneau? Charlie Spikes? Steve Olin?

Or how about Herb Score? Not the broadcaster—the pitcher.

This franchise is haunted by tragedy, disappointments, even death.

The only major-leaguer to ever die on the field was Ray Chapman, who played for the Tribe back in 1920. He was killed when he was hit in the head with a pitch.

This is not to dwell on the negative.

But if you were ever to try and sweep all the mess that is a part of Tribe history under the rug—well, you'd run out of rug.

To fully appreciate what this team has done, we must keep in mind where they have been.

Then go ahead, curse Manager Mike Hargrove.

But remember many Tribe fans did the same to Al Lopez in the 1950s—and he remains the most successful manager in the history of this franchise.

Go ahead, get mad at John Hart.

Like Hargrove, there are days when the general manager deserves it.

But just remember this guy is no Frank Lane . . . Gabe Paul . . . or even Phil Seghi.

Hart and Hargrove are not perfect. Heck, there are many times when they don't even agree with each other. But they will be remembered as the best management team in the history of this franchise.

Especially with Dick Jacobs as the owner.

Never forget that the Indians were once owned by a dead man.

True story.

In 1983, major owner Steve O'Neill passed away, and for three years the team belonged to the O'Neill estate. Meanwhile, they did everything but put a "FOR SALE" sign in front of the Stadium, trying to find a new owner.

Finally, Dick Jacobs showed up in 1986, a man with a heavy bank account and big plans.

The Indians would never be the same—thank heavens!

The next time you go to Jacobs Field, think about all this.

Then think how the Indians should remain contenders for the rest of this decade.

Contention in Cleveland, year after year. For most of us, that is still hard to believe.

From 1960 through 1993, Tribe fans never had a real pennant race. They never had a team that played an important game in September. It was summer after summer of depressing nights down on the lake, fighting off the yawns and the gnats.

Then came the move to Jacobs Field, and a new house never had such a positive effect on a family as it did with the Tribe.

If there was no strike, the Indians would have been in the playoffs in 1994.

It was the World Series in 1995, the playoffs last year.

Again, more playoffs.

To a real Tribe fan, this is almost too much. Nothing in our lives really prepared us for all this success. Maybe that is why we are quick to complain. We are just so accustomed to things going wrong, we imagine a mugger lurking in every dark corner.

But believe it or not, we are safe with the Indians.

There will be more October baseball, more sellouts and more reasons to care about this team.

In the end, that's all a real Tribe fan can ask.

9/24/1997

Let's all just enjoy this team for now

I'M NOT GOING TO EVEN GUESS if the Indians can beat Baltimore.

Right now, I really don't care.

I want to live in the present.

I want to tell you about the Indians team that beat the Yankees, the team that won two of the biggest games in the history of this franchise.

I want to tell you about the team that could have folded after Game 1 in New York.

They were up 5-0 in Yankee Stadium and blew it?

The Indians' Mr. October, Orel Hershiser, can't make it through five innings? The bullpen brings back memories of a Victor Cruz Missile when it served up not one, not two—but three home runs?

This team came back to win the best-of-five Division Series against the defending World Champions?

For a while, it seemed that the Indians might be swept—or at least never live to see the fifth game. Now they are in Baltimore for tonight's opener in the best-of-seven American League Championship Series.

OK, some of them have headaches and bloodshot eyes.

So what?

To the winners go the hangovers, and if any Tribe team deserved to celebrate, it is this one.

You know what happened in the games. You know how the Indians were eliminated by Baltimore in the first round of the playoffs last year.

So let's talk about the people.

There is Jose Mesa.

He finished what Jaret Wright started in Game 5. At this time last October, his life was beginning to fall apart. Remember Game 4 of the 1996 playoffs against Baltimore? The 12th inning at Jacobs Field?

Mesa was on the mound. Roberto Alomar at bat.

Alomar homered. The season was over for Mesa and the Tribe.

Then Mesa lost his rudder, his sense of balance. He began showing up in night clubs in the Flats—ended up in court during the spring, facing a rape charge.

Mesa was acquitted, but the details of his life became public, soiling his image with many fans.

Against the Yankees, Mesa held the lead. He gave up a shot similar to the one Alomar hit in 1996, only this one, off the bat of Paul O'Neill, banged off the center-field wall for a double—instead of going over for a home run.

A few feet was the difference between winning and losing.

For Mesa, this is a second chance. Not just with the Indians, but in his life. He insists he'll make the most of it, that now he heads home, not to the bars.

The Indians are counting on it. So is his family.

There is Jaret Wright.

In October of 1996, Wright was watching the playoffs on TV while working out with the Tribe's Instructional League team in Arizona, pitching against a bunch of other 21-year-olds. Only those kids were headed to Burlington, Kinston and Columbus—as in Columbus, Georgia.

Wright was just another baby face in that crowd of prospects. He figured that if everything broke just right in 1997, he could end up pitching in . . . drum roll, please . . . Akron!

Now, he's the anchor of the pitching staff—in Cleveland.

He's a young man who said before Game 5: "Do I want to be in this spot? Of course I do. Little kids all over the country will be watching this game. They all want to be in my shoes. Why should I be any different?"

Got to love that.

Just like when he said: "Am I scared? No, that's not me."

The most confident pitcher on the baseball planet today is Jaret Wright. He beat the Yankees twice in five days. He has a great arm and even greater self-esteem. He was dropped straight into the pressure-cooker that is Yankee Stadium, and then the final game of the playoffs at Jacobs Field.

And he emerged with a winning smile and a couple of notches in his belt.

Wright is still a baseball infant, but he has known nothing but success and pats on the back. Unlike someone such as Charles Nagy, he hasn't had his nose bloodied, his courage questioned.

Eventually, that will happen.

But when it does, he can look back on these days. Wright will know he was a great pitcher in games when it meant the most.

That is why Jaret Wright can be so good, it's scary.

There is David Justice.

A year ago in October, he was watching the Braves in the playoffs. He was in street clothes, recovering from major shoulder surgery that threatened his career. Then he was tossed aside by Atlanta, because his seemingly perfect body is too frail. Too many broken bones and strained tendons. Too many aching elbows and kinky knees.

He was supposed to be a little moody, sort of a prima donna who married actress Halle Berry.

Instead, he plays hard, he plays hurt and he signs as many autographs as any player on the team.

He is a sometimes left fielder, but his engaging personality makes him the anti-Albert Belle.

And the man can hit, even with that knee pad and his elbow brace.

He also is a player not afraid to speak up in the dressing room, the kind of guy who can say he played on four division winners in Atlanta, and this is how things ought to be done.

Then he goes out and does it.

There is Sandy Alomar.

A year ago in October, he was explaining why his brother (Roberto) spat on an umpire. He was explaining why the Indians were ambushed by Baltimore in the first round of the playoffs. He was even explaining why he had been injured for so much of his career.

Did anyone see this season coming for Alomar?

The 30-game hitting streak . . . the homer winning the All-Star Game at Jacobs Field . . . the homer off Mariano Rivera that tied Game 4.

Sandy Alomar has gotten as many big hits as anyone on this team.

"That's because Sandy worked harder last winter than any player we've ever had," said General Manager John Hart. "Every day, he was at the ballpark, in the weight room and the batting cages. He took a body that has had a lot of injuries and surgeries, and made it strong again. He did it with sheer sweat and desire."

There is Orel Hershiser.

A year ago, even a week ago—it has been the same for the Indians veteran right-hander.

"They're always about to put me in the glue factory," Hershiser said.

But in his last nine starts of the regular season, Hershiser was 5-1 with a 3.14 ERA. He was bombed in Game 1 of the playoffs, but came back to pitch seven sterling innings in Game 4.

It was Hershiser's heroics in Game 4 that bought the Indians time to come back and win. It was his grit that seemed to rub off on the team, to make them believe they really could beat the Yankees.

Hershiser is 18 years older than Jaret Wright. He looks at the kid in awe, not just because of his talent—but his youth, his future.

Hershiser is like a lot of us. He wishes he could take what he knows now as he nears his 40th birthday and then put it on a 21-year-old body.

Think about this: When Hershiser was 21, he was a marginal prospect at Class AA San Antonio in the Dodgers' farm system.

His record was 5-9, and he was being used in relief.

There is Matt Williams.

A year ago in October, he thought he'd be a San Francisco Giant for the rest of his career—and a married man for the rest of his life. A few months later, he was traded to the Indians.

Then his wife filed for divorce.

Then he went through the agony of any father who has three children in one part of the country . . . while he is working somewhere else . . . and the lawyers are dividing up the assets.

For Williams, much of this season was the most miserable year of his life.

But this man persevered. By the end of the season, he was hitting home runs.

He was wearing his socks high like his good friend Jim Thome.

He was a Gold Glove at third base.

Most of all, Matt Williams felt like a ballplayer again.

There is Jim Thome.

A year ago in October, he thought he would be the Indians' starting third baseman for the rest of his career.

Then John Hart called. The general manager said he had a deal in the works for Matt Williams. Would Thome be willing to move from third base to first base?

"In today's baseball, most guys in that situation call their agents or flat-out say they won't do it—at least not without a new contract," said Hart.

"Jimmy told me if it was a good move for the team, it was a good move for him."

To prove it, Thome reported to spring training 10 days early to get a jump on learning his new position.

And who makes the Play of Game 5, the one Manager Joe Torre said broke his team's heart and shattered the Yankees dreams?

A first baseman by the name of Thome.

And who became best friends?

Thome and Matt Williams.

There is Omar Vizquel.

A year ago in October, Vizquel was in a daze.

He still couldn't figure out why the Indians were at home after one round of the playoffs. He thought they'd go back-to-back, a World Series in 1995 and 1996.

He watched so many of the players from the great 1995 team leave—Albert Belle, Kenny Lofton, Carlos Baerga, Eddie Murray and Dennis Martinez.

He worried about the Tribe's future.

The Indians' front office told Vizquel that he was a leader, that a lot of new players were on the way and he had to be the glue in the clubhouse, just as he is in the infield.

"It took a long time for us to get to know each other," he said.

"We didn't know how to make jokes, or when to laugh. We wanted to do so well, but didn't know how to play as a team."

Then came the socks.

You've heard more than you want to about those stupid high socks, how Vizquel and Williams decided the team should celebrate Thome's birthday on August 12th by pulling up their socks—as Thome always does.

And the socks have stayed up.

"It's a little thing, but it brought us together," Vizquel said.

"It made us feel like a real team."

A team that is very easy to love.

10/8/1997

Has baseball ever been quite this fun?

THEY ARE MAGIC MOMENTS.

They are stories we will tell our kids.

Heck, they are stories our kids will tell their kids.

The heroes are beginning to pile up, the improbable and impossible is becoming the expected.

It is happening, night after night.

Welcome to the Indians' postseason, 1997.

If you are a longtime Tribe fan, has there ever been anything quite this much fun?

Marquis Grissom hitting a home run off Armando Benitez to beat Baltimore in Game 2?

Only 24 hours before, Grissom was so sick, he could barely get out of bed. They hooked him up to an IV so the poor guy wouldn't end up with pneumonia.

Here is a player who has battled injuries and slumps all year.

Here is a guy who had a needle in his arm before Game 1, then played and nearly knocked himself out running into the center-field wall. He didn't catch the ball, but ended up with a huge headache—as if he wasn't feeling rotten enough.

Now, I'm going to tell you about Grissom's homer off one of the most feared pitchers in the American League. It sounded like an explosion.

I was in the press box at Camden Yards. I wasn't even watching the pitch. I was typing.

But I'll never forget the sound, the whap.

The fattest part of the bat on the center of the baseball.

Whap!

That's what I'll tell people about Grissom's homer—the *Whap!*, the sheer shock of knowing this little guy just hit something shot out of a cannon.

I'll remember seeing the ball disappear deep into the Baltimore night.

I'll remember Benitez throwing his glove up in the air, catching it and then shaking his head as Grissom jogged around the bases.

I'll remember this as the first moment when I really thought, "You know, this team just might go to the World Series."

I'm here to tell my own Indians story.

One from 1995.

One about Tony Pena.

As Grissom rounded the bases in Baltimore, I thought of Tony Pena.

Grissom had about as much chance of hitting a home run to win Game 2 as . . . you got it, Pena did in Game 1 of the Boston series of 1995.

That was a magic moment for the Tribe in 1995, Pena's homer in the bottom of the 13th inning at 2:30 A.M.

Dreams are really stories such as these.

I'm here to remind you of what the Tribe has done already.

Jaret ("I'd rather be surfing") Wright has the makings of a young Dennis Martinez.

Give me the ball.

Give me the spotlight.

I'll give you a show.

Jaret Wright is only 21 years old. This is his first season (make that half-season) in the big leagues, and he has already won two playoff games.

I'm here to tell you that Wright is not a fluke. He did not sell his soul to the devil. He can do this, year after year.

I'm here to remind you of how Wright beat the White Sox twice within a week. That was in September, and in those games, Albert Belle and Frank Thomas were a combined 0-for-11 off the kid.

Talk about surf's up, this California kid can mow 'em down—anyone, anywhere.

I'm here to talk about the fans.

The Indians are playing the Orioles in Game 3 today at Jacobs Field. Orel Hershiser is on the mound.

I fully expect the Tribe fans to do for Orel what they did last week.

If you were at Jacobs Field for Game 4 of the New York series, you witnessed one of the most heart-rending moments in Tribe history.

It happened before the game.

Hershiser had just completed his warmups in the center-field bullpen. The gate swung open. Hershiser walked out, a towel over his left shoulder, dragging his Tribe jacket behind him with his right hand—almost like Linus clinging to his security blanket.

He looked all of his 39 years, and he had yet to throw a pitch.

Then the fans stood.

And cheered.

And cheered louder.

They gave Hershiser a standing ovation as he walked from the bullpen to the dugout—all for just warming up.

It was as if the fans knew Hershiser is, to use his own words, "in the twilight of my career."

But they were going to bring some sunshine to that night in Cleveland, they were telling Hershiser they believed in him.

And the old man went out and held the Yankees to two runs in seven innings, doing it more with stubbornness than stuff.

I'm hear to tell you about Sandy Alomar.

It was his home run in Game 4, a blast off Mariano Rivera, that changed everything. Tied the score. Kept the hope alive.

On that night, I thought Alomar might do something. This has been his year, from the 30-game hitting streak to the All-Star Game heroics.

But his was another *Whap*.

Another power pitcher seeing the ball go out even harder than he threw it in.

And what I'll remember is Alomar running the bases, arms over his head—a man remembering this is a boy's game.

No Little Leaguer could have been happier.

I'm here to talk about Omar Vizquel.

Some Tribe fans will always remember Albert Belle's homer in Game 1 of the 1995 Boston series, and how Belle pointed at his bicep.

Or they'll even remember Belle's grand slam off the same Benitez (maybe he's getting a phobia about Cleveland?) in the Division Series against Baltimore last year.

But I'll take Omar Vizquel.

Vizquel is everything a ballplayer should be.

Graceful in the field.

Pesky at bat.

Warm with the fans.

He is in love with the game, in love with being a ballplayer.

And it was his pingpong single that beat the Yankees in Game 5, his hit that banged off the pitcher's glove and rolled right where the shortstop should have been standing.

A little luck, of course.

But every team needs a little luck if it hopes to have a lot of magic.

10/11/1997

They drive us crazy, but they win!

I GREW UP WITH THE INDIANS just like most of you, but never with an Indians team quite like this one.

We have just watched the Indians and Baltimore play for nearly four hours and 11 innings. We watched a guy for the Orioles named Mike Mussina, who was downright unhittable.

No way the Indians would beat Mussina on this day.

And they didn't.

But they didn't lose to him, either.

That is the difference between this Indians team and so many others. Somehow, they hang on—and hang around.

They drive you crazy. They keep you up all night. They force you to throw things at your television set and curse the manager.

But you don't give up on them, because they are a team that doesn't quit on themselves.

That is what we have learned this October of all Octobers. It is what we saw when the Indians beat Baltimore, 1-0, yesterday to win the American League pennant.

This was a game where the Indians never even put a runner on third base until Tony Fernandez touched the bag during his home run trot.

This is a team where Marquis Grissom was named the American League Championship Series MVP—and Grissom struck out in all four of his at-bats yesterday. Marquis Grissom didn't even hit a hard foul all day (much less a fair ball), but he is your MVP for this fairy-tale six-game series.

If you are a true Tribe fan whose childhood heroes were flawed folks such as Sam McDowell, Joe Charboneau or even an aging Rocky Colavito—you can relate to Grissom.

You also can appreciate Charles Nagy.

Yes, Charles Nagy is one of the reasons the Indians will be in Florida on Saturday for the World Series.

Charles Nagy, the man riddled with doubt. Charles Nagy, the pitcher who has been wilting under the bright lights of October baseball.

Charles Nagy who talks in such a drone, he sounds like a man on the witness stand convinced he is heading to the gas chamber.

This Charles Nagy took the mound in Camden Yards yesterday and matched Mussina, inning-for-inning.

Who would have ever dreamed that?

Probably not even Nagy, who spent most of his postgame interview talking about Mussina's great performance.

Nagy even said, "My heart goes out to Mike, pitching like that and seeing your team lose."

That is the kind of person we have in Charles Nagy.

Even in winning, he feels bad for the losers.

He sounds like a true blue Cleveland Indian.

But never underestimate what Nagy did on this afternoon.

Mussina threw pure smoke, while Nagy survived on a little smoke and mostly mirrors.

Mussina allowed only one hit in eight innings and struck out 10.

Charles Nagy was surrounded by more runners than a track coach.

He spent more time in the stretch position than an aerobics teacher.

But when Charles Nagy walked off the mound in the eighth inning, the Orioles had yet to score.

Nagy walked off with his head down, as he usually does—win or lose.

But he also left the mound with his reputation beginning to heal.

As teammate David Justice said, "We were just glad to see Charlie get some of his confidence back."

In other words, we weren't the only ones worried about Nagy yesterday—and relieved when he survived.

What a team.

What a month of baseball.

What other team ever won a big game on a botched suicide-squeeze bunt?

Or because Bip Roberts didn't play?

That's right. Do you realize the Indians are going to the World Series because Bip Roberts was scratched from yesterday's lineup?

Because Tony Fernandez hit a line drive in batting practice that severely bruised Bip Roberts' thumb.

Because Bip had the bad thumb, he was bumped from the lineup.

Because Bip couldn't play second base, the aforementioned Tony Fernandez did.

And Fernandez hit the home run in the top of the 11th inning.

Just like everyone figured it, right?

Tony Fernandez, a switch-hitter, who had not had a hit from the left side this month—until yesterday.

Tony Fernandez, known more for his glove than his bat.

Tony Fernandez steps to the plate in the 11th inning with 50,000 people cheering against him and a pitcher throwing 100 miles an hour—and he hits a home run.

Someone, somewhere is wearing Wahoo red and white these days.

I want to introduce you to yesterday's winning pitcher.

His name is Brian Anderson.

He is one of us.

He grew up in Geneva, an hour's drive from Cleveland.

Anderson and his family made that drive a lot—to see the Indians at the old stadium.

Anderson is a guy who says his favorite movie is *Major League*, where a rag-tag group of players wins a pennant for Cleveland.

Brian Anderson was so highly regarded by the Indians that he was left off the postseason roster for the first round against New York.

Then he was added for the Baltimore series, figuring to be the last pitcher.

Instead, he pitched in three of the six games against the Orioles. He pitched 6 ⅓ innings against the Birds, allowing only one run.

Like Tony Fernandez, Brian Anderson wasn't supposed to play yesterday.

Then again, the Indians weren't supposed to be here, either.

10/16/1997

We're used to it, but this loss really hurts

HEARTS BREAK AS NICE GUYS FINISH SECOND

You are a Cleveland Indians fan, so you should be used to this.

You should expect to have your heart ripped right out of your chest.

You just knew if your team ever made it to the Seventh Game of the World Series, something like this would happen.

You'd cry.

You are an adult, but you can't help it.

Your life has revolved around this baseball team for the last month. No October in your lifetime will be quite like this one.

You'll love this Cleveland Indians team forever, a team that surprised everyone just to reach the Seventh Game of the World Series.

It's a team of good guys. A team that plays with dignity and respect for the game.

But you still cry.

You'll remember how your team had this World Series won—and let it get away when Florida won, 3-2, in the bottom of the 11th on Edgar Renteria's bases-loaded single just past the ear of Charles Nagy that landed softly in shallow center field.

You'll remember how Jaret Wright gave you shades of Bob Feller, in this, the biggest game of his life—the biggest game of anyone's life.

You'll remember how Manager Mike Hargrove said his team has no reason to feel sorry for themselves, how they overachieved in the playoffs to force a seventh game.

All of that is true.

But it wasn't enough.

You'll remember how Tony Fernandez drove in both runs to put the Indians in position to win this game in the ninth inning—and how his error in the 11th inning helped give it away.

You'll remember how Jose Mesa couldn't hold a 2-1 lead in the bottom of the ninth. You'll remember how Charles Nagy (of all people) was on the mound in the bottom of the 11th inning.

And you'll remember how you knew what would happen.

You just knew they'd lose it the moment Charles Nagy came in from the bullpen.

This is not Charles Nagy's month. This wasn't even supposed to be his game, as Hargrove wisely chose to start Wright instead.

Yet, Nagy ended up back on the mound because there was no one else ... because it was fated to happen ... because these are the Cleveland Indians.

If you are an Indians fan, you spent 11 innings and over four hours watching this team last night—and you'll swear you never took a single breath.

You can spend months, even years, performing an autopsy on this last game.

The Indians lost it when they left six runners on base in the first six innings.

They lost it when they had a runner on third in the top of the ninth. They still had a 2-1 lead. One out, Sandy Alomar was only 90 feet away from home plate.

Marquis Grissom (a man with a .400 career batting average in the World Series) could not bring him home.

Maybe you'll be upset at Grissom, or at Hargrove for not calling a squeeze play to add that crucial third run.

Maybe you'll take the name of Jose Mesa in vain, because he couldn't save the day.

Hopefully, your brain will just shut off when you hear the name of Charles Nagy. He was the Tribe's winningest pitcher in the regular season, but seemed to lose more than some ballgames in October.

He lost his sense of self. He had a couple of weeks that caused Hargrove to say, "Charlie looks as if he doesn't want to be on the face of this Earth."

You hate to hear those words about anyone, especially a dedicated athlete and truly a fine man.

But that is what it means to be an Indians fan—it is watching bad things happen to good people.

You'll shake your head at how that ground ball in the 11th inning went right under the glove of second baseman Fernandez. The guy was a Gold Glove shortstop. He is a terrific second baseman, and has made

one clutch play after another in this playoff drive, hitting .471 in the
World Series and sweeping up grounder after grounder hit to the right
side of the infield.

This wasn't even a difficult play.

He just missed it. In fact, Fernandez said he didn't know how he
missed the ball—he just did.

The Indians reached the Seventh Game partly because of their tight
infield defense.

And an error cost them the game.

You don't even have to Go Figure.

You are an Indians fan. You just know these things happen to your
team, and you know better than to ask why.

If someone told you 25 years ago . . . or even five years ago . . . that
the Indians would lose in the Seventh Game of the World Series . . . .

Well, you'd take it.

You just wanted a taste, and you'd welcome the heartbreak.

After all, you have waited for the Seventh Game about all of your
baseball life.

Then it happens.

They come this close . . . they lose like this . . . and you feel as if your
best friend just died.

You tell yourself that baseball shouldn't be this important. You tell
yourself it's just a game and finally there is a team in this city worthy
of your attention, a team that pays you back for all the years (how
about decades) of misery.

But you still feel empty.

If they had lost to the Atlanta Braves or some other National
League power, it might be a little different.

But the Florida Marlins?

The Men In Teal?

This group of mercenaries who came together when their owner
spent $89 million in six weeks last winter?

Now the same owner wants to dump the team, because it hasn't returned as much as he'd like on his investment.

Is this baseball or mutual funds?

They lost to a team that has been in existence for exactly five years.

There was a newspaper story about this Florida team's success that
ran under the headline "Patience Finally Pays Off."

You'd like to tell these people in South Florida something about
waiting and the price of patience.

You'd love to tell them how life and baseball isn't fair.

But you can't.

You are an Indians fan and you have a lump in your throat and a heart that just won't stop aching.

10/27/1997

A genuine team, even in defeat

In Northeast Ohio, we know how to lose.

We know how to embrace those who come so close, then come up so agonizingly short at the end.

Brian Sipe will always be a hero, despite Red Right 88.

Earnest Byner returned to town later in his career and received standing ovations, despite The Fumble.

Mark Price, Brad Daugherty and the rest of that Cavs team will always be loved, despite Michael Jordan and The Shot.

So we know what to do for the 1997 Indians.

We do what GM John Hart did to Tony Fernandez in the Tribe dressing room. With tears in his eyes, Hart hugged his second baseman—just as Coach Sam Rutigliano threw his arms around Sipe after Sipe's pass (and the Browns' Super Bowl dreams) were intercepted in that snowy end zone.

"I love you, Brian," Rutigliano told his quarterback.

You can love a guy who makes a huge mistake. You can love a team even if it doesn't win the ultimate championship. Your mother was right. You can love them for how they played the game, not because they won or lost.

Tribe fans should open their hearts to Tony Fernandez. You should write him letters. You should know that he was once an 11-year-old who played shortstop with a limp in the Dominican Republic, a kid who needed a knee operation but whose parents couldn't afford it.

You should know that Fernandez learned to play baseball in his bare feet, that he once played a game for the New York Mets while passing a kidney stone. You should know this man doesn't make excuses, and that he is very sincere about his Christianity.

You shouldn't forget that Fernandez drove in both of the Tribe's runs on Sunday night, just as he was the guy whose error set up the 3-2 loss to Florida in 11 innings in Game 7 of the World Series.

So now we have The Boot, to go with The Fumble, The Shot and all the rest.

We have another flawed but admirable hero in Fernandez, whose homer in Game 6 of the Baltimore series is the reason why the Indians were in the World Series.

We also have another team that will go down in Cleveland sports history, a team that will live in infamy for Tribe fans.

But we also have something else.

This is a team truly worthy of its name, a team that earned your respect.

As Manager Mike Hargrove said, "I was glad to see the fans embrace this team, because we really have a lot of good people."

Amen to that.

In fact, they have a lot of players who also take religion very seriously. They have players who work hard at their jobs, players who stay out of trouble.

This really was a team with character, and just because they lost in the 11th inning of the seventh game of the World Series—they still remain worthy of your respect.

Not all of these guys belong on church windows. Jose Mesa has a lot of work to do on the homefront. Manny Ramirez is still trying to figure out what those red, yellow and green lights mean as he drives down the road.

But, in an age of pampered athletes and mega-million-dollar contracts creating some of the most noxious, cruel and self-indulgent people you'll ever meet—most of the Indians come across as regular guys.

I still remember this story from veteran baseball writer Jim Ingraham of the Lake County News-Herald Ingraham was trying to carry three bags as he stepped off an airplane.

He felt a tap on his shoulder.

It was center fielder Marquis Grissom.

"Can I help you with the bags?" he asked.

Ingraham feels as if he's been covering the Tribe since the first Rocky Colavito trade, but a player never offered to help him with his bags.

Not until Grissom.

Not until this guy—one of 14 children, the son of an auto worker who knows that everyone has to work together or nothing gets done.

I think of left fielder David Justice in the lobby of the hotel in Toronto. It was a Sunday morning, early in the season. Justice had missed the game on Saturday because of the kind of flu that had him in a very close relationship with the bathroom fixtures.

On that Sunday morning, Justice was still sick.

How do I know?

He looked sort of green.

All he wanted to do was check out of the hotel, get to the park and lie down in the trainer's room.

Fans spotted him. About 20 of them surrounded him. They wanted autographs. Justice looked at me and rolled his eyes. At that moment, he would rather drink motor oil than sign those slips of paper.

But he signed.

I think of Matt Williams, a man who seemed to spend the summer looking as if someone had just whacked him in the face with a frying pan. Williams was absolutely tormented, first by the trade to the Indians and then a divorce that ripped him away from his children.

He spent as much time this summer figuring out how to keep his three children close to him as he did solving the new pitchers he was facing in the American League.

But Matt Williams never blew his cork at strangers. He never loshed out, even when Manager Mike Hargrove pulled him from a game in favor of Casey Candaele. Imagine being Matt Williams, an All-Star. Imagine watching Casey Candaele bat for you. That is like Pavarotti being pulled off center stage for some guy who banged on a garbage can and belched.

Imagine how that had to tear Williams apart.

Now realize Williams never complained. Remember how he played down the stretch, how his defense at third was the best this franchise has ever seen.

Now think about these new players—Fernandez, Grissom, Justice and Williams.

Two blacks, one Latino, one white.

Four reasons to feel very good about the Indians.

Will we ever have a baseball October quite like this one?

Consider the Indians won six consecutive one-run games in the playoffs to reach the World Series.

This was a team with a 19-19 record in one-run games in the regular season.

But they won six in a row in the playoffs.

Then came the World Series.

Two more of those nerve-wracking, nail-chewing one-run games.

What happened?

They lost them both.

You'll say, "What else do you expect from the Indians."

You'll talk about teases and broken hearts.

You'll curse the day you first embraced this franchise, and you'll wonder if there is something to this Curse of Rocky Colavito business.

Just look in the broadcasting booth.

There was Herb Score, calling his final Tribe game on Sunday. Score spent 34 years behind the microphone and never saw a Tribe team win the World Series.

Or how about this?

In 1954, the Indians won 111 games, which still stands as the most victories by an American League team in a single season. OK, they were swept by the New York Giants in the World Series, but we won't drag that up.

Anyway, Score came to the Tribe in 1955.

You saw Jaret Wright on Sunday. That was Herb Score in 1955, only he was left-handed and threw even harder.

Then in 1957, Score was hit in the eye by a line drive off the bat of the Yankees' Gil McDougald and never approached his previous greatness.

If anyone ever deserved to watch the Indians win this series, it was Herb Score.

But they didn't, and Score probably wasn't surprised. After all, his old roommate and best friend in baseball is Rocky Colavito.

Being an Indians fan is understanding that there are powers greater than all of us, that things just happen to this franchise—and there is nothing you can do about any of it.

Just like you knew Charles Nagy some how, some way was going to end up in Game 7. Even though Mike Hargrove intentionally skipped over Nagy in favor of Jaret Wright, you still knew Nagy was going to have a hand in that game.

And you knew it wasn't going to be pretty.

So the bottles of champagne stayed on ice in the Tribe dressing room. The Tribe caps and T-shirts proclaiming 1997 WORLD SERIES CHAMPS stayed in the boxes.

Instead of cheers, there were tears.

And down deep, none of this surprises you.

10/28/1997

Is this heaven? No, but close

IF YOU CAN REMEMBER the old Stadium and Rocky Colavito, this will never get old.

If names such as Joe Charboneau, Jerry Dybzinski, Andy Allanson and Chico Salmon mean something to you, then you're smiling today.

Once again, October baseball has its fist around your baseball heart, and it's getting a good squeeze.

Isn't this sweet?

Didn't you love every moment of the Tribe's 2-1 victory over the Red Sox at Boston's Fenway Park yesterday?

Maybe you're still sweating a bit, because postseason ball is a time for aspirin and a strong serving of your favorite adult beverage.

Your stomach probably churned as you watched Tribe hitters flail away at Pete Schourek like a bunch of guys trying to kill a buzzing fly with an ax.

They grunted. They lunged. They swung hard enough to drop a redwood with one swing.

But they missed.

They were absolutely dumbfounded by a junkball lefty with a bum elbow and a losing record—a guy who never should have started this game.

If you have spent your life with the Indians, you probably sat there, your throat sandpaper dry, expecting the worst.

Pete Schourek, for heaven's sake, you said.

But the Indians stayed close. They kept the faith. Bartolo Colon didn't pitch so much as he fired bullets. This 23-year-old kid, making his first playoff start, showed he was ready for prime time.

For five innings, it was fire and ice.

Colon's heat, Schourek's snowflakes.

The difference was a homer by Boston's Nomar Garciaparra (who else?) in the fourth inning.

It seemed as if the Red Sox had that 1-0 lead for about six weeks. You had to keep telling yourself, "This can't hold up."

But in your Wahoo heart of hearts, you wondered if it just might. Suppose the Indians lose 1-0. Suppose they go into a decisive Game 5 at Jacobs Field with Pedro Martinez on the mound for Boston.

If you are a veteran Tribe fan, you had to be creating worst-case scenarios in your head.

Only this is a different era.

As Manager Mike Hargrove said: "You don't get to the postseason by being lucky. You don't go as far as we have in the postseason by being lucky."

So true.

The Indians didn't win three games in a row over Boston because of the fickle finger of fate, the Curse of the Bambino or any other ghosts of Red Sox horrors past.

The Indians were better. The same Indians who have been to the World Series in two of the last three years.

When they needed a key hit, David Justice delivered a two-run double in the eighth inning.

It wasn't a broken-bat bloop. It wasn't a flare between a couple of confused outfielders.

It was a rocket, a laser, a whap!

If you were at Fenway Park, you heard it—whap!

It's the sound of the bat hitting the ball exactly right. It's what you hear when you take a guy with a Picasso swing like Justice, and he makes perfect contact.

Whap!

Smash to deep center field. Pinballing around the nooks and crannies of this wonderful, quirky old ballyard. Runners kicking up dirt with their spikes, running faster than they have all year.

Whap!

One swing, two runs.

"You get used to seeing guys like David Justice come through in those spots," Hargrove said.

That's right, guys coming through—doing it in October, when it means the most. Believe it or not, that's Tribe baseball as we head into the millennium.

You can go on and on.

Justice's double. Justice throwing out John Valentin in the sixth inning. Justice playing the Green Monster in left as if he were born in its shadows and tutored by Jim Rice and Carl Yastrzemski.

But there was more.

How about the bullpen?

Jim Poole, a scoreless inning. Steve Reed, two up and two down. Paul Shuey, no runs allowed.

"I know there was some concern about the guys who pitched before me, but you can see what they did," closer Mike Jackson said.

Ah, yes, Mike Jackson.

Before the game, there were whispers about Jackson. He's tired. His back is sore. His elbow is aching. He didn't have it on Friday, when he gave up two runs.

But here came Jackson, cap pulled down low over his eyes and the kind of stare that would melt a railroad spike. Mike Jackson was out there with a 2-1 lead. He needed three outs.

He got 'em, and not even one ball left the infield.

So now, we move on to New York, on to the Yankees and the next round of the playoffs.

If you're a veteran Tribe fan, you probably are still coming to terms with a team that has been in the postseason the last four years. You never thought you'd live to see the day.

Tribe fans, welcome to baseball heaven.

10/4/1998

Respect for the Tribe—at last

I ALMOST CALLED for the smelling salts when I heard it.

"To beat a team like Cleveland, that has been to the World Series so often lately, well, that says a lot," said Yankees manager Joe Torre late Tuesday night.

A team that has been to the World Series a lot?

Beating that team—the Indians—says a lot? This comes from the manager of the New York Yankees?

He's talking about our Indians?

Believe it or not, that was one of the first things out of the mouth of Torre after his Yankees eliminated the Tribe from the American League Championship Series on Tuesday night. He didn't say it with a smirk. He didn't say it to be patronizing.

He meant it.

The Indians had the Yankees worried, a Yankees team that won 114 games.

I never thought I'd live to see this day, a day when the Yankees view the Indians as the one team between them and the World Series.

It's still hard for me to believe that these guys in Wahoo red, white and blue . . . this team that is a fixture in the postseason . . . that these really are the Cleveland Indians.

As Mike Hargrove said the other day, "Times have changed."

Hargrove played on those awful Tribe teams in the early 1980s. And he's managed the Indians in 1995 and 1997, when they've gone to the World Series. He's managed them to a 25-22 record in the postseason.

I thought about this when I was looking for something buried in my desk, and I found a stack of faded Tribe baseball cards.

The first one was Joe Lis.

This was a 1975 card. It revealed that Joe Lis batted .202 for the Tribe in 1974. But those old cards always tried to turn your frown upside down.

"Acquired from the Twins at midseason, Joe filled in ably at first base for the Tribe," someone wrote.

Ably? Hitting .202?

Excuse me?

The next card was of Fred Beene, and it reads: "Fred is equally effective as a starter, middle reliever or late reliever."

So true. He could do None of the Above as his 4.93 ERA in 1974 attested.

Shuffling through the cards was a revelation, the perfect tonic for the day after the Indians had been eliminated from the postseason by the Yankees.

There was a card of John Lowenstein looking like a cross between Charles Manson and Serpico, with a mop of black hair nearly to his shoulders, a droopy mustache and a black stubble of a beard.

"He is the only major-leaguer born in Montana," reads Lowenstein's card in an attempt to turn that year's edition of the Tribe into something special.

Well, what was the card supposed to say? That Lowenstein was the only player of his era to hit exactly .242 in 3-of-4 seasons from 1974–77? Yes, Lowenstein beat the incredible statistical odds by doing just that—.242, year after year after year.

Next up, Leron Lee.

"Leron joined the Indians during spring training in 1974 and provided timely hitting as an outfielder and designated hitter," says his card.

Maybe it was timely, but his watch was stuck as he batted only .233.

As I flipped through the cards, I suddenly stopped grousing about the Tribe not hitting with runners in scoring position, about Omar Vizquel (of all people) making a critical error and about Manny Ramirez being Manny Ramirez when he forgot to turn around on a fly ball that nearly hit him in the back of his foot.

Hey, I was looking at a card of Larvell Blanks, who played for the Tribe in the middle 1970s. It says, "Larvell comes from a sports-oriented family, his uncle being Sid Blanks, a former halfback with three professional clubs."

The card didn't tell you that one day Blanks was so angry at Manager Frank Robinson for not putting him in the lineup that he burned his uniform.

Torched it in the clubhouse.

Jose Mesa set a lot of fires with the Tribe, but never one of that magnitude.

I think of Enrique Wilson and Joey Cora trying to play second base in the postseason, and I come to a Tony Martinez card.

In the mid-1960s, Martinez was a middle infielder, one of the Tribe's alleged hot prospects. "Once Tony proves he can handle major-league pitching, he'll have a steady job with the Indians," reads his card.

This was from 1964. The card says Martinez hit .217 at Class AAA Jacksonville in 1963. It says he batted .156 in 43 games with the Tribe in 1963.

The card didn't say what you can probably guess by now—Tony Martinez never did hit, never would hit and never got that steady job with the Indians.

Now that we have a team that has won the last four Central Division titles, a little perspective is in order.

As Hargrove said after Tuesday's 9-5 loss at Yankee Stadium: "There is no comparison between now and when I played for the Indians (in the 1980s). There were some seasons when we were out of the pennant race by May."

There were no seasons in which the Indians marched into Fenway Park and took two games from Boston to win a playoff series. There were no players like Ramirez, who hit 45 homers and drove in 145 RBI. There weren't even any pitchers like Charles Nagy, who took his lumps (and the loss) on Tuesday.

He might drive you crazy, but Nagy has won at least 15 games in each of the last four years.

In 1987, no Tribe pitcher won more than seven games.

In 1985, no Tribe pitcher won more than nine games—thank you, Neal Heaton and Bert Blyleven. Yes, they combined for 18 victories, but they also chalked up 29 losses.

In 1983, Dan Spillner led the team in saves—he had a grand total of eight!

I flip through some more cards. There's Steve Arlin, who became a better dentist than a pitcher. There's Frank Duffy, the Indians' starting shortstop in 1976, when he batted .212.

There's Charlie Spikes, the Bogalusa Bomber whose career blew up with the Tribe. There's Duke Sims, who had a great name for a catcher. There's Chico Salmon, who slept with the light on because he was afraid of ghosts.

I look at these cards and realize I have a part of my youth in my hands. I think of the old Stadium, which smelled like a small animal had curled up in the corner and died—as did many of the ballplayers who passed through the Lakefront.

Then I think of Jacobs Field, of a team perpetually in contention. And I have to admit, I remain amazed by it all.

10/15/1998

Don't take playoff game for granted

THE INDIANS HAVE MADE OCTOBER RELEVANT.

Never forget that. Never forget how tonight will feel, the October air baring its teeth with an autumn chill. Never forget what it means to see the Indians in the postseason, the Indians trying to go to the World Series for the third time in the last five years.

Don't take a playoff game for granted, especially not a game where the Tribe sends Bartolo Colon to the mound against Boston's Pedro Martinez.

It could be a game for the ages.

In this Era of the Hitter, an era when Jay Bell hits 38 homers—Jay Bell, for heaven's sake!—and a guy with an ERA under 4.00 is a star, Martinez brings order to the mound.

He's a legitimate Hall of Famer, his ERA of 2.60 being nearly two runs under the average American League starter. He strikes out eight batters for every walk. He won 23 games and lost only four times.

It's almost like seeing a dinosaur come strolling down East Ninth Street. You pause and say, "I thought those things were extinct."

Then there's the 24-year-old Colon, a future Pedro Martinez. Don't think so? Just ask Martinez, who once said, "Bartolo reminds me of me."

For proof, I submit this piece of evidence: Only one American

League pitcher won more games than Colon—and you'll see him tonight, too.

Martinez vs. Colon.

As I sit here and savor tonight's game, I think of my Indians. I still marvel at Jacobs Field, at the sellouts night after night and at the toilets that actually work.

Most of all, I'm stunned by Indians teams that are so different from my Indians.

There was Larvell Blanks, whose temper ran so hot, he took off his uniform and burned it in the middle of the clubhouse as a sign of protest when he wasn't in the lineup.

There was Joe Charboneau, who drank beer through his nose and ate raw eggs with his mouth—when he wasn't pulling out his own teeth with a pair of pliers.

There was Jerry Willard, who had a sore throat and was told to gargle with lukewarm water and salt. He paused and asked, "How do you get lukewarm water?"

There was Chico Salmon, who always slept with the lights on because he was afraid of ghosts, and Rico Carty, who always played with his wallet in his back pocket because he was afraid someone would steal his money out of the clubhouse.

There was Kevin Rhomberg, who never would let you touch him—not unless he touched you back. And if you managed to sneak away without him touching you last, then he'd mail you a letter and count you as touched. There was an old stadium that smelled like some animal died in a distant corner, and no one ever found it. It was a place with football yard markers in the outfield beginning in September, and Rick Manning would signal for a fair catch while camping under fly balls in center field.

My Indians were always on the second year of a five-year plan; they were always trading pitchers for hitters or hitters for pitchers—and ending up in sixth place in a seven-team division.

Which is why I can't wait for tonight.

It's a game where the stakes are high, where this team is trying to make it back to the World Series for the third time in the last five years.

That still amazes me—the Indians in the World Series.

For all of us who loved Rocky Colavito, he never had a year like Manny Ramirez has had in each of the last two seasons.

Kenny Lofton is certainly an upgrade over Alex Cole. Omar Vizquel doesn't make you pine away for Tom Veryzer, and can you think of any Tribe player in your lifetime who has had a better all-around season than Robbie Alomar? Name another team that has a Gold Glove second baseman batting third in the best lineup in baseball?

When this team was healthy, it was the best Indians team I've ever seen. They scored more runs than the legendary 1995 team. They catch the ball better than the 1997 team. They run the bases better than any Indians team since, well, maybe ever.

I know, the pitching.

Boston has Pedro; the Indians don't.

But I also know that Bartolo Colon ain't exactly Dave Van Ohlen or Tom Hilgendorf. If any pitcher is capable of warming up this October by matching heat with Martinez, it's Colon. As Tribe assistant general manager Mark Shapiro said, "What a lot of people don't know is Bartolo wants the ball in a game like this; he thinks he's a big-game pitcher."

He showed it by allowing only two runs in two postseason starts last year, including a complete game, 6-1 victory at Jacobs Field in Game 3. He showed it with an 11-2 record after the All-Star break.

So before you think about showing up for tonight's game wearing black and humming Taps because Martinez is pitching, remember how far this franchise has come in the last five years—and how far it still can go.

10/6/1999

Indians crowds have come a long way

DID YOU EVER THINK you'd see the day when the big news of the day was the Indians didn't have a sellout?

Not if you remember old Cleveland Stadium, where some nights it was so quiet, you could hear a batting average drop.

The Tribe's batting average, of course.

Or nights when that silence was broken only by the lonely drummer in the bleachers, having all the fans around him—yes, both of them— reach for the aspirin by the fifth inning.

Or nights when the guy who sat behind home plate and bellowed, "WHO-LEE-OO!" for former Indian Julio Franco, the futile battle cry echoing all the way down to the Lakefront.

"We'd draw 60,000 for the home opener," said former Tribe center fielder Rick Manning. "Then we'd have 6,000 for the next game."

And most games thereafter.

That was Tribe baseball for 35 years, when the team's motto was, "Good Seats Available."

Lots of seats, 74,483 to be exact—about 20,000 of them were behind poles.

"What I would have given to play in a park like this in front of crowds like these," said Manning, staring out of the TV booth at Jacobs Field.

Here's what Tribe baseball has become: last night, the crowd was announced at 32,763 and that's considered a disappointment.

In the last seven years at the old Stadium, the average crowd was 17,284—and those counts must have included about 5,000 people who spent the entire game in the rest rooms, because you never saw them in the seats.

Jeff Overton, the team vice president who deals with ticket sales, admitted as much. He joined the Tribe in 1989.

"There were games when I never wanted to leave our office because I knew there were only 4,000 people in the stands," he said. "It was too depressing."

That's why last night was a cause for celebration, even though the Tribe's sellout streak ended at 455.

It began on June 12, 1995, and it lasted for 2,122 days. For five consecutive years (1996–2000), the Indians sold out the entire season before the first pitch!

No other team can come close to matching that. The other significant sellout streak was 203 by Colorado in the middle 1990s. Right now, the San Francisco Giants have the longest current streak—83 games.

Since moving to Jacobs Field in 1994, the Indians have played to 98 percent capacity in front of nearly 22 million fans.

That's why the row of empty bleachers and the barren sections of green seats in the upper deck in right field were so shocking last night.

There will be more nights like this when you can actually walk up to a window and buy a ticket, but the Indians have already sold 2.8 million tickets and expect to draw at least 3 million fans this season.

So it's not like the old days, when former Tribe manager Frank Robinson said, "Indian fever is a 24-hour disease."

He meant those rare flash crowds that came to old Municipal Stadium for the opener, for the Fourth of July fireworks, for bat day.

And the next day, it was business as usual where the Indians had 4,000 season tickets compared to about 27,000 now.

"What has happened here is awesome," Manning said. "The players, they are almost spoiled by the crowds, the facility. You should see the weight room. It's amazing. At the old stadium, our weight room was three dumbbells under the trainer's table."

There's more.

"One year, they put in a batting cage under the old bleachers," said Manning. "But no one would go out there because the rats were as big as dogs."

It was former Tribe executive Gabe Paul insisting, "Cleveland is a sleeping giant."

For more than three decades, it was more like a coma.

That's why this is a good day for fans to give themselves a standing ovation—because more than anyone else, they deserve it.

4/5/2001

Tribe fans should savor the moment

TRIBE FANS, ENJOY THIS.

Never take a championship—any championship—as your rightful inheritance. Don't fall into the trap of thinking every Indian summer will be like this one.

Because it won't.

This Tribe team yesterday clinched the American League's Central Division title and its sixth postseason trip in seven years. It's a team that has won 13 games at Jacobs Field in its last at-bat. It's a team with an MVP candidate in right field, an MVP candidate at second base and a possible 50-homer muscleman at first.

What a lineup with Robbie Alomar, Juan Gonzalez and Jim Thome as its heart!

It's a team with perhaps the best young left-handed pitcher (C.C. Sabathia) in the major leagues, a team with maybe the greatest defensive shortstop (Omar Vizquel) ever to wear a glove, a team that makes you care about Cleveland baseball.

Not a perfect team, but a fun team.

A team that, in the words of GM John Hart, "gives us something to talk about around the coffee maker in the office."

It's a team where no lead is safe, the opposition's or its own. It's a team that has blown countless five-run advantages, yet has come back from 12 runs behind to win—and did it against Seattle, the best team in baseball!

It's Hart's last Tribe team, and it reflects the personality of the man who deserves the monster share of the credit for a great baseball revival that began with the move from the old Cleveland Stadium to Jacobs Field in 1994.

Some of us read that and just shrug.

Some say, "Well, they never won a World Series, so if you ask me, they ain't won nothin' yet."

Some people don't have a clue.

If that's you, I'm asking if you remember when the Indians had a pitcher named Jim Kern who had to leave a game because he swallowed a bug, believed to be a wasp?

Or when the Indians had a catcher named Jerry Willard who once asked, "Where do you get lukewarm water to drink?"

Or a first baseman named Broderick Perkins who brawled with Rick Sutcliffe in the shower because he didn't like Sutcliffe's country music.

Or a designated hitter named Cliff Johnson, whose idea of practice was to sit on the bench, sipping coffee from a foam cup in between puffs on a cigarette.

They once had a pretty good third baseman named Toby Harrah, who fell off the roof of his house while trying to be a handyman. And, oh yeah, it was that Cliff Johnson who broke a finger while unloading a barrel of oats from a truck.

Why didn't these guys just pay someone to do the chores around the house?

They also had a pitcher named Jamie "The Rat" Easterly, who injured his back one day when he decided to go for a run—backward—and fell into a hole. Don't ask why.

And they had another pitcher named Victor Cruz who once said, "All umpires are vampires." Don't ask why.

They had yet another pitcher named Juan Eichelberger who didn't want to sit next to the window on a plane because he thought it would hurt his arm. Don't ask why.

They had a couple of pitchers (why so many pitchers?) named Jack

Kralick and Gary Bell, who once got into a fight over what channel to watch—and that was back when there were black-and-white TVs and only three channels from which to pick.

They had a manager named Mike Ferraro who once said, "We're not a baseball team, we're like the traveling circus. We just go from town to town, providing entertainment for the other team."

Ferraro had that epiphany after watching a first baseman named Mike Hargrove (Yes, that Mike Hargrove) lead the Indians off the field after only two batters came to the plate in the first inning of a game. Somehow, he thought two batters had made three outs, and Hargrove convinced eight of his teammates to follow him.

You probably have your own lovable loser story about the Tribe, your own memories of Stadium Mustard, thousands of empty seats and drummer John Adams' relentless banging away in the bleachers, his lonesome bass echoing around the park, as you watched Alex Cole lose fly balls in center field.

"But there is an entire generation of fans who are growing up knowing nothing but the Indians are a contender," Hart said. "That's what means the most to me, to see the kids wear Tribe shirts and jackets and knowing that every year, they have a terrific team to watch."

From 1960–94, the Indians never played a meaningful game in September. Forget their last World Series appearance being in 1954, this team never even came close to contention until the strike-marred season in 1994, followed by the season-long 100-victory celebration that was the 1995 World Series team.

"Other than 1995, this team means the most to me," said Hart, who took over the Tribe in 1991. He is quitting at the end of the season because he knows it's hard to sustain a winner, that sometimes it's wise to leave while people still want you to stay.

Hart also was stunned by some of the harsh criticism last winter when the team lost Manny Ramirez and Sandy Alomar to free agency. He also was attacked for hiring Charlie Manuel to replace Hargrove, for not obtaining a dominating starting pitcher, and finally, for not winning the World Series despite advancing that far in the 1995 and 1997 playoffs.

"Some of the stuff was so personal, so vindictive, I wanted us to come back and win again just to prove some people wrong," he said.

Under Hart's leadership, the team went from 105 losses in 1991 to becoming the only American League team other than New York to play in the World Series since the 1994 strike.

As he likes to say, "We raised the bar," but there's no doubt he has been affected by the ever-increasing fan and media expectations.

So Hart decided it was time to step down, time to turn the team over to his protege, Mark Shapiro.

But Hart wanted one more playoff team, and many of his moves during last year's winter of discontent have made this a very enjoyable summer.

Hart lost Ramirez as a $160 million free agent signee with the Boston Red Sox but he then signed Juan Gonzalez to a one-year deal— and the Tribe's Gonzalez has been better in every respect than Ramirez with the Red Sox.

He lost catcher Sandy Alomar, the fan favorite who played only 70 games and had two knee surgeries this season with the Chicago White Sox.

In place of Alomar, Hart and Manuel handed the catching position to Einar Diaz, whose energy, throwing arm and clutch hitting have made him one of the league's more underrated players.

Hart gambled on signing Danys Baez to a 4-year, $14 million contract, and in only his second year in the United States, the Cuban import often has saved the bullpen.

He found Marty Cordova in a baseball rummage sale. Out of work and written off, Cordova signed a one-year contract worth a mere $500,000. And he responded with a career year, hitting .304 with 19 home runs.

He traded power-hitting prospect Richie Sexson to Milwaukee last summer for Bob Wickman, who has been brilliant in the bullpen. And the Indians now are getting some mileage out of left-handed relief specialist Ricky Rincon, who had represented one of Hart's worst deals as he came from Pittsburgh for emerging All-Star outfielder Brian Giles.

Not everything has worked. The starting pitching remains shaky. Hart's last trade, Steve Karsay for John Rocker, saw both pitchers lose jobs as the closer with their respective teams. Also, no one has been thrilled by the bat of reserve outfielder Wil Cordero.

Yet, here are the Indians bearing down on 90 victories for the fifth time in seven years, a streak that began in 1995.

Consider the previous 90-win season was in 1955.

And for that, Tribe fans should be thankful.

10/1/2001

Players

Williams knows where he comes from

SORRENTO IS A ONE-STOPLIGHT, three-junkyard town in southeastern Louisiana, halfway between New Orleans and Baton Rouge.

To most, Sorrento would be the middle of nowhere. But to Cavaliers forward John Williams, it will always be home.

"People tell me that I put it on the map," Williams said. "Makes me feel good to hear that."

Sorrento is a town of trailers, shacks and a couple of nice but unpretentious brick houses. Chickens, dogs, goats and cars on blocks share yards with statues of the Virgin Mary, a sign of the French-Catholic influence.

It is the edge of Louisiana bayou country, five feet below sea level. Water seeps from the ground almost as if the ocean were trying to reclaim the land. It's a great place to see huge white herons overhead and to watch for alligators sunning themselves on the side of the road. The air is hot, heavy and humid. The joke is that the mosquito is the state bird.

Sorrento is where you'd guess people are born poor and stay that way.

But not John Williams. Sorrento is where Williams grew up with nothing—now he wants his family to have everything.

Williams is building houses here—yes, more than one house—and you can bet this sleepy Southern hamlet's 1,139 folks have never seen anything quite like his 11,000-square-foot palace-in-the-making.

Sorrento became the home of the NBA player with the richest contract 10 months ago, when Williams received an unprecedented seven-year, $26.5 million offer sheet from the Miami Heat, and the Cavs matched it.

"I always said that once I got some money I was going to take care of my Mama," Williams said. "She lived most of her life in a trailer. She never had her own house, so I told her I'd build her one. She didn't want me to, but I'm doing it anyway."

And a nice home it will be—3,000 square feet, four bedrooms and baths and a kitchen big enough to feed the New Orleans Saints, if they come marching in.

"It will be ready by the end of the summer, just like my house," Williams said. "I wanted my Mama to live next door to me, but she wanted to stay right where she always lived. I'm five minutes away."

Ah, yes, the Williams home.

One day, Williams strolled into the office of Fairlawn architect Gerald Rembowski with sketches of his dream house. Together they developed a design that is in the final stages of construction.

The home is in an upscale development, but nothing comes close to Williams' place—six bedrooms, six bathrooms, four-car garage, tennis court, game room, guest house, swimming pool with waterfall, and mud room.

Mud room?

"That's my idea," Williams said. "The kids and I can get real dirty playing outside. You don't want to mess up the house, so you come in and go right to the room next to the door to wash up."

The house also has bathroom counters at two different heights— the tall one for Williams, the other for his wife, Neicy. It has eight-foot doorways and 10-foot ceilings so the 6-foot-11 Williams won't have to duck.

Of course, there's the gym, a 6,750-square-foot job.

"Official, NBA half-court with a 28-foot ceiling so I can go out there and work on my game anytime I want," Williams said. "I also have a full weight room in the house."

People from Sorrento drive by to see what all the fuss is about. Its construction has become a local event. (They had best get a good look now, because when completed the home will be surrounded by a wall.)

The cost?

"If I built it back in Cleveland, it probably would be at least $3 million, maybe more," Williams said.

On the West Coast, maybe even Williams couldn't afford it.

But in Sorrento, Williams will pay less than $2 million for the two homes because he is overseeing much of the work and has known many of the construction people all his life.

"A man named Joe Martin—a friend of my Mama's. I've worked

with him on carpenter's jobs ever since I was 10 or 11 years old," Williams said. "The cabinets in the cafeteria of my high school were built by my friend and myself when we went there.

"I am good with my hands. I love building things and I've built about 10 garages around here and worked on houses. I've been thinking about this house for three years, making lists, drawing up sketches, working with architects.

"I talked to Neicy. She told me a couple of things she wanted. She's picking the furniture inside, but the house is all mine. I planned it."

There is nothing left of the home where Williams was born—just an empty lot between modest wooden houses, one on stilts to keep it above soggy soil and away from termites.

"That's where my Mama saved me," he said.

There once was a small house on the spot, actually little more than a shack with a rickety front porch. Williams lived there with his mother, father and blind grandfather. His mother died when he was 7 months old; his father left Williams on the porch and never returned. The blind grandfather was helpless to comfort the wailing, frightened infant.

"My Mama heard me crying, came and took me in," Williams said.

The woman, Barbara Colar—Mama, a neighbor—named Williams "Hot Rod" when he was a preschooler because he liked to make motor sounds while pushing his toy cars on the floor. Her relationship to Williams is one of the heart, not blood.

"We weren't any kin that I know of," Williams said. "My Mama just felt sorry for me. But she is my Mama, always will be. The only time I ever saw my father was when I was 11. He showed up with a document that he needed signed to prove he had a son.

"From what I understand, it was the settlement for a lawsuit and he got a lot of money. He took off after that and I never saw him again.

"But I heard that he knows who I am now," Williams said matter-of-factly. "I couldn't have had anyone better than my Mama. She worked as an elementary school janitor in the morning, then as a cook at a seafood place in the afternoons. She worked so hard, she almost worked herself to death for me."

Williams says that he has at least 200 relatives in Sorrento and nearby Gonzales (population 7,778).

"That's why I stay. People have known me here all my life," he said. "I'm just Hot Rod around here."

Williams feels a sincere sense of community. Baby sitters are every-where as children wander from one house to another—everyone is a cousin, an aunt, a neighbor. As Williams drives around town, he waves at every policeman; they call to each other by name.

"My family will be as safe here as it would be anywhere," Williams said.

John and Neicy Williams have three children—John Jr., 8; John-francis, 4; Johna, 18 months.

While they will grow up in the same place—on some of the same streets—as their father, their world will be completely different.

Williams' first basketball rim was an old bicycle rim. He knocked out the spokes and nailed the rim to a pecan tree. His court was sand; his ball was slicker than a billiard ball.

His children will have their own official NBA floor.

Williams knows hunger. He speaks in reverent tones of his high school coach, Tommy Wall, who was white, "who proved all the folks around here wrong. They said he came from a real racist town and couldn't work with black kids.

"About all of our team was black and we loved that man."

Wood died of cancer at age 45. As Williams spoke of Wood, he pointed to the "R&B SuperWarket" sign (the "M" was turned upside down) on the side of a building that was no more than a glorified coun-try store.

"Coach Wall told the owner that if any of his players came in there for food, give it to us," Williams said. "He'd pay for it. He understood how it was for us, how poor some of us were.

"When we lost in a state tournament by a point, Coach Wall cried in front of the whole team. Not because we got beat, but he told us, 'They said I couldn't coach black kids, but you did everything I could have asked. You were great to me.'"

Williams said that his Tulane coach, Ned Fowler, used to tell peo-ple that he—Fowler—taught Williams how to play basketball. "Not true," Williams said. "It was Coach Wall."

Williams' kids will have a full refrigerator and the best coaching. Nor will race be the overriding issue it was for their father. And odds are they won't have to face anything like the Tulane point-shaving scandal of 1985, in which Williams was charged, but exonerated.

"What happened at Tulane is another reason I want to stay in Sor-rento all my life," Williams said. "I had friends on the police depart-ment saying that they would bet their careers that I was innocent. Peo-ple here said how I would take care of their kids.

"It's just like why I have Mark Bartelstein as my agent. We have nothing written down. If I leave him tomorrow, he doesn't get paid anymore. But we don't need things in writing. We trust each other. That is how it is down here, too."

Williams talked about crawfishing as a child, an experience he plans to share with his children. He is buying the chunk of land where he fished.

"I want to turn it over to the city for a park so kids have a woods to play in. I want it to be better for them than I had it. My family is all that matters. I've known Neicy since we were in high school and we've been together for 11 years. She stood by me when I had the trouble at Tulane. She is a full-time mother, a great mother. I'll be there for my kids.

"I've heard people who moved from Sorrento say how great the big cities are. I say, 'Listen, I've been to those cities. I know you're telling a fib.' That is why I want to keep my family in Sorrento, at least in the summer. They go where I do when I play, [and] if we always come home here, then we'll be OK."

6/16/1991

Growing through the pain

SOME QUESTIONS HAVE NO ANSWERS.

Why do some people get cancer and some don't? Why would Cavaliers guard Craig Ehlo's sister die at age 34? Or his father-in-law die at 57?

What do you say to someone you know is dying?

Ehlo learned this year.

"I remember looking at my father in-law [Ron Webb] in bed," Ehlo said. "He had cancer and it had spread to his back. The doctors said his spine and pelvic area were like peanut brittle. Every move he made meant pain. He couldn't get up. He couldn't change his own clothes.

"Ron was an active guy. He hated being a prisoner in that bed. He'd tell me, 'Craig, I can't look at these four walls for another day. Tonight, I'm going to beat this and tomorrow I'm getting out of bed.' I agreed with him, but I knew from what the doctors said that it would never happen.

"That's the heartbreaking part—not being able to help, or even to stop the pain."

Ehlo is 31 and starting his seventh year with the Cavs. For most of his career, he was the team's perpetual teenager, a guy who played more on guts than smarts, someone liable to forget a play but then win a game with his sheer courage and desire.

Sometimes absent-minded, Ehlo often is the target of criticism from Coach Lenny Wilkens. Yet the shooting guard is one of Wilkens' all-time favorite players, "because he puts so much of himself into the game. He's a lot of fun to have around, too."

And Ehlo still is . . . to an extent.

"I do think I've grown up some this year," he said. "I had to."

Last November, Ehlo learned that his sister, Carrie Bell, had breast cancer. It was detected too late, then spread to her brain.

"She was in a coma for four months," Ehlo said. "She loved basketball and coached a youth team in Lubbock [Texas] called the Little Cavs. I couldn't believe she got so sick so fast and that she never came out of it.

"I remember being on the road, waiting for the phone to ring to find out she had died. Part of me dreaded the call, but part of me wanted to hear that it was finally over. I saw her not long before she died.

"You see movies where someone is on their death bed. Well, those actors can't come close to how it is to see someone you love laboring for that last breath. It just tears you up."

Ehlo's sister died on Feb. 14.

Ehlo had known Ron Webb for 11 years.

"I met Jani [Ehlo] when I was a junior at Washington State," Ehlo said. "We dated throughout college and got married seven years ago. Ron was more than a father-in-law to me. I always told people that I was lucky, I had two fathers."

Ehlo's father was victimized by arthritis for much of his life.

"There were times when I had to help him get dressed and just get around," Ehlo said. "He had four operations and is better now than ever. But he wasn't able to go fishing, play golf and do things that a son likes to do with his father. Well, I did those things with Ron."

Ron Webb was a pitcher in the St. Louis farm system in the 1950s.

"He became my biggest booster because he understood pro sports," Ehlo said. "Jani loved her dad—she's a Daddy's Girl just like my daughter Erica is a Daddy's Girl. When I needed to work out or do the things athletes have to that take them away from home, Ron would tell Jani not to worry.

"He was a great support system for me and he made things easier in our marriage."

Ehlo said that when Michael Jordan scored 35 points in the first half of Game 1 of the 1992 NBA Finals, his phone rang.

"It was Ron saying, 'Did you see what Michael did to Drexler? He never lit you up like that,'" Ehlo said. "That was Ron just trying to cheer me up."

The closeness of Ehlo and his in-laws was demonstrated in 1988 when Craig and Jani went to Webb's home in Spokane, Washington, for the summer so the entire family could be together for the birth of their daughter.

"Ron bought me a membership to the Spokane Athletic Club because he knew I needed a place to work out," Ehlo said. "Even when he was real sick this summer, he told me to go the health club. He was always looking out for me." Webb had been battling prostate cancer for a few years.

"They thought they had it stabilized," Ehlo said. "But in June, it went out of control and really took over his whole body. That's the scary thing about cancer—they can't tell you why certain things happen. They just happen."

For the second time in four months, Ehlo found himself on a death watch as he returned to Spokane after the Cavs' season. He joined with Jani and his mother-in-law to care for Webb.

"The hospice people were great. I can't say enough about them," Ehlo said. "They taught us how to pick up Ron so we could change his bed. We gave him sponge baths, helped feed him. I just had such a hard time accepting the fact that such an active guy was so sick."

Ron Webb died on Aug. 9.

Anyone who believes that the suffering ends when someone dies never lost anyone close to them. Ehlo remained in Spokane for several weeks after the funeral.

"Husbands and sons like to think they can make things better," Ehlo said. "When my daughter's bike breaks, Jani tells her that I'll fix it when I get home and then I do. I like to fix things, to make people happy.

"But this year, I couldn't do that. Jani and I would be in bed and she'd say, 'I don't want Dad to die.' Or she'd say, 'Why does he have to die?' Those are tough conversations."

Ehlo said that he went to the gym every day, for a few hours to lift weights and practice his shooting.

"It was great therapy for me and it was something Ron wanted me to do," Ehlo said. "I never thought about my problems there, but the minute I put the ball in the bag and headed out the door, my thoughts were back to him and the family.

"You never realize how you can become so wrapped up in it when someone is sick. It's all you think about and all you talk about. Then when they don't get better, you just feel empty.

"But I try to find the good side of everything. This brought Jani and I closer. My sister was dying, but I kept things inside. It was strange. I can watch a movie and cry, but I wouldn't let my emotions out when it came to my family.

"But at Carrie's funeral, all the pent-up things . . . I just let loose. I'd never let myself go like that. Then Ron got sick, I found that I had to talk about it.

"Jani has been wanting me to open up to her for years. When things were touchy, I'd cut off the conversation or we'd end up in a fight. Now, we talk it through. We're really starting to tell each other how we feel and that's the one good thing that came out of this summer."

10/8/1992

Belle plays by the numbers

ALBERT BELLE CAN TELL YOU what he hit last season when he swung at the first pitch—.479.

"The only guy in the American League who was better was Kirby Puckett," he said. Belle can tell you that Al Rosen has the Indians' single-season home run record—43 in 1953.

"I really thought that I had a chance to break that—until the strike came," said Belle, who had 36 homers when the season ended last August 12.

Belle even can tell you about the only player ever to have 100 RBI by the All-Star break.

"That's Hank Greenberg," he said. "I really think that record can be broken. I had 84 at the break last year—and I got off to a lousy start and didn't really begin to hit until May."

Actually, Belle hit .333 in April—but he hit .416 in May. So Albert is right again. At least by his standards, he didn't hit until May.

Why all this talk about numbers? It is part of what drives the Indians' biggest bat—as does his prospective place in history.

In a sport where some players don't know anything about Jackie

Robinson . . . where they never heard of Ty Cobb (unless they saw the movie) . . . where they think of Babe Ruth as an old-time candy bar . . . it's refreshing that Belle knows the names and numbers of the game.

"I try to pay attention to those things," he said. "I like to read."

He also likes to break records.

If Belle again leads the Indians in homers, it will be for a fifth straight season—something no Tribe player has done.

Heard of "shoeless" Joe Jackson? He did it from 1911–14—but he also did it by hitting seven, three, seven and three home runs. Yes, three home runs a year could lead a team in home runs during that deadest of the dead ball era.

Maybe you've heard of Jackson, if not from history books, then from the movies *Eight Men Out* and *Field of Dreams*—and when it comes to home-run hitters, you have to put an asterisk next to his name.

But what abut Hal Trosky? He did it from 1934–37, averaging 35 homers a season as a Tribe first baseman at old League Park. Trosky is one of the forgotten sluggers of the game, a man who might have attained true greatness but was haunted by severe migraines.

Then came Belle, averaging 34 homers from 1991–94.

"Shoeless" Joe Jackson . . . Hal Trosky . . . Albert Belle.

That's it—three guys in Indians' history . . . a history that spans the entire century.

"I want to finish my career in Cleveland," Belle said. "If I do that, I'll probably lead the team in home runs."

The record now belongs to Earl Averill, who hit 226 while playing for the Tribe from 1929–39.

Belle has 144 in five seasons. He is only 28. He is a better hitter than ever, and is in the middle of what might be the most potent lineup in the history of the franchise.

Why can't he break Rosen's record of 43 homers? If not in this 144-game season, then maybe next year? Why wouldn't he again lead the team in home runs?

Can we say that this man—not Rocky Colavito, Trosky, Averill or Andre Thornton—is destined to be the greatest slugger ever to wear a Cleveland uniform?

"I don't know about that," Belle said, "but what I want to be is the best run producer, the guy who drives in more runs than anyone else. That is what means the most to me."

OK, more numbers.

Averill leads the Indians with 1,085 career RBI, Belle has 477. He'll probably need five more years to claim that mark as his own.

"Something else I've been looking at," Belle said. "Joe Carter has the [team] record with six straight seasons of at least 30 homers and 100 RBI."

Belle didn't say any more, but you know what he was thinking—I can break that record, too.

The reason for this history lesson about Albert Jojuan Belle of Shreveport, Louisiana is that with all the explosions and suspensions, it is easy to forget that Belle is no longer a prospect—he is a producer.

Yes, he'll snap and do something that will earn him a spot on the bench—be it charging a pitcher, throwing a ball at a fan or using a corked bat. But he'll also hit.

"You know, I needed two hits on the last day of the season to win the batting title; I got only one," said Belle, who batted .357 last season. New York's Paul O'Neill won the title at .359. "It would have been nice for the season to have gone just to see where my numbers would have ended up," he said. "I was in contention for the Triple Crown."

Belle's final numbers were staggering: .357 (second in the American League), 36 homers (third) and 101 RBI (third).

"My brother kept talking to me about the Triple Crown—and I talked to him every other day," Belle said. "I'd say, 'Hey, I'm glad you reminded me,' like I really needed to hear about the Triple Crown all the time."

The most remarkable aspect of Belle's season was the .357 batting average. He never had hit higher than .290 before.

"I see myself as a .300 hitter," he said. "I'm still an aggressive hitter, but when I came up [to the majors], I was an aggressive, out-of-control hitter. I got upset when a pitcher wanted to walk me, and I'd swing at bad pitches. I kept trying to force things."

And now?

"Now I'll take a walk if I have to," he said. "I'm forcing the pitchers to give in to me, instead of giving in to them. I also don't let a couple of bad at-bats carry over. I don't dwell on them as much."

Some may suggest that Belle's numbers were tainted because he used an illegal bat early in the season—and was suspended for seven days in late July.

"If you want to know why I hit, don't bring up the bat," Belle said. "The big difference last year from the others, was that I had a great player in Eddie Murray batting behind me. I know that I got better pitches to hit because Eddie was there. Besides, what did I do in my other three years? You can't bring up the bat when talking about that."

As if to prove his point, Belle can enter even more numbers into evidence. After the corked bat caper, he came back to hit .476 (30 for 63) with 10 homers in 20 games. Then the season ended abruptly.

So what about this year?

"I'll say that I'm going for .300, 30 homers and 100 RBI," he said. Why not more?

"Well, suppose I say that I'll hit 50 homers—and then I hit only 40?" he asked. "For most guys, 40 homers is a great year. But if I say I'm going to hit 50, then everyone will be mad at me if I hit only 40."

Unlikely—except, perhaps, for the relentless Belle himself.

4/25/1995

A career night for Murray and family

EDDIE MURRAY had to be thinking about a lot of things as he stood at first base last night, his helmet off and arms raised to the crowd.

Cheers? Yes, he heard them.

Tears? Yes, he had to feel them.

He'll never admit it, but 3,000 hits will do that to a man, even a guy who believes in putting on the same mask every day to keep the world from getting too close, from knowing too much.

As Murray was mobbed by his teammates, he had to feel as if he were back in East Los Angeles. That was where the 12 Murray children—and countless cousins—got together for baseball games.

To him, baseball will always mean family. It will mean his father, Charles, who worked 30 years as a mechanic for the Ludlow Rug Company. It will mean his mother, Carrie, who ruled the family with huge hugs, and sometimes an iron hand.

It will mean being the eighth of a dozen children, and having plenty of older brothers and sisters telling you that the world does not revolve around you and your wishes.

Three thousand hits always will remind him of a family that played baseball with rubber balls and tennis balls. They even tried to hit the plastic lids from Crisco cans when they ran out of balls.

One year, the Murray boys drew the wrath of their mother when they took the heads off their sisters' dolls and used them for baseballs.

Three thousand hits began on a "diamond" where the telephone pole was first base . . . a hole in the ground was second . . . a clothesline pole was third . . . and a slab of cement was home plate.

Despite 3,000 hits, Murray will tell you that he wasn't the best ballplayer in the family. That distinction went to Charles, the oldest brother who hammered 37 homers and drove in 119 runs at Class A Modesto.

But that was back in 1964. That was Vietnam, and Charles Murray had his baseball career submarined by two stints in the military. He leveled out at Class AAA and then worked as a prison guard.

Murray's next older brother was Leon, who played one year of pro ball, suffered a major arm injury and was released. Leon Murray also gave his brothers haircuts. When Murray was with the Orioles and they played in Southern California, he would take some of his teammates to his home and Leon would cut their hair, too.

Eddie and his brother, Venice, were high school teammates. They also played on two summer teams at the same time, and their parents drove them from one game to the next as the boys changed uniforms in the back of a car.

Venice signed a pro contract, but blew out his knee after one year of Class A ball, his pro career ending in Cedar Rapids, Iowa. Eddie Murray's career will conclude in Cooperstown, New York.

His youngest brother, Rich, made the majors. Rich finished 2,956 hits short of Eddie. Rich Murray had 204 at bats with the Giants in the early 1980s, hitting .216 with four homers.

Eddie thought Rich was a terrific athlete, too. Willie McCovey agreed, saying that Rich Murray would be the right guy to take over for him at first base with the Giants—and McCovey became a Hall of Famer. But it just didn't happen. Now Rich Murray is a coach in the Tribe's minor-league system.

So Murray can look back at family and see what can stand between a ballplayer and 3,000 hits—wars, injuries, lousy luck and bad timing.

To Murray, this day wasn't just about him. It was about Charles, Leon, Venice and Rich. It was about his mother who died in 1985, and whom he wished could have been in Minnesota last night.

This also was about his early days in the big leagues with the Orioles when his father would make ribs for the entire team, serving them in the Orioles' clubhouse.

Things like that don't happen anymore. Baseball is more business than family. But it was different on April 7, 1977, the date of Murray's first hit and his first big-league game. Bert Blyleven was the pitcher, and Murray slapped that curveball back up the middle.

How long ago was that? Mike Hargrove was the starting first baseman in that game—for the Texas Rangers.

Blyleven pitched for the Rangers, Jim Palmer for Murray's Baltimore Orioles. The game lasted 10 innings, and both pitchers went the distance. You don't see that anymore, guys pitching 10 innings.

It was so long ago that Murray had just turned 21, but in the eyes of the Orioles, he was still a kid. When Murray started to say something, veteran first baseman Lee May would say, "Shut up, rookie."

No one talks to rookies like that today.

May eventually would become Murray's mentor and best friend. Ever notice how Murray is the only man on the Indians who wears his batting helmet over his regular baseball cap? Well, Lee May was the only guy on the Orioles to do that—until Murray followed.

By the end of the 1977 season, Murray would have 173 hits on his way to 3,000. He would be the 1977 American League Rookie of the Year and have $19,000 in the bank.

That's right, the man who earns $3 million today started at $19,000.

When *Sports Illustrated* visited the Murray home in Los Angeles, mother Carrie showed the reporter 21 scrapbooks filled with stories about all her children.

That was 13 years ago. Now the Murray family probably has 21 more scrapbooks—all about Eddie. "I'm starting to run out of wall space," Murray said, mentioning his silver bats, gold gloves, honorary plaques and pictures of himself and favorite teammates.

But the family, it is always there.

"After all these years [19 in the majors], my brothers still call me with batting tips," he said. "They tell me not to lunge, to take pitches—things like that. They keep me in my place."

7/1/1995

A Brown in Earnest

IF WE ARE JUDGED on how we act when things are at their worst, Earnest Byner belongs in the Hall of Fame.

For Byner the football player, the bottom was Jan. 17, 1988, at Denver's Mile High Stadium. It was the Day of the Fumble, the day the Browns' Super Bowl dreams died.

The Browns were on Denver's 3-yard line when Byner lost the ball with 72 seconds left. The Broncos recovered and hung on for a 38-33 victory. If Byner hangs on to the ball . . . if the Browns score . . . well, you know the drill.

When it was over, Byner had a choice. But he'll tell you that he really didn't. If you are Earnest Byner, you don't hide. You stand up like a man and say you made a mistake.

Byner did that over and over, for wave after wave of reporters. He talked about how the play was supposed to be run . . . how it broke down . . . how he had a Super Bowl ticket in his arms—and dropped it.

Some reporters wanted to know how the Cleveland fans would treat him. Another wanted to know if he could sleep at night. A third asked how it felt to let his teammates down.

In that game, Byner carried the ball 15 times for 67 yards and caught seven passes for 120 more. Without Byner, the Browns never would have been in position to win. There was no reason to apologize, especially since Byner is a classic, blue-collar overachiever—a 10th-round suspect out of East Carolina. At 5-foot-10 and 210 pounds, Byner had neither the size nor the college pedigree to be a star, or even a starter.

But he didn't say any of that. He patiently and honestly answered the questions.

Then a reporter asked, "How does it feel to be the Bill Buckner of Cleveland?"

"That's OK with me," said Byner, who isn't a baseball fan. "I don't know who Bill Buckner is."

Finally, laughter broke the tension. For Byner, it was a relief because his heart was breaking.

Byner played one more year with the Browns, then was traded to Washington for a guy named Mike Oliphant. "One of the worst mistakes I ever made," Browns owner Art Modell said. That covers a lot of ground. Modell obviously has pulled some real beauties.

Byner went on to become a Pro Bowl back in Washington, and Mike Oliphant, well, he remained Mike Oliphant.

Some said The Fumble made Byner timid in his last year with the Browns, that it rocked his confidence. He became the guy some fans blamed for their Super Bowl frustrations. There were few tears when he was traded.

Six years later, Byner was the one Brown most fans wanted to touch during last week's finale at the Stadium.

"I'll never forget these fans," he said. "They were crying. They were telling me that they loved me and they didn't want me to leave."

The second time around, the fans know Byner as a player to remember, a man worthy of respect. He is a Cleveland Brown in the truest sense, a link to the days when football was fun and the Super Bowl was so close you swore you could touch it.

Byner is now 33 years old. He has the face of a man of 40, a man who has seen more than his share of pain. He has a body that sometimes feels like it is 50—but most of all, he has the wisdom that many of us could use.

Perhaps the best thing about the last two seasons is that Byner was able to come home again.

"I've really appreciated how the fans have treated me, especially how they have welcomed me back the last few years," Byner said. "It means a lot to me."

That is because he means so much to them.

At least he played on a team that was a legitimate Super Bowl contender. He was there with Bernie Kosar, Kevin Mack and the birth of the Dawg Pound.

"The thing that struck me when I came to the Browns was the history," he said. "I was playing on the same field and in the same stadium where Jim Brown, Leroy Kelly and Ernie Green played. You can feel that history, and the fans are a big part of that legacy."

After listening to knuckleheads such as Dana Hall, Andre Rison and Pepper Johnson pop off about the Browns' fans and show their disdain for the legacy of this team in other ways, Byner stands even taller today.

Then came last Sunday's game against the Bengals, probably the final Browns game at the Stadium.

Leroy Hoard was hurt. Lorenzo White was so deep in Bill Belichick's doghouse that a bloodhound couldn't find him.

"The night before the game, [offensive coordinator] Steve Crosby asked me how I was feeling and if my body was ready," Byner said. "I told him I was fine."

Then Byner called a meeting of the Browns' running backs.

"We got together in my hotel room, knelt down and prayed for God to give us strength in this last game," Byner said.

The prayers were answered.

Byner touched the ball on 13 of the Browns' first 15 plays. He carried the ball 31 times, the crowd roaring as he chewed up every one of his 121 yards on the ground.

When he wasn't running the ball, he caught it—seven passes from

Vinny Testaverde, another man whose classy conduct deserves your respect.

The coaches will tell you that Byner is a tremendous blocker, a shrewd player who doesn't forget assignments and sacrifices his body.

He teaches younger players, players who might take his job.

"A lot of people tell me that I'm crazy because I'm helping someone who may push me aside one day," he said. "But it is something I've always done. I've always wanted to be a coach."

But for now, he can still play.

Guess who leads the Browns in pass receptions? Sorry, Andre, it's Byner with 55 catches. He's second on the team with 380 yards rushing, and the man just doesn't get hurt.

Older members of the Browns organization will tell you that Byner was crucial in convincing Kevin Mack to stay with his drug rehabilitation program, and then was a one-man support group for the Browns' fullback after he returned to the team.

Byner is a Christian like Andre Thornton and Mark Price, an athlete whose faith is so well-known that he doesn't need to preach a word to deliver a powerful message on how one should live his life.

As Byner met the fans in the bleachers last Sunday, there were tears in his eyes, too.

Know what words meant the most to him?

"When the fans told me that I would always be a Cleveland Brown," he said. "That last game at the Stadium is something I'll always cherish. I'm getting a [video] tape. I never want to forget any of it."

12/24/1995

In Manny's neighborhood

YOU HAVE TO REMIND YOURSELF this is still New York City.

Still the United States.

On the street, all you hear is Spanish.

From the cars cruising Amsterdam Avenue, it's the relentless beat of salsa music.

From the brownstone tenements, you smell rice and beans simmering on the stove.

This is Washington Heights in northern Manhattan. It also is the home of the Tribe's Manny Ramirez.

You walk the streets and suddenly begin to feel as Ramirez must in Northeast Ohio.

You are a stranger in a strange land.

You see a man selling gold watches and necklaces out of a trash bag.

You see stores called bodegas, not Dairy Marts.

You see storefront churches, and all the signs are in Spanish.

You see young teenagers hanging out on the corners.

This is a school day. You wonder why they are out here. You try not to think the worst, but can't help it.

Washington Heights is more than New York's version of the Dominican Republic—it is one of the city's most notorious drug areas.

"Going to Washington Heights?" says a policeman.

"Well, they'll figure a white guy up there is either undercover [cop] or out to make a drug buy."

Or maybe a baseball scout.

That is the other story of Washington Heights.

Baseball.

It is the home to thousands of kids who want to be Manny Ramirez, kids who can barely speak English, but who understand the summer game perfectly.

Baseball is all that matters here, or at least that is what so many people tell you.

In the daytime, you feel safe in Washington Heights.

People smile at you as they pass on the sidewalk, a rarity in New York.

They will try to help you with directions, even if their English is terrible and your Spanish is far worse.

Yes, there are a lot of drug dealers here.

You know it from the gang graffiti on the walls.

You know it from the hollow eyes from some wasted souls nodding on street corners.

But there are people working two, even three jobs. They are trying to pay the bills, to make a life in this country.

You ask a stranger where to find George Washington High, and she takes you there. Leads you to the door. She reminds you that there are a lot of good people here.

At the school, there is a guard named Lou.

He checks your identification.

Everyone has a picture ID card—teachers, students, administrators.

You can't walk the hall by yourself, a teacher escorts you.

Want to use the bathroom?

The teacher opens it with a key, then stands outside, waiting.

This huge, stately school was built in 1923, and it appears like an old opera house with its marble floors, high ceilings and chandeliers.

Its alumni include Henry Kissinger, former New York Senator Jacob Javits and broadcaster Edwin Newman.

Also, Hall of Famer Rod Carew and Manny Ramirez.

On the windows, there are bars.

On some spots of the roof, there is barbed wire.

In the halls are 15 policemen in uniform, others undercover.

You walk out to the baseball diamond (it's Astroturf, believe it or not), and a plain clothes security man approaches you.

He wants to see some identification, even though you are wearing a big red sticker proclaiming, VISITOR.

"No disrespect," he says. "But a lot of stuff goes on out here. We try to keep everything cool."

Say this much for those running George Washington High—they are determined to make it a safe place.

And the 3,000 students and teachers appreciate it.

You find Steve Mandl in the gym.

He was Ramirez's high school coach. He is still the baseball coach and a good one.

Last year, his team had a 44-2 record and was the best in New York City.

Mandl has about 60 kids in his gym class. All are sitting in assigned spots on the floor as attendance is taken.

No one talks. Everyone knows the drill.

His baseball teams are coached the same way.

In a world where so much seems like chaos, Mandl not only wins— but he also brings order.

"It used to bother me when people talked about Manny's lack of fundamentals and his mistakes," Mandl says.

"People wanted to know if he was coached. But he has been playing pro ball since 1991 . . . "

And the blunders have continued.

Point being, it's not anyone's fault. It's just Manny.

"I really believe Manny has a learning disability, attention deficit syndrome," he says. "I have seen other kids with it. That is the source of some of Manny's problems."

The Indians are aware of this. They won't discuss it publicly. They don't want to embarrass their star right fielder. They just say they are trying to work with him.

"When we drafted Manny, we were aware of his situation," says Tribe general manager John Hart.

"But we also know Manny is a good kid. He is street smart. He is from a tough neighborhood and has had few academic advantages. Believe me, we do all we can for Manny, and understand there are some problems."

Ramirez did not graduate from high school, something all too common for kids at George Washington High.

Books in English were impossible to read, and what he heard from his teachers had little relevance to his life.

"Manny is misunderstood," Mandl says.

"People don't know him like we do. He was obsessed, absolutely obsessed with baseball. He had great talent, but his work ethic was tremendous."

Ramirez would awake at 5 A.M. He tied a rope around his waist and attached the other end to a tire. Then he ran up and down Amsterdam Avenue—for miles, rain or shine—dragging that tire behind him.

"If I told Manny to be there for a game at 1 P.M., he was there two hours early," says Mandl. "If I said the team picture was at 1 P.M., he'd forget and not show up. Baseball is really all he cares about."

Ramirez came to Washington Heights from the Dominican Republic at age 13. His father was a cab driver, his mother a seamstress. They were separated.

The youngest of four children (the other three are sisters), Ramirez sometimes lived with his mother, other times with his father.

He showed little interest in learning English, and his neighborhood offered him little incentive to do so.

Spanish is the music of these streets, which are a replica of any city in the Dominican Republic. In fact, 90 percent of the kids at George Washington High are from the Dominican.

"I've been coaching youth baseball for 25 years," says Mel Zitter.

"I've had over 20 kids sign pro contracts. I've had 20 other kids with the same talent as Manny, only they didn't make it."

Why?

"Too scared to leave the neighborhood," he says. "Not as dedicated and disciplined as Manny. You have to give this kid a lot of credit for accomplishing what he has in Cleveland. A lot of these are street kids, and the street often gets them before they can get out."

Zitter coached Ramirez for three summers.

"He would talk to me after about every at-bat, about the pitches he hit and what he missed," Zitter says.

"I always wish he could carry over the sophistication he has when hitting to the rest of his life."

Ramirez batted over .600 in his final two years of high school. During his senior year, the *New York Times* called him "The Hit Man," his nickname from school.

He batted .615 with 14 homers in 22 games, enough to inspire the Indians to make him their No.1 pick in the 1991 amateur draft.

Despite the wealth and notoriety that he has received, Ramirez is perceived as friendly and humble by those who have known him the longest.

"He is more sensitive and more aware of the criticism coming his way than you think," Zitters insists.

"Most players think they are much better than they really are—with Manny, it's the other way. Behind that smile is a good kid who is not a very confident person."

Both Zitter and Mandl are demanding coaches.

Their practices take hours. They insist upon a lot of running and stretching, in addition to baseball.

They raise money to help their players buy equipment.

Mandl's high school teams have to travel to road games by subway. The coach uses his own money to buy players gloves and bats.

High school coaches like Mandl in schools such as George Washington are real heroes. They know they are bucking the odds. They see too many of their kids end up dead or on drugs, kids whom they worked with for years.

Yet, they come back for more.

Not just hoping for another Ramirez, but for kids who actually make it through college. Kids who become responsible adults in the neighborhood, and these kids are his real success stories—as Mandl proudly ticks off their names.

Ramirez could do more for his alma mater. But he is too shy to speak to the students (or even the baseball team), and apparently not savvy enough to let his checkbook do the talking.

"I've never asked him to donate money to the program," Mandl said.

"It wouldn't be right to bother him. He has enough people pulling at him.

"A few years ago, he gave us $1,000 he won in a home run derby. He has given kids in the neighborhood gloves and shoes."

Ramirez promises his high school coach and old teammates tickets—then forgets to leave them.

Instead of being angry, the friends of Manny just assume it's Manny being Manny.

"For years, he'd show up at the school unannounced," Mandl says.

"He'd eat with the kids in the cafeteria.

"He looked like just another student, and was happy to be considered like that."

But now, Ramirez is a 25-year-old man.

He is 6 feet tall and 200 pounds of muscle.

He wears glittering jewelry and sharp clothes.

"Heads turn when he walks into school now," says Mandl.

"People know who he is. They know he has made something of himself and he has stayed out of trouble.

"We have every reason to be proud of him."

10/2/1997

Vizquel is truly an all-star

EARLY THIS SEASON, OMAR VIZQUEL was huddled in the corner of the Tribe's dressing room with rookie Enrique Wilson.

"Now write the word—socks," Vizquel said.

Slowly, Wilson wrote S-O-C-K-S.

"Good," Vizquel said.

Wilson smiled.

"Now, try—pants," he said.

Carefully, Wilson wrote the word, making a mistake.

Vizquel corrected him. Wilson tried it again.

"P-A-N-T-S," Vizquel said. "That's good."

"I have been around baseball dressing rooms for a long time, but I've never seen a player teach English to another player like Omar was doing," said Allen Davis, the Tribe's community relations director

Tribe manager Mike Hargrove has a list of players he plans to pick for the All-Star Game—and Vizquel's name is on it.

All the names are written in pencil.

It's a hard job, picking an All-Star team. Names will be added and erased. The shortstop position is loaded with young, powerful hitters such as Nomar Garciaparra, Alex Rodriguez and Derek Jeter—all are .300 hitters with more homers and RBI than Vizquel.

But somehow, Hargrove has to make sure Vizquel is an All-Star. No Tribe player deserves it more.

Not just based on this season, either.

Vizquel is the best defensive shortstop ever to wear a Cleveland uniform. Veteran sportswriter Hal Lebovitz has seen them all since the middle 1920s, and he even ranks Vizquel ahead of Lou Boudreau.

As Hargrove said the other night, "I'm awestruck by how Omar plays. I don't think anyone in the history of the game has ever played shortstop like him."

The man has five Gold Gloves. He has only one error next to his name. That's one error in the last 112 games.

He's never made an error in the postseason.

But this isn't about hits, runs and errors. It's about a man who has been an All-Star in the clubhouse ever since he joined the Tribe in 1994.

Hargrove knows this better than anyone. It's why the Tribe manager must find a way to make a statement for defense and for character, and he can do that by naming Vizquel.

In his locker, Vizquel has a calendar.

It's where he keeps track of all his personal appearances, his things to do. Most other players have a hard time knowing what they'll be doing tomorrow, much less six weeks from now.

They'll say, "Ask my wife."

They'll say, "Ask my agent, he keeps track of things."

Not Vizquel. He has it all there, in his own precise writing. He does it so he can find the time to speak at the Old Stone Church in downtown Cleveland, as he did recently to raise money for Rainbow Babies and Children's Hospital.

He does it so he can raise money for arts in the schools, a passion of his—Vizquel loves to draw.

He does it because he's an adult, and it's the right thing to do.

Three weeks after he joined the Indians, Vizquel had his worst day in the majors.

Three errors.

Three errors in one game.

He still shakes his head, thinking about it. He booted a grounder. He dropped a pop-up. He bobbled a throw.

This from a man who came to Cleveland as a Gold Glove winner.

When it was over and the Indians lost, Vizquel stood in front of the unforgiving glare of the TV lights. His teammates watched in respect as Vizquel never flinched, over and over admitting his mistakes.

"I made a mess of the whole game," he said. "I cost us seven runs. No excuse for that."

And he offered none.

He could have, because he played that game with the stomach flu and a fever. Some of his teammates knew that, too.

But there were no alibis from Omar.

"That taught me a lot," first baseman Jim Thome said. "It taught me that I have to face the writers and fans even when I have a bad day."

Ballplayers can be spoiled. Ballplayers can be nit-pickers. Ballplayers can act as if their job was to dig the Suez Canal with a teaspoon.

Not Vizquel.

He loves the game. He loves infield practice. He loves the interviews. He loves the fans.

"He makes time for so many good things," said Davis, the liaison between the front office and the players. "Several times a week, I get requests from sick and/or dying children who say Omar is their favorite player. I get their phone numbers and Omar calls them back."

It's not easy, talking to kids who are dying—or visiting them, which Vizquel also does.

"I also know he raises money for the Cuyahoga Board of Mental Retardation, and he visits the people at the adult-training center," Davis said.

Vizquel looks at those sick kids. He looks at the adults who haven't been as blessed as most of us.

He fights back the tears and smiles.

He thinks about them when little things go wrong. He thinks about them when the Indians ask him to break in yet another guy at second base, a guy who never played the position before.

Omar Vizquel thinks about more than himself, more than baseball.

Mike Hargrove knows all this.

He also knows that a strong case can be made for Rodriguez, Jeter and Garciaparra. He knows they are better hitters than Vizquel. They are not his equal in the field, but they are very close.

He knows they are three shortstops who might be All-Stars for the next 10 years.

Vizquel is 31. He is at his peak. He is batting .299 with 14 stolen bases. He plays shortstop like Picasso paints.

Finally, Vizquel has never been an All-Star.

If it doesn't happen this year, it might never come to pass. Not with all those young shortstops in the American League.

"All I'll say is Omar is having an All-Star season," Hargrove said. "And I know what he means to this team."

Hargrove seems prepared to take the heat if he has to leave one of the star shortstops off his roster and keep Vizquel.

"That would mean so much to me," Vizquel said. "I mean, I want it so much, I'm afraid to talk about it."

On Vizquel's calendar, he has an opening for July 7. It's when the All-Star Game is in Denver, and he deserves to be there.

6/30/1998

Tough times have changed Lofton

To KENNY LOFTON, he'll always be "Uncle B."

Uncle B., the steel worker. Uncle B., the card player. Uncle B., the man who could talk to Lofton in a way that a woman never could.

He'd tell Lofton: "Lofton, here's the deal. You can keep doing what you're doing and end up in big trouble, or you can stop. The choice is yours."

B.F. Collins didn't yell. Didn't have to.

Uncle B. was bigger than screaming, bigger than needing to take off his belt and take it to Lofton's rear end.

Not in size, just bigger in Lofton's eyes.

That's because Uncle B. was the father Lofton never had, the man who helped Rosie Person to raise the Indians center fielder on the mean streets of East Chicago, Indiana.

Rosie Person is Lofton's grandmother. When she needed someone who could talk to a young Lofton, it was Uncle B.

"He was the male role model for a lot of us in the family," Lofton said. "He never beat us. He never had to."

It seemed as if Uncle B. never would die, but he did. Died at 51. Died of lung cancer. Died a long, painful death.

The man of the family—gone too soon.

Last month, Lofton helped to bury Uncle B.

"It was hard to believe," Lofton said. "It's still real hard for me to talk about. The emotions start to come up, and some of them, I really don't want to feel again."

Lofton dropped his voice as he talked about Uncle B. This conversation took place in the Tribe dugout, about 90 minutes before a game. Lofton was thinking about the funeral, thinking about looking around the church and realizing that he was one of the oldest men left in his family.

At the wake, Lofton spoke. To this day, he's not sure what he said, or even how he managed to say it. He just prayed, and the words came.

He found himself stepping into Uncle B.'s shoes at age 33.

"So much has happened this past year," Lofton said. "Nothing in my life prepared me for this."

It began in October, when Lofton ripped up his left shoulder while sliding head-first into first base in the final playoff game of the 1999 season. Lofton never had any type of surgery before.

His fleet feet . . .

His incredible hand-eye coordination . . .

The physical gifts that enabled him to dunk with ease at the University of Arizona, or leap over the center-field wall to rob a slack-jawed opponent of a home run at Jacobs Field . . .

He found it impossible to imagine life without them.

Then came injury, sickness, death.

"Right before my operation, my great-aunt died," Lofton said. "She also had cancer. That really hurt me, because she was close to my grandmother and me. We used to go to her house all the time."

Meanwhile, Uncle B. was dueling cancer.

And Lofton was heading under the knife.

The remarkable part of this story is that Lofton was back in the lineup on Opening Day, coming back faster from that kind of reconstructive rotator-cuff surgery than any major-leaguer ever had before.

In the middle of it, Lofton was losing two people who had been very close to him, two people who joined with his grandmother to make sure he had a home. A home that was safe. A home that made sense.

"It's hard to explain what it's like to go through something like this," Lofton said. "So many things happened at once."

Lofton said that this season has been about so much more than baseball.

It's about just getting healthy, trying to deal with a shoulder that is cranky, sometimes sore, sometimes more than sore.

It's about being dropped out of the leadoff slot for the first time in his career, about having the worst season of his career—in terms of batting average (.262), 48 points below his career mark of .310.

It's about reclaiming his spot at the top of the order, about growing spiritually and emotionally.

"I guess it's about dealing with life," Lofton said.

A kind of life he never knew before.

8/27/2000

Nagy gives Indians his all . . . as usual

YOU'RE CHARLES NAGY, and you've heard the whispers.

Your elbow is like a cracked peanut shell, your fastball a fading memory.

You're a nice guy, a gritty competitor, a three-time All-Star—blah, blah, blah. You hear the front office talk about you, and it sounds like they're paying you respect—as in last respects, practicing their lines for your baseball funeral.

You're Charles Nagy, and you're 34 years old. The doctors have told you that you have no cartilage in your right elbow after having season-ending surgery last summer, meaning every time you throw, bone grinds against bone.

You're not supposed to be able to throw hard enough, not supposed to be able to withstand the pain. You're certainly not supposed to do what you did yesterday at Yankee Stadium, limiting New York to one run in seven innings.

But you did.

You took the mound and became the first Tribe starter in 11 games to pitch into the seventh inning—in the previous 10 games, the starters had a 7.52 earned-run average.

You took the mound two days after Chuck Finley grabbed the back of his neck and headed for the disabled list. And Bartolo Colon clutched his elbow, and headed back to Cleveland for X-rays, and perhaps a spot on the shelf to rest.

You took the mound on the sunny Sunday afternoon in a park where the subway clicketyclacks by, where the Yankees have chewed up one pitcher after another while winning the World Series in four of the past five years.

Everyone expected New York to spit you out by the fourth inning.

Instead, you bit your lower lip. You reached back for a little more zest on the fastball, a little more sink on the sinker, a little more life in an arm that had been prematurely pronounced dead.

You're Charles Nagy, and you're the reason the Indians took 2-of-3 in New York this weekend, the winning pitcher in yesterday's 4-3 verdict.

If you weren't Charles Nagy, you'd gloat.

But you're Charles Harrison Nagy of Fairfield, Connecticut. You're "the original stoic New Englander," according to Tribe GM John Hart.

You don't whine. You don't make excuses. You take everything to heart but show virtually nothing on your face.

So you don't grab the horns of the doubters and engage in an oral argument. You just say, "I don't care what people think. I don't care what they say. If I can pitch, I'll pitch."

So you pitch.

You pitched well in spring training, a 2.08 ERA. But your fastball rarely was above 85 mph, well-below the major-league average of 90 mph.

They left you behind in Winter Haven to throw against some rookie kids in Florida on diamonds in the back where only a few scouts and radar guns watched.

You pitched well.

Then you went to Class AAA Buffalo, where your ERA was a sparkling 1.00 in your last five starts, where you didn't allow a home run in 38 innings, where you won five games in a row.

But they still talked about the radar gun.

You're sick of radar guns, but you don't say that.

Instead, you tell the writers, "I never was a guy who overpowered people."

At least not since 1993, when you had that major surgery to rebuild your shoulder—something that was career threatening. But you came back to make 192 consecutive starts, pitching with sore muscles, head colds, aches and pains.

When they hand you the ball, you take it.

"I don't know any other way," you say.

You don't want to hear about the radar gun, about the difference between an 89 mph fastball and 87, or 85.

You don't deny that it's part of the game, that speed helps, but speed isn't everything.

You say, "I can change my motion and drag and drill it up there

about 91 mph, but that wouldn't help me. I'd lose my sinker, my movement. Any hitter will tell you that an 86 mph fastball that moves is
much tougher to hit than a 91 mph fastball that's straight."

Yesterday, the Yankees said the same thing as they could only dent
you for Derek Jeter's opposite field home run. Twelve of your 21 outs
came on ground balls, which is how it should be when you're pitching
like the Charles Nagy who won 90 games between 1994–99.

You're Charles Nagy, and you're doing this your way.

The right way.

You keep your feelings to yourself. You stay patient. You work hard.
You wait for your team to need you, and you keep telling them you'll
do anything they want—start, long relief, just name it.

You tell yourself that if you just keep pitching, it will work out.

Yesterday, it did.

You smile, at least inside, when you hear Manager Charlie Manuel
say, "Nagy surprised me with his fastball. He blew it past a couple of
guys. He gave us exactly what we needed."

You like that.

Being needed. Being relevant. Being a part of the organization that
drafted you back in 1988.

You're Charles Nagy, and today you're a major-league pitcher—
again.

And for that, the Indians should be very grateful to you.

6/4/2001

Big Games

Three seconds is plenty for Jordan

THREE SECONDS.

That was long enough for the Cavaliers to seemingly beat the Chicago Bulls, yet long enough to lose to Michael Jordan.

For most of the Cavaliers, it was the longest three seconds of their young lives. For Jordan, three seconds was just long enough to make a statement that silenced the sellout crowd of 20,273, who saw Jordan's Bulls defeat the Cavs 101-100 to advance to the second round of the NBA playoffs against New York.

Three seconds.

"That's a long, long time in an NBA basketball game," said Chicago coach Doug Collins.

So it is. Just ask Cavs center Brad Daugherty.

"This game was really hard to take," he said. "We knew what they were going to do. We knew they were going to swarm around our big men and we knew to get the ball out to our guards for 3-pointers.

"And the thing was, our guards were hitting the shots, 3-pointers, everything. At the end of the game, we needed a great out-of-bounds play to win and we got it. I'm telling you, we had the perfect game plan and then The Guy goes and makes a shot like that."

The Guy is Jordan, whose 18-foot jump shot at the buzzer gave the Bulls the victory—and that's one whopping understatement of this shot, this game, these two teams who "made more clutch plays than I ever remember seeing in a playoff game," said Cavs coach Lenny Wilkens.

It was Wilkens who set the stage for Jordan's heroics. With six seconds left, the Bulls took a 99-98 lead on a Jordan (who else?) jumper from 12 feet on the left wing.

The Cavs called timeout. Wilkens is a master of the out-of-bounds play, and he came up with a corker—the old give-and-go.

He put Larry Nance on the left side of the court and all the other Cavs on the right. Craig Ehlo took the ball out and passed it to Nance. Then Ehlo cut to the basket and caught a pass from Nance for a layup.

Three seconds. That's all it took, and it gave the Cavs a 100-99 lead.

The only fault that could be found is that the Cavs scored too fast, the play worked too well. But if Ehlo had passed up that highway to the basket, he would have a lot more explaining to do today, than he does as the guy who couldn't stop Jordan at the buzzer.

"Even after Ehlo's shot went in, I still knew we had three seconds," said Jordan. "Three seconds is plenty of time."

Especially if you're Michael Jordan.

The Cavs knew Jordan would get the ball, and they knew he would take the last shot. Jordan knew they knew. The question was what would they do about it.

"I needed three fakes to get that last shot off," said fake-a-second Jordan. "One to get open and away from Ehlo so I could catch the in-bounds pass, one after I caught the pass to dribble away from Ehlo again and then one more fake so I could get the shot off over Ehlo.

"Ehlo . . . I just couldn't shake the guy."

So he shaked-and-baked over him.

Jordan caught the ball about 30 feet from the basket, faked right, drove left and ended up in the middle of the floor.

"That's when I had this bad feeling," said Wilkens. "Michael won't miss too many shots in the key."

Jordan pulled up a step behind the foul line.

"From the beginning, I knew I'd take a jumper," said Jordan. "I just didn't know from where."

Or how.

"When I went up for the shot, there was Ehlo again with his hands up," said Jordan. "I knew I had to hang there awhile to get my balance and everything right. So I pumped. I mean, it's not a shot you practice. It's a shot you just do."

With the clock clicking off that last, seemingly everlasting second, Jordan hovered. Both he and time seemed to be suspended in air.

"I sort of shot it on the way down," he said. "I barely saw the rim, I don't know how it went in. It's funny, I didn't see it go in, but I just knew it would."

The ball sort of circled the rim, yet it never seemed in real danger of being coughed out. The shot did show how two basketballs can indeed fit inside the rim, because Jordan needed every inch.

"I just don't see how Michael stayed in the air that long," said

Daugherty, who played with Jordan at North Carolina. "But it is the most outstanding shot I've ever seen."

It also was points 43 and 44 for Jordan, who averaged 39 for the 5-game series.

"I said all along, that a 1-man team couldn't beat Cleveland," said Jordan. "I said we—the Chicago Bulls—could beat Cleveland, not just Michael Jordan. Today, we beat them. I hit the last shot, but I had plenty of help." The gracious Jordan talked about Bill Cartwright's tip-in with 1:35 left and Scott Pippen's 3-pointer with 1:05 remaining, both shots giving the Bulls leads.

But in the end, Cartwright was the Bulls' second-leading scorer with 16 points, and Jordan accounted for 44 percent of his team's offense while taking 39 percent of the shots.

Meanwhile, the Cavs had three 20-point men—Ehlo 24, Mark Price 23, and Ron Harper 22. Those players also combined for 7-for-12 from 3-point range.

5/8/1989

It's enough to restore a man's faith

I NEVER THOUGHT I'D SEE THIS DAY.

I never thought I'd see the Indians in the World Series. Even this year. Even when they were clearly the Best Team In Baseball.

Somehow, I feared that the best wouldn't be good enough. Something would happen. Something always did.

The Indians last won a pennant in 1954. I was born in 1955.

I heard about Indians' teams like this. I heard about Lou Boudreau and 1948, and I heard about 1954, and the Indians' team that won more games than any American League team before or since.

But those were like family folk tales, passed down from one generation to the next—growing more mysterious and incredible with each passing year. Those were like days when the dinosaurs roamed the earth. We'd never see it again.

Then came last year and the new ballpark. Then came this year and these Indians, who seem to never lose. And last night came the American League pennant with the 4-0 victory over Seattle.

I see it. I know it's real. But somehow, I can't believe it.

I feel like Manager Mike Hargrove, who said, "I still have this feeling of disbelief. Like it is happening, but it can't be happening. I still am pinching myself to make sure that this is what is happening to Mike Hargrove and the Cleveland Indians."

Hargrove invested 14 years of his life in this quest, starting when he joined the Tribe as a player in 1979 and continuing as he managed at every level of the farm system—and then taking over a team that lost 105 games in 1991.

He said he always wanted to be here when the Indians finally won— but he had to wonder when that would happen . . . if it would happen . . . or if it did, would he be alive to see it?

Last night was all those things to Hargrove or to anyone else who spent decades waiting and praying for this day.

To fully appreciate what the Indians did on Oct. 17, 1995, you had to be here in the Kingdome. You had to hear the 58,489 fans shake this building and cheer against the Indians on every pitch, trying to carry the Mariners home on a wave of raw emotion.

To be here is to know why Mike Hargrove called the Kingdome, "The Mouth of the Lion."

I sat here in the teeth of that lion, and I watched Dennis Martinez do something even Bob Feller couldn't. He won a game in the post-season, and he did it against a pitcher who was like Feller in his prime.

Dennis Martinez is 40 years old. His knee hurts. His shoulder hurts. But more importantly, his pride was taking a beating when he stepped on the mound last night because he believed no one gave him a chance against Randy Johnson, a man at the height of his powers who hadn't lost a game since Aug. 1.

Martinez is like many Indians fans. He has a feeling that time is running out.

To Martinez, it seemed that no one expected him to deliver a pennant on this night.

But last night, he pitched the game of his life.

In the words of Seattle manager Lou Piniella, "Dennis went inside and outside with his pitches. He changed speeds. He threw to spots. He was like a surgeon out there."

Yes, and he cut the heart right out of the Seattle Mariners.

He went to the mound believing that this was the game the Indians had to win—that they couldn't take a chance on a seventh game on enemy turf.

Knowing that he had to be as perfect as any 40-year-old pitcher could be, he went to Hargrove before the game. He asked for his personal catcher, 38-year-old Tony Pena, rather than scheduled starter Sandy Alomar.

Some managers would say, "Hey, no one makes out the lineup but me." Some would argue with Martinez.

But Hargrove looked into those piercing brown eyes and at the leathery face that has seen so much pain and come back from the depths of alcoholism.

Hargrove knew that Martinez was going to war and wanted Pena in the foxhole. Proving why he deserves to be Manager of the Year, he wrote Pena's name in the lineup.

"When Dennis asked for me, it made my heart feel so good," Pena said. "We were in this together."

Playoff MVP Orel Hershiser talked about "the sense of urgency surrounding this team."

That is what Martinez and Pena brought to the game.

"Dennis was so intense, he didn't hear the noise," Pena said. "It was like we were the hand and the glove, working together. If we had to win that game, 1-0, we could have done it."

Instead, Martinez left after seven scoreless innings. He left with his team leading 4-0 when 22-year-old Julian Tavarez took over in the bottom of the eighth.

He shut them down in the eighth. Then Hargrove handed the ball to Jose Mesa for the ninth, who threw another zero on the scoreboard to put his exclamation mark on history.

Hargrove managed like he had all season—he made his plans, he stuck to them.

But that makes this game sound too cold, too clinical.

Think about what happened on this night.

Kenny Lofton drove in the Tribe's first run with a single to left field in the fifth inning.

Then think about the eighth inning—when Lofton scored from second base on a passed ball.

"They weren't watching, so I just kept running," Lofton said.

Think about a pitcher born in 1955, the year after the Indians last pennant—and how this pitcher had won 231 big-league games, but none in the postseason.

Think about what happened to him three hours before last night's game.

Martinez sat in the lobby of the Crown Center Hotel. He was waiting for a friend, and Bob Feller stopped by. They talked a little bit.

Feller is the greatest pitcher in the history of this franchise. His one disappointment in baseball is never having won a postseason game.

Martinez was facing those same demons last night. He had the history of this franchise and of his own postseason failures on his shoulders.

Feller wished Martinez luck, and Dennis said he'd take all the luck he could get.

But he didn't need any. Neither did the Indians. Great ones never do.

10/18/1995

For once, silence tells Indians' story

SO THIS IS HOW IT ENDS.

This is what it's like when 44,000 people are so silent, it hurts.

This is what it's like when Jacobs Field looks like a cemetery, the same stadium that shook with cheers and chants of AL-BERT only 18 hours before.

Now it is empty, except for a few white hot-dog wrappers fluttering in the wind like miniature surrender flags.

This is how it ends when a usually boisterous locker room is a tomb. Its grown men shaking their heads while staring at nothing. It is 25 players in a room, but most of them feeling so alone.

"It feels as if someone just stepped on my heart," said Omar Vizquel.

Vizquel is the Tribe's graceful shortstop. He tried to explain the Indians' 4-3 loss to Baltimore in 12 innings. He tried to talk about what was won, what was lost—and how the Indians will play no more games this year.

He talked strategy and breaks.

He talked about how Roberto Alomar came to home plate with the tying run on second base.

"We had two strikes on him and two outs," he said. "Jose [Mesa] was pitching with a [3-2] lead. Ninety percent of the time, we win."

Not this time.

"Two strikes on Robbie Alomar," Vizquel repeated. "Jose threw a pitch. It was strike three, down the middle. They called it a ball. I couldn't believe it. He was struck out, but they called it a ball. You'd think that the umpires were mad at us instead of at him."

He meant that the fallout from Robbie Alomar's spitting incident nearly led to an umpire boycott. He thought of how the umpires were outraged by Alomar's presence on the field, believing Alomar should have been immediately suspended.

Vizquel thought they would keep Alomar on a short leash and grant him only a big strike zone, because Alomar should not have been in uniform (at least according to the umpires).

Yet he caught a break from the umpires. He beat the Indians.

"He stuck his bat out and dropped that single into left-center," Vizquel said. "He was fooled on the pitch, but he got a hit, anyway."

That made the score 3-3. That led to 12 innings of agony, and Alomar winning it all with his 400-foot homer.

Nothing lucky about that hit.

"It was like it was just not meant to be for us," said Vizquel.

Jim Thome sat in front of his locker, staring at his right hand.

"Broken," he said. "A stress fracture [of the hamate bone]."

Thome is the Tribe's third hitter, a man who hammered 38 homers this season.

"I hurt it in the first game in Baltimore," he said. "I fouled a pitch straight back, and that was it."

What kind of luck is that?

Thome swings at a pitch . . . fouls it off . . . and breaks a bone in his hand? He played two more games. By yesterday, he could barely grip the bat.

So instead of having Thome at third base in the most important game of the season, there was Jeff Kent. Kent batted four times and left four runners on base. He was shaky at third, although his glove at least didn't cost the team a run.

But if you are an Indians fan, you had to know this was a bad omen—seeing so much of Jeff Kent in the playoffs. What next, the return of Jeff Manto?

"You have no idea how frustrating it was for me to just sit and watch," Thome said. "Nothing I could do."

It was that way for the Indians. No matter what they did, it wasn't enough. Somehow, they found a way to strike out 23 Oriole hitters—and still lost.

They found a way to lose even with Cal Ripken (of all people) pulling a boneheaded move and being thrown out by Manny Ramirez (of all people). They lost even though four Oriole infielders couldn't catch one crucial pop up.

They received a courageous, six-inning, 12-strikeout performance from Charles Nagy—but lost.

This is what 99 victories gets a team. You win a marathon by two miles—and then they tell you to run a sprint. You stub your toe and stumble. The race is over.

You end up with this key matchup with the winning run on second base in the bottom of the ninth inning—Jesse Orosco vs. Jose Vizcaino.

How can it come down to that? But it did.

The Indians know Orosco. They know he's no Sparky Lyle—but he was yesterday as he retired both Vizcaino and Kenny Lofton .

They watched the Orioles' Todd Zeile play third base like the reincarnation of Brooks Robinson. They saw left-hander David Wells pitch like a young Dave McNally. They could have sworn that Albert Belle would savage Armando Benitez, just as he did Friday night. Only this time, Belle was fooled by a slider.

They were inspired when Sandy Alomar drove in two runs with a clutch hit, yet younger brother Robbie came along to steal Sandy's thunder.

Sandy was the first member of that family to make the All-Star team, but now it is Robbie who is the real hero back home in Ponce, Puerto Rico—because Robbie keeps doing things just like this.

Robbie spits on an umpire ("a terrible thing my brother did," according to Sandy) and brings embarrassment to the family name— and he ends up the hero.

That was why the Indians sat stunned in the dressing room. That was how it ended for them after 12 innings and 4 hours, 41 minutes.

There was so much to talk about, yet so little to say.

10/6/1996

Dream dies hard for Zips

THE WALLS WERE WHITE CEMENT BLOCKS. They were sweating, water oozing from the cracks. The floor was a hard gray, like a table in a morgue.

The place reeked like a damp old sock. This wasn't so much the visitors locker room at Virginia Tech, as it was a bunker, a tomb in the bowels of Lane Stadium.

It was cold and hot at the same time, the humidity so thick, you swear you could see it. You certainly could feel it sucking the breath

right out of you, a warm, wet fist around your throat, sweat breaking
out on your forehead.

But the cold came from the rain. The unrelenting rain coming from
the clouds hanging so low, the nearby mountains were nothing more
than a rumor.

It was more like water torture for the Akron football team, which
had just lost 52-23 to Virginia Tech. It was feeling the walls closing in,
the ceiling dropping down on them.

This is what it feels like when dreams die.

The Zips came to Virginia Tech knowing they would face the 11th-
ranked team in the country and the favorite to win the Heisman Trophy in quarterback Michael Vick—and that they were supposed to be
31-point underdogs.

But Akron took the opening kickoff and drove to Tech's 23. Field
goal blocked. Second possession, all the way to the Tech 3. Settled for
a field goal.

"We can do it," screamed the players on the bench. "Come on now,
this is our day."

Their day.

Before the game, several players heard a sermon from The Chapel's
Mike Arnold. The theme was "Going Through the Door." It featured a
parable from the gospel of Mark, about a man who tells Jesus, "I believe, but help me with my unbelief."

How this team wanted to believe.

How this team truly listened as head coach Lee Owens sent them
onto the field with these words: "You want respect? You get it on the
field. You get in their face. You rip it away from them. You have prepared nine months for this game, nine months! This is your day."

How this team ignored it when, in the middle of Owens' rousing
speech, the Virginia Tech cannon roared.

They didn't know it would be like that all afternoon: Boom. BOOM.
BOOM! KABOOM! Seven times, one for each Tech touchdown.

That's because Akron still believed.

The Zips had their game plan. They had a confidence that came from
their 7-4 season last year and 45 upperclassmen in uniform, from being
picked as the second-best team in the Mid-American Conference.

"The last time we played here [1995], it was awful," Owens told a
couple of his team captains the night before the game. "I heard that
cannon 11 times, one for each TD. Fans were yelling, 'What's a Zip?
What's a Zip?' I never want to hear that again."

The players began telling stories.

"I remember when we played at LSU [1997] and a 6-year-old kid mooned us and kept screaming: 'Tiger bait. Tiger bait,'" senior defensive back Rich Reliford said of the game in which Akron was spanked 56-0.

Quarterback Butchie Washington talked about a pep rally a few years ago. "All that showed up was us, the band and [kangaroo mascot] Zippy."

They talked about a training camp in 1996 at Camp Chof, where the flies were so thick, they swarmed anything that resembled food. They talked about the stench that came from the manure spread on nearby fields.

"We did have some sanitary issues back then," Owens said.

The players laughed.

And they believed. After games at Nebraska, at LSU, at Penn State. They had been through so much, this group.

Most came in when Akron was the second-worst Division I team in the country, and they survived to see the team come back from a 23-9 deficit to win at Navy last year.

Maybe, just maybe, they could deal with Virginia Tech.

As the players left the dressing room, they chanted: "Do You Want To Get BIZ-EE? Time To Get BIZ-EE!"

And they chanted, "BLOOD! SWEAT! CHAMPIONSHIP!"

Over and over.

BLOOD! SWEAT! CHAMPIONSHIP!

The words on their lips as they headed onto the field, their cleats going SCRAPE, SCRAPE, SCRAPE on the cement.

"They think we're a joke," yelled Akron defensive back Brad Detwiler. "They're laughing at us."

BLOOD! SWEAT! CHAMPIONSHIP!

This team was David, looking for a few stones for its slingshot.

The problem is, Goliath wouldn't stand still long enough to be a target. The giant was a 6-foot-1, 215-pound eel of a quarterback with a rocket launcher for an arm and feet quicker than snake tongues.

During the week, the Akron defensive coaches handed out copies of Vick's picture, a bull's-eye on his chest.

"Watch his eyes," the Akron coaches told their players.

But how can you keep track of his eyes, when all you see is the back of his No. 7 jersey?

Fast?

You say Michael Vick is fast?

Well, he's so fast, Florida State couldn't catch him last year, and Florida State was supposed to be the quickest team in the country.

Contain Michael Vick?

It would be easier to dam up the Missouri River with a couple of toothpicks.

Akron thought it had Vick sacked for a 10-yard loss.

It became a 16-yard TD dash.

It thought it had flushed Vick out of the pocket.

Sure did, only it turned unto a 63-yard TD gallop.

And then Vick threw a 59-yard TD pass and a 34-yard TD pass.

All this in the first half, when Virginia Tech took a 35-17 lead.

Vick did this on a field that went SQUISH, SQUISH, SQUISH under every footstep. He did it when others in Akron blue, gold and white were slipping, sliding, sucking mud.

"WARM UP THE BUS," Virginia Tech fans screamed as the Akron players returned to their dungeon for halftime.

"WARM UP THE BUS! WARM UP THE BUS!"

The Akron defensive coaches met in the tiny shower area, drawing up more futile plans to try to lasso Vick. In a small office, the offensive coaches scrawled their Xs and Os, trying to figure out a way to outscore Vick and an offense ranked No. 1 in the nation a year ago.

Players sat on the concrete floor, sweating, muttering, guzzling water, crushing paper cups, their eyes wide but not really seeing much. Some of the players, especially the underclassmen, looked a bit shell-shocked.

"It's not physical," pleaded Owens. "It's mental. It's blown assignments. We need to focus. One lapse of concentration, and it's over. He's gone."

No need to say *his* name.

Michael Vick.

"He's even faster in person than on tape," said Butchie Washington, the Akron quarterback who played so well, throwing for 248 yards, moving the offense, holding his own against the best defense he'll face all year.

Before the game, Owens kept telling people, "Butchie is our Michael Vick."

It sounded good, but at halftime, everyone knew better.

No one is Michael Vick.

Vick was 7-for-11 passing, 186 yards. He ran the ball eight times,

102 yards. He had either an arm or a leg in four TDs. He averaged nearly 20 yards per play.

No matter how hard they had prepared, how many weights they had lifted, how many sprints they had run, how long they had studied films and scouting reports—none of it mattered. Not when Goliath disappeared from sight in what seemed to be a wink of the eye.

Yet, Owens told his team: "We just have to fight them a play at a time, a series at a time. We can't cheat ourselves. We can't cheat the program. We can turn this thing around."

No they couldn't.

More cannons boomed.

More appearances by the maroon turkey, the Tech mascot that ran onto the field after every Hokies TD and did a bench press for each point with a phony barbell set. More rain.

More *squish, squish, squish*, mud flying from Vick's cleats into the faces of the Akron players.

Akron's offense had some nice moments. Jimmy Gray—all 5-foot-7, 165 pounds of him—zigged and zagged and racked up 80 yards in 12 carries. Lavel Bailey caught five passes, including a 34-yard Picasso from Washington.

Punter Andy Jerdon.

This freshman with blond hair, freckles and the face of a 12-year-old who just earned a scholarship.

This kid "who milks cows, takes care of chickens and all that farm stuff," according to senior Rich Reliford.

This young man whom Owens had put black dye under his eyes so he'd look older, meaner.

Jerdon didn't panic when faced with the bare teeth of Tech's infamous rush, punting six times for an average of 43 yards.

So there was good news, and that was what Owens stressed when it was over, when he saw the dead stares of his players.

Coming into the game, Owens had two speeches ready.

One if his team played well.

One if they didn't.

"You can't lose your whole season in the first game at a place like this," he said, meaning Lane Stadium/Worsham Field, which proudly proclaims, HOME OF THE FIGHTING GOBBLERS!

This is where the fans are so close, you seem to feel their warm breath on the back of your neck as you stand on the Akron sideline. You hear every insult, every sarcastic laugh.

A game such as this can make a season for a team. Or ruin it.

"We will have no finger-pointing," Owens said after the game. "I know one of our goals was to beat a ranked team. I know we could play better. I know it hurts."

He paused, staring at the blank faces of some of his players, faces hiding the pain.

"But we have to turn the page," he said. " . . . That's what we do now, we turn the page."

The next chapter is a game at Central Michigan next week.

"A game we can win," Owens said. "So we start thinking about them, right now. We leave this game right here, right in this room."

The tomb where Akron's dream died.

9/3/2000

Massillon-McKinley means everything

IT WAS A QUIET FALL AFTERNOON, one of the few where Lee Owens slipped away to spend time with his kids.

They were in the middle of a lake, in a boat, far from the pressures of coaching football.

Then he heard a voice echo over the water, seemingly from nowhere, "Hey, Coach, we gonna beat McKinley?"

The mood was shattered; the guilt poured down.

Owens was the new coach at Massillon. The McKinley game was weeks away. He already was working 12-hour days, virtually seven days a week. He just wanted a few hours with his family.

But how dare he not spend every waking moment thinking about Canton McKinley?

"When you coach at Massillon, every day of your life, you hear something about McKinley," Owens said. "Either what you did wrong in the last game, or people wanting to know if you'll beat them the next time."

It's 12 years later, and Owens is the head coach in college at Akron.

"The Massillon-McKinley game is the biggest game I've ever been involved with, and even bigger than Ohio State–Michigan," he said. "I was an assistant at Ohio State, so I can say that."

Owens paused, then laughed.

"The best thing I did in my four years at Massillon [1988–91] was go 3-1 against McKinley," he said. "To survive at Massillon, you have to consistently beat McKinley."

Kerry Hodakievic will never forget the parade.

The year was 1998, his first as McKinley's head coach. He beat Massillon, and there was a caravan after the game, from Massillon's Paul Brown Tiger Stadium back to McKinley.

"These people lined the streets, up and down Lincoln Way and Tuscarawas," he remembers. "They yelled and held signs, mostly for us. A few against us. It was the greatest feeling I've ever had as a coach."

And it made Hodakievic feel accepted in Canton.

"People came up to me after we beat Massillon and said, 'You're a real Bulldog now,'" he said. "It's like you can't be a Canton McKinley Bulldog until you beat Massillon."

And when you lose?

"You just thank God that you have a family who loves you, because it seems no one else does," said Hodakievic, who was 1-1 vs. Massillon. "You don't want to go out in public. You don't want to talk to anyone."

Now an assistant at Walsh University, Hodakievic still aches from last year's 35-7 spanking he received from Massillon.

"It was only 7-7 at the half," he said, his voice trailing off.

Then the game got out of hand, and Hodakievic felt as if someone had just ripped out his heart and fed it to the Massillon tiger.

Jack Rose understands.

Now the head football coach at GlenOak, Rose had a 1-6 record vs. McKinley during his six years at Massillon.

To this day, he can barely speak about the rivalry because there are so many painful memories.

"You lose, and it's like a death in the family," he said. "It just stays with you, and it erases everything else your team has done. I remember us going into the 1996 game. We were 9-0, ranked No. 1 in the state. They beat us, and I'm serious, it was like someone died."

Rose only smiles when he thinks of the 100th Massillon-McKinley meeting. It was such an event, even *Sports Illustrated* covered it.

"We were undersized and certainly not the favorite," he said. "But we played magnificently that day."

If only the season could have ended right there.

Unfortunately, Massillon and McKinley squared off again two weeks later, this time in the state playoffs. McKinley won.

"I didn't even get a chance to say, 'We got 'em,' for more than a few weeks," said Rose, who has revived GlenOak's program.

"Coaching at Massillon was one of the great experiences of my life," he said. "There's no better place to be on a fall Friday night than Massillon when the Tigers are playing at home, there's a sellout crowd and you hear the roar of the fans as you come out of that stadium tunnel."

What is it about Massillon and McKinley? What is it about these two schools and their fans?

"From Massillon's point of view, you feel like McKinley is the big city [Canton] and they're looking down at you," Owens said. "When you coach at Massillon, you sense football keeps the town on the map, that it truly is the lifeblood of the community. As the coach, you are more well known than the mayor, the priest, the president of the steel company or anyone else in town."

Owens then recalled how there was a school levy on the ballot when he first took the job. It had failed a few times before that, and he spent a lot of time campaigning for the levy.

"I had people telling me if we could beat McKinley, it sure would help the levy pass," he said. "I didn't know if that was true, but it sure put even more pressure on that game because I felt a new school was at stake."

In 1989, Massillon did win. The levy did pass. A new high school was built. Was there a connection?

"All I know is that beating McKinley didn't hurt," Owens said.

Massillon-McKinley is like no other high school rivalry, "because there's a real hatred between the fans. Not the players and coaches, but the fans," said Owens.

Rose and former McKinley coach Thom McDaniels (1981–97) were cordial, chatting at clinics, not afraid to shake hands and say respectful things about each other and their teams.

"But the fans didn't like that," McDaniels said. "They held that against me, the fact I like Jack Rose."

Or as Rose said, "It's not like Thom and I would go out to dinner, but I guess some fans thought we shouldn't even speak to each other."

Owens now admits the rivalry did not bring out the best in him.

In his first year, he refused to trade game films with McKinley because he thought his films were of better quality. That created hard feelings on both sides.

Then on game day, he didn't want to bring his team out of the dressing room first. Neither did McKinley.

"So we both just sat and waited and waited," Owens said. "Finally, after about 20-30 minutes, the officials convinced both teams to come out together."

Owens then was silent, thinking about those times, those games.

"The fans loved it when I wouldn't trade films, but now, I wish I hadn't acted like that," Owens said. "As a coach, you just get caught up in it. In Massillon, everyone tells you that food tastes better, business is better, the economy is better, the schools are better, everything is better if you beat McKinley. You feel like you just can't lose."

The week of the game is a blur of pep rallies, banquets and booster club meetings for coaches on both sides.

"It's like your first nine games of the season didn't mean anything," Owens said. "I barely slept during McKinley week. You do ask yourself if this is healthy, if the game isn't too big. But in the end, all you can do is think about the game. And when you win, it's the ultimate high. It's one of those red-letter days, right after the date of your marriage and the birth of your children."

Of these four coaches, McDaniels lasted the longest in the spotlight, 16 years at McKinley. He still has hundreds of nasty fan letters. He knows about the FIRE MCDANIELS signs some fans brought to games.

He had an 11-6 record vs. Massillon. He won a Division I state title and the *USA Today* national title in 1997.

"It's a little different at McKinley," he said. "They tell you if you just beat Massillon, that's enough. Well, it's not enough. If you lose to Massillon, it's miserable, but you can still beat Massillon and hear you didn't win a state title."

Now the coach at Warren Harding, McDaniels said the hardest part was in 1996, when his son Ben was the Bulldogs' quarterback. He was criticized for playing his kid, and then told he'd never beat Massillon with a sophomore quarterback.

"When we won that game, I was so proud of our team," he said. "Then Ben became the leader of those great teams [1996–98, including two state titles] and was 3-0 against Massillon. But my family went through a lot, even though we dominated Massillon in the 1990s. It still wasn't enough for some people."

McDaniels paused for a moment.

"The longer you have that job, it seemed like you made more enemies and had fewer friends," he said. "The way people view you and your team should never come down to just one game. That's wrong."

Yet, McDaniels said there was the tremendous satisfaction of coaching his two sons at McKinley, of leading that 1997 team to the mythical national title.

"I don't regret any of it," he said. "My kids became better people, tougher people, because of what they were exposed to and how they learned to handle it."

McDaniels just hopes tomorrow's game is a clean one, which he says wasn't the case last year.

"The Massillon-McKinley game is bigger than any coach, any player, any one thing," said McDaniels. "It's been around for 106 years. It's about tradition and respect. You want to have a good game, and you want to win with class, because that's what this rivalry should be about."

10/27/2000

KSU leaves us lasting memories

MOST KENT STATE FANS will remember how their team won this year, how they went to the NCAA Elite Eight, how they dominated the Mid-American Conference, how they had a 30-6 record.

But I'll always remember how they lost.

I'll remember how the Golden Flashes were as dignified and as classy in defeat as victory. I'll remember how they didn't lash out at officials, at each other. I'll remember how Coach Stan Heath lined up his players after the 81-69 loss to Indiana and made sure they shook hands and congratulated the winners.

I'll remember how they played the game with no trash-talk, no chest-thumping, nothing but five players on the court working together like fingers on the same hand.

I'll remember how Indiana swished its first eight jumpers from beyond the 3-point arc, how the Hoosiers acted like they were shooting in the driveway, and how it appeared Kent State wouldn't just lose, but be embarrassed as the Flashes trailed 34-14.

I'll remember how they came back, how they cut Indiana's lead to seven points with 6:37 left, how the issue really wasn't decided until Eric Thomas missed a 3-pointer with 40 seconds left, a shot that would have cut the Hoosiers lead to six points.

I'll remember how they weren't intimidated by the sellout crowd of 22,435 fans at Rupp Arena. I'll remember how my reaction was the same as Kent State's Heath, who said: "I saw a sea of red out there. Indiana did a great job of getting tickets to their fans."

I'll remember how a Bloomington, Indiana, writer told me, "This place is louder than [Indiana's] Assembly Hall."

I'll remember the Kent State fans, about 5,000, wearing gold shirts, waving signs, especially the one reading: THE ROAD TO THE FINAL FOUR COMES THRU KENT! And I'll remember thinking, "Who'd ever believe that?"

There is so much more about this Kent State team.

Understand that no opponent defended senior Trevor Huffman as well as Indiana. Coach Mike Davis sent two pit-bull defenders at the Kent State guard the second he touched the ball.

Understand that Huffman came from Nowhere, where he had zero major-college offers and had to beg Kent State to sign him, only to become Kent State's all-time leading scorer. Don't remember that last image of Huffman, sitting despondently on the bench, staring hopelessly at the court after fouling out.

Understand Indiana had just too much firepower for Kent State, that Heath had a decent game plan. He noticed Indiana was only 2-of-10 from 3-point range against Duke, but the Hoosiers destroyed the defending national champions inside. So he decided to take away the shots near the basket, but the Hoosiers guards got hot.

Understand that some nights, the other team has more talent that just plays better, and there's not much else you can say.

Understand that Antonio Gates plays more like an NBA prospect every week, that he is a lot like Anthony Mason, and he scored 22 points against Indiana's Jared Jeffries, who is 6 inches taller and expected to be a first-round NBA Draft choice.

Understand that 20 years from now, Kent State fans will be talking about this team and that Huffman, Andrew Mitchell and Demetric Shaw should all have their numbers retired.

Understand that this Kent State team didn't just win, it made history.

I hope you really appreciate not just what Kent State accomplished this season, but how the Flashes did it.

I hope you realize that it's nearly impossible for a school such as Kent State to advance this deep into the NCAA Tournament. Most Kent State fans probably don't know the Hoosiers had five athletes who were high school players of the year from four states. There was Dane Fife (Michigan), Donald Perry (Louisiana) and A.J. Moye (Georgia) while Jeffries and Tom Coverdale were Mr. Basketball in Indiana. And Jeffries was a National High School Player of the Year.

I hope you realize Kent State was playing in a different basketball universe, that some college teams have McDonald's High School All-Americans—and other teams have kids who had part-time jobs at Mc-Donalds, over-looked kids who had to work for everything.

I hope you realize that's the Kent State team that made you proud.

I hope you know that Thomas and Mitchell already have their degrees. That had Kent State won, Shaw was going to have to postpone taking his entrance exams for medical school. And that the star, Huffman, is expected to graduate at summers end.

I hope you realize that when a "mid-major" team such as Kent State comes out of nowhere, it sometimes happens because the school had some players who were more likely to end up on a police blotter than the honor roll.

I hope you realize Kent State took no shortcuts to get here, that its one academic gamble paid off in Gates. I hope you realize what Heath, a rookie, did was truly amazing, taking over a team from the popular Gary Waters, enduring a 4-4 start to win 26-of-27 games.

I hope high school kids watched this Kent State team, pattern themselves after this Kent State team, and play like this Kent State team.

I hope you know that's the greatest compliment of all.

3/24/2002

Coaches

Wilkens a man of faith, family, friends

FATHER PAUL SCHINDLER has been the pastor at St. Bernard's for 14 years. He is the kind of guy who watches all the local pro teams on TV and keeps track of their games on the radio and in the newspaper.

That is why he was so stunned to see Lenny Wilkens in the pews one morning.

It was 10 years ago, and Wilkens had just become coach of the Cavaliers. Schindler was saying a 7:10 morning Mass. It was the middle of the week, and there were only a few folks in the huge church.

"I just looked up from the altar and I saw Lenny," Schindler recalled. "Then I started to see him all the time. If the Cavs were in town, he was at morning Mass.

"If they played a Sunday afternoon game, somehow he got out of the Coliseum and made it to our 4:30 afternoon Mass. I never figured how he did it."

Wilkens is in town with the Cavs again tonight. Only now, they play in downtown Cleveland at Gund Arena—and he is coach of the Atlanta Hawks.

For seven years, he lived on Ghent Road in Akron. He was a regular at such restaurants as Jack Horner's, Papa Joe's and The Courtyard in Brecksville.

The man who won his 1,000th game last week . . . a coach who has won more games than anyone in NBA history . . . well, the key to his longevity might be found in those quiet mornings at St. Bernard's.

"Lenny usually sat near the back," Schindler said. "The people who saw him knew that Lenny was there to pray and think. It was not for show. He wasn't there to be seen. Our people didn't bother him, except maybe to say hello. They respected why he was in church."

It was there that Wilkens met Sister Kathy McIntyre.

"I went to the morning Mass at St. Bernard's," she said. "I started to see Lenny there—a lot. At first, I just wished him and his team luck."

One morning, Wilkens invited Sister Kathy to have breakfast with him and his wife. Soon, Marilyn Wilkens and Sister Kathy had become close, and the nun visited the Wilkenses in Atlanta last summer.

If you want to know why Wilkens has survived for 23 years as an NBA coach, consider the company he keeps. His friends are priests and nuns. They are people such as Akron Judge James Williams and former teammate Barry Clemens. It's not a star-studded cast, but Wilkens isn't a Hollywood kind of guy.

"Lenny always has both feet on the ground," Clemens said. "When you are around him, you sense this inner peace. As my wife says, he is a very quiet, but a very sweet, man."

Clemens is now a stockbroker in Cleveland. He played with Wilkens in Seattle in the 1960s and with the Cavs in the 1970s.

"When Lenny broke Red Auerbach's record [938 career victories], he sent me this [plaque] to hang on the wall," Clemens said. "In each corner is the name and logo of the fours teams he coached—Cleveland, Seattle, Portland and Atlanta. In the middle, he wrote that I helped him to a lot of those victories."

Clemens insists that Wilkens never will be truly appreciated. Part of the reason is that he has coached in NBA backwater towns.

"When Pat Riley does something, we all know about it because he has coached in L.A. and New York," Clemens said. "Now he's in Miami. He's part-owner of the team and on the cover of *Sports Illustrated*. Pat is very colorful. He knows how to attract attention."

Wilkens knows how to survive in a profession littered with divorces, paranoia and basket cases.

"He has a very spiritual side," Sister Kathy said. "That is his secret."

To Wilkens, a fun night on the town is eating at a good Italian restaurant with a few friends, then heading home to read a book.

Wilkens devours everything from Tom Clancy to American history, although he seldom reads sports books or the daily sports page.

"He hardly sleeps, maybe two to three hours a night," Sister Kathy said. "Marilyn told me that he'll lie in bed very still, but he won't be sleeping. His mind is on something, or sometimes he just prays."

Sister Kathy and Wilkens exchange books through the mail. The latest is *Joshua*, a spiritual and inspirational account of a man's search for truth.

Wilkens is now a 58-year-old grandfather.

"He is thrilled about that," Sister Kathy said. "I got a picture of his granddaughter [Ashley]. The nun I live with, Sister Carol Joy, made a shirt for Lenny with a picture of his Ashley, and Lenny wore it to practice."

And the awards have kept coming his way. He's in the Hall of Fame, he's led his teams to 1,000 victories and he will coach this summer's Olympic team.

"He loves it, but he's also embarrassed by the attention," Sister Kathy said.

Said Clemens, "To Lenny, each time something like that happens, he becomes so self-conscious that it is as if it is happening to him for the first time."

When Wilkens announced that he and the Cavs had reached the end of the road back in the summer of 1993, Father Schindler spotted him in church.

"I thought it might be the last time we'd see Lenny at Mass, so I told the congregation that someone special had been with us for seven years and was leaving—and that we should say goodbye to Lenny Wilkens," he said "I had never done anything like that before, but I just felt something must be said."

The people in church stood up and applauded. It brought tears to Wilkens' eyes. To him, that meant as much as any award.

3/7/1996

Manuel's heart

THE NIGHT BEFORE HIS BYPASS SURGERY, Charlie Manuel stared at the ceiling.

He thought about being 54 years old and already having suffered a third heart attack.

He thought about all the relatives he knew, and how so many of them had died from heart disease—a lot of them before they were 60.

He thought about how doctors were going to saw his chest in half, rip it open—stop his heart—and how this was supposed to make him better.

The Indians' batting coach thought about a lot of things on the night of July 6, as anyone would when you end up staring death straight in the eye.

They put you in one of those stupid hospital gowns that never fit right and leaves some of your body parts flapping in the wind.

They tell you to sleep, but every 90 minutes someone is coming into your room, poking at you.

They tell you everything is going to be fine—right after they tell you all the things that could go wrong in the surgery.

What Charlie Manuel did was tell himself that he had so much for which to live. He thought about his fiancee, Melissa Martin, who has been battling breast cancer. He thought about how he admired her courage, how she was right in the middle of chemotherapy and how he wanted to be strong for her.

But now he was the one in the hospital.

He thought about baseball.

He thought about the many players, coaches and baseball people who called. He thought of the call from Eddie Murray that surprised and delighted him. He thought of the note from Manny Ramirez that brought tears.

He thought about what it meant for him to be in the batting cage, talking hitting with Jim Thome or anyone else with a bat in his hands and an ear willing to listen.

The night before his quadruple by-pass, Charlie Manuel thought of everything for which to give thanks.

"But I didn't think about dying," he said. "I just didn't believe it was my time. Now, I won't kid you. I was scared. But I just knew deep inside, it would be all right."

It is five weeks later, and it's more than all right.

It's pretty close to a miracle that Manuel is back with the Indians, back in uniform. It's an astounding recovery, one that has amazed his doctors and delighted his teammates.

This was a man whose chest was torn apart, whose heart was stopped, who had four arteries replaced and then put back together.

And it worked.

"I'm not even sure of everything they did," he said. "Sometimes, my chest still feels so sore. And my back, it kills me. But it's not the heart."

He smiled.

No, the heart is fine.

It's the pounding the chest and back took from the surgery—all that cutting and moving him around. It was the fluid that filled part of a lung about 10 days after surgery, and how he had to go in and get it drained.

"They stick a big needle into your lung," he said. "Now that is scary."

But the heart, it's fine.

"About as good as new," he said.

As Manuel told his story, he sat in front of his locker in an empty
Tribe clubhouse. He held his baseball cap in his hand, twisting and
folding and churning it around—as if the cap were how his stomach
felt during the time his life was in the balance.

Manuel can kick himself now.

In 1991, he had two quick heart attacks during spring training. His
chest felt as if a horse was kicking it. He went to the hospital, where
they did an angioplasty, put him on a strict diet and told him to be
careful.

This was much better than heart surgery.

"I had a warning," he said.

And he was careful—for a while.

But then he began to feel better. He began to eat whatever was
around, especially the free food in the clubhouse. He began to gain
weight.

"At the start of this season, I stood on a scale," he said. "I figured I
weighed about 235."

He was at 258.

Manuel is a big man, 6-foot-4. He has one of those Jim Thome bodies, the kind with shoulders broad enough to lift a John Deere tractor
and carry it on his back.

So 220 pounds was a good weight.

But 258?

"I started watching my diet and the weight came off," he said. "I
went from 258 to 217 by the All-Star break."

While watching the All-Star Game on TV, Manuel felt numbness in
his right shoulder and arm. Up and down, a tingle and then numbness.

"It didn't feel like my other heart attack," he said. "But it didn't feel
right, either."

The next morning, he went to the hospital. Doctors become very
engaged when you start talking about numbness in the arm. Tests revealed he had four arteries blocked at least 90 percent.

"I was a time bomb," he said.

As he talked, Manuel's voice stayed strong, his eyes calm and clear.

But that cap. He kept twisting that cap. Watching his strong hands
working on that cap, that gives you a clue of what Manuel endured
during the time of his surgery.

He thought of his fiancee, how Melissa Martin juggled three kids
and battled cancer. How she went from her chemotherapy treatments

straight to the hospital to visit him, and how she refused to let either one of them mope.

"Melissa is an extraordinary person," said Sandi Hart, wife of Tribe general manager John Hart. "She told me, 'I wish I could take this pain for Charlie.' And she really meant it. Her mother died of cancer. She has a lot of cancer in her family, but she was mostly worried about Charlie."

Manuel knew that. He didn't accompany Tribe manager Mike Hargrove and the other coaches to the All-Star Game in Denver because he wanted to be with Melissa, to help her.

And he had the heart attack.

Go figure.

Manuel always has been strong. As a player, he was much like the Tribe's Jeff Manto—a minor-league power hitter who never stuck for long in the majors.

He is a high-character, hard-working guy from the Blue Ridge Mountains near Roanoke, Va. The son of a preacher. He played six years in Japan, where he set several home run records, including the most by an American player. He also was able to handle the Japanese demand for rigorous physical conditioning, which chased many American players home.

So Charlie Manuel knew he had grit. He knew he could discipline himself.

"Some people thought I had the heart attack because I lost too much weight, too fast," he said. "The doctors said different. They said losing that weight may have saved me."

Manuel is in his fifth season as the Tribe's hitting coach.

"I used to think that I was a tough guy," he said. "But having something like heart surgery, you find out that you're not that tough. Not when they have all those tubes sticking in you. Not when they want you to get out of the hospital bed, and all you want to do is lay there and moan."

Manuel gave his cap a good twist.

"Find out you're not that tough at all," he said.

John Hart and those who know Manuel well say otherwise. They talk about his determination, how his dedication to the Indians and baseball seemed to speed the healing—and how they have a hard time telling Manuel to take it easy.

"All I know is that I need baseball a lot more than baseball needs me," he said. "It was nice when the players said they missed me. But I'll tell you the truth, I missed them even more."

8/14/1998

My old coach

MY OLD COACH still writes with pencils the size of his pinkie finger. He still scrawls out his practice plans on the back of an old school announcement. He still wears sweaters that seem to date to his days at Notre Dame.

My old coach is now 82 years old.

He's still at the same school where he coached me in baseball 25 years ago. Still at the same school where he coached my brother, Tom, 35 years ago. Still at the same school where he coached his own grandson.

Still at Cleveland Benedictine High—and still coaching.

Augie Bossu is the John Glenn of coaches. He just completed his third undefeated season as coach of Benedictine's freshman football team.

That's three perfect records in five years as freshman coach.

This comes after a coaching career that landed him in the National High School Coaches Hall of Fame, a career with four state titles.

Now, he coaches a bunch of 14-year-olds with stick-like arms and legs that seldom seem to operate in any sort of orderly fashion. Yes, this man who also is in the Ohio High School Coaches Hall of Fame for both football and baseball now works with kids who barely know how to wear shoulder pads.

My old coach still goes to Mass every morning at 7. He still says nothing stronger than "Hell's Bells, boys." He still spends time in prayer each day. He still digs in his garden and goes for long walks.

Oh, he's had two hip replacements.

Oh, he still gets the water ready for practice. Yes, the water.

"We don't have a manager," he said. "Besides, I like preparation."

My old coach has been at Benedictine since 1953. He coached his first high school game in 1939, at Mineola, New York. He never made any real money, because Benedictine is a private school.

For what seemed like decades, he drove an old yellow station wagon with no radio, no automatic transmission and a heater that worked on its own whim.

Yet, my old coach sent all eight of his children to college, six to graduate school. My old coach is just that—a coach.

He thinks of nothing but tomorrow's practice and the next game. He revels in his routines. He relishes being around the kids, even kids who won't be seniors until after the millennium.

"They'll question you more than they used to," he said. "But they still want to play, they still want to be coached."

So he coaches them, at least those who show up. At a recent practice, he was missing four key players.

"Two are in detention, one is visiting relatives in Texas and one got hurt playing football with his dad in the backyard," he said.

My old coach shook his head. You'd think, at 82, he'd prefer not to worry about kids with detention, kids not doing their homework or kids just being kids.

"Son, the goal post is that way," he said to an obviously confused receiver.

Bossu smiled and shook his head again.

"Freshmen," he said. "You don't have any seniors to teach them. You don't even know who will be your best players, because they all come to you as unknowns. This is a challenge."

Watching Bossu at practice is Tony Russ, who played for Bossu and now is an assistant with Benedictine's varsity.

"I don't know how Coach does it," Russ said. "I've been coaching for 28 years and, I swear, there are some days when all I can do is just wring my hands."

Or as Benedictine athletic director Frank Novak said, "We all believe that the day Coach dies, he'll be whisked straight up to heaven."

In case you didn't guess, Novak also played for Bossu. So did Charley Reynolds, the school's principal, who was watching a couple of Bossu's freshmen players in detention last week.

My old coach seldom loses his temper. Only once did he ever take the Lord's name in vain in front of his players.

"He stopped right on the spot, made the sign of the cross and then apologized to the entire team," Russ recalled. Bossu grew up during the Depression. That's part of the reason for the pencil nubs and the paper that's never wasted. It's part of the reason he stayed at Benedictine so long. If you find a good job, stay with it. That was the creed of his generation.

"Coach has many virtues, but he may be the most disciplined man that I've ever seen," said Rev. Dominic Mondzelewki, a history teacher at Benedictine who once played baseball for Bossu.

For nearly 20 years, Bossu's summer job was as a milkman. Then, he was the head of a cleanup crew at Sea World.

"Coach is just a truly humble and righteous man," Al Hodakievic said. "He walks with the Lord."

You guessed it, Bossu also coached Hodakievic. The twist is that Hodakievic became the man to replace Bossu as Benedictine's coach in 1994.

"He could not have been more gracious, more helpful," Hodakievic said. "He went out and scouted our next varsity opponent every Friday night for me."

Now the coach at Chamberlin High in Twinsburg, Hodakievic still sounds amazed by the fact that Bossu would scout for him. That Bossu would treat him with the respect due a varsity coach—while Bossu remains the most influential coach in the history of thousands of young men who passed through Benedictine in his 45 years. My old coach's office is nothing more than a big closet with a little desk and lots of helmets and shoulder pads. He likes to fix equipment in his spare time.

My old coach considers being in charge of the freshman football players and the junior varsity baseball players as "semi-retirement."

He doesn't have to teach anymore. He doesn't have the pressure of winning varsity games at a school where winning is as important as breathing.

"As long as my health holds, I'll keep coaching," he said. "With this job, I don't have to be here until 2 P.M. Besides, if I started staying home, I'd drive my wife crazy. We've been married for 52 years and she still gets up at 5:30 A.M. to play tennis."

So my old coach—well, he keeps coaching. He coaches kids who know he is somebody, but really have no idea.

As freshman lineman Matt Wilson said: "I think he's coached for something like 60 years. I think he's one of the best coaches in Ohio. I know he's old school."

My old coach uses the same eight basic plays he always has. But in this, his 45th year at Benedictine, he did something new.

"We rotate quarterbacks on every play," he said. "Never did it before. But I've got two I like, and I want to play them."

My old coach beat Lakewood St. Edward 30-6 last Thursday to end the season with a 7-0 record. When the game was over, he embraced his wife. Then he gathered the players together, said a few words—and the kids roared.

"All he said was to tell us we did a good job," said freshman Jason Madden.

From my old coach, there's no better compliment.

11/4/1998

Winner and Winner

IT'S 20 MINUTES BEFORE GAME TIME.

Two high school coaches sit next to each other, two coaches in their first year at their schools. Two coaches whose teams haven't won a game, two coaches knowing this may be a very long year.

There is John Malinowski of Ellet, and Steve White of East High.

White is 31 years old, an African-American. Malinowski is 47, a middle-aged white man. As you listen to them talk, you realize both have so much in common.

"We've played three games and lost them all," White said. "I coached the junior varsity at Buchtel, and we only lost three games in the last two years!"

White shook his head.

"I've been married for a year," he said. "My wife [Margurite] is expecting our first child in early January, and I'm out here chasing my basketball dream."

White has been a coach in the Akron school system for 10 years, but this is his first season as a head coach on the varsity level. His brother in-law, Troy Jackson, is his assistant. He is a social studies teacher at Goodyear Junior High.

"I never thought being a head coach would be like this," he said. "I have kids who are upset when they don't play enough. I have parents telling me that their kid is better than some other kid."

He shook his head again. He talks about his team making 27 turnovers against Walsh. He talks about threatening to kick a kid off the team because he wasn't going to class. Then the kid got his studies in order, but stopped going to practice.

He kicked him off the team.

"And just the other night, I had to kick another kid off," White said. "He missed practice last week. Then he finally came to practice, mouthed off and refused to run. I told him to run our drills, or get out. He just up and left, walked right out of the gym."

Then White smiled.

"But you know what, I love this," he said. "The kids sticking it out, they're good kids. In a couple of years, we'll be all right."

White says he has four kids who are at least "B" students—Vance Summers, Chris Glasper, Andre Walton and Lance Rodgers.

"We'll build with good people," he insists.

Ellet has its fine students, too. Dion Sams is senior class president. Mike Jackson, Kyle Carpenter and Eugene Lowery are at least "B" students.

None of these kids in this game were averaging more than 12 points. None of them were especially tall. None will receive major college basketball scholarships.

But these kids are sticking it out, and there's much to be said for that.

Malinowski was hired seven weeks ago, replacing Bruce Moore who had been Ellet's coach for the previous 20 years.

Malinowski had been the head coach for two seasons at Central-Hower, but mostly, he has been an assistant. His last stop was Cuyahoga Falls.

"I'm 47 years old, and sometimes it's hard to me to understand why some kids would rather take 20 shots than win the game," he said. "So far, this has been a real test of wills between the coaches and the players."

Malinowski is a business teacher at Ellet. He has his own story of telling a kid to leave the team, a kid who wouldn't run drills or listen.

"Then we lost two kids [Carpenter and Justin Walker] to injuries," he said. "We have nine kids on the team. To have 10 for practice, [assistant coach and former Kent player] Craig Glenn has played."

Malinowski heard White say his team made 27 turnovers in a game.

"Well, we did that, too," Malinowski said. "And we shot 27 percent in a game, too."

White and Malinowski are good men in tough spots. Their players don't know them. They assumed teams that combined for a 10-30 record last year. They were 0-5 heading into last night's game.

As one veteran at the scorer's table said right before tip-off, "Well, tonight someone has to win."

The Ellet coaches were worried.

"Did you see our kids during the JV game?" asked Malinowski. "They were talking to their buddies, their girlfriends, doing everything but concentrating on the game. We called them into the locker room a little early, but I don't know if we got their heads back in the game."

Both teams knew this was a game they could win. Both teams were nervous.

It took White 34 seconds into the game to scream, "What are we doing out there?"

It took Malinowski 45 seconds to yell, "Pay attention, stay with your man."

It took 66 seconds for the first shot to be taken—a glass ball from 10 feet. Then came a flurry of turnovers. Bodies were all over the floor. The ball was flying everywhere—but through the rim.

Coaching these teams is not for the weak of heart.

By halftime, the score was 25-25.

White's first words to his team were, "Why do we keep making an easy game so hard? We do that, week after week, make an easy game hard."

Then he held his head and took a deep breath.

He didn't really yell. He pleaded. He preached. He taught. He made adjustments.

In the Ellet dressing room, Malinowski had lost his voice. He had been fighting the flu for days—and losing.

He spoke about not rebounding, not boxing out.

"Do we want this game?" he tried to yell.

It came out like a feeble rasp, his throat already raw.

The second half was much like the first, kids with skinny arms and legs and endless enthusiasm racing up and down the floor, often with more heart than head.

The coaches worked hard. More than once, they drew up fine plays and yielded wide-open shots for their kids—only the kids got too excited and missed.

Ellet had an inside player named Mike Jackson, a 6-foot-4 senior who powered his way to 14 points.

But East countered with a kid named Andre Walton, a relentless 6-3 forward who pounded the boards and scored 22 points.

East also had a kid named Sunni Wallace, who had arms and legs like twigs and could run like the wind. He scored 10 of his 14 points in the third quarter to help East take a lead it never relinquished.

Final score, 61-57.

In the Ellet dressing room, Malinowski had no voice and a broken heart.

"This could have been our game," he said in a rasp. "But we were too worried about talking to girls, talking to our buddies. We lost our focus. We had no one to blame but ourselves."

Then assistant Craig Glenn spoke. A star at Central-Hower who made Kent State's team as a walk-on and worked his way up to a starter as a senior, he sees a lack of effort and dedication from these kids.

His voice shook the metal lockers, "Mike Jackson was the only one who gave 110 percent." Then he went around the room, pointing at players and saying, "Did you give 110 percent? Did you?"

Malinowski loves Glenn. Believes Glenn will make a great high school coach because of his passion, his knowledge of the game.

"If any of you don't like it, you can turn your uniforms in tomorrow," Glenn bellowed. "You can leave right now."

No one moved.

Then Glenn said to Malinowski, "Sorry, coach."

"That's OK," said Malinowski. "You said what had to be said. But hey, we're young. We'll come around."

But that didn't make the loss any easier to accept.

In the East dressing room, there were smiles. There was White saying, "The elephant is off our backs, we've won." There were a couple of players pouting because they didn't play enough, and that led to a quiet but passionate discussion led by White about teamwork, and how some kids will play more on some nights than others.

Then White said, "On Dec. 23, we're going to Ponderosa for a team dinner. I got some money donated, so we'll have steak."

The coach then said he'll have a team gift exchange.

"We'll all draw names out of a hat," he said. "You buy a present for whatever name you draw. But no gifts for more than $5. Get them a cap or something."

White paused, then smiled.

"Gentlemen, walk out with your heads high," he said. "Tonight, you are winners."

12/16/1998

"You just expect to win"

THE WINNINGEST COACH in college football history had a luncheon date on Tuesday—with the guys who take care of the field, his way of saying thanks.

The winningest coach in college football usually answers his own office phone. He likes to listen as much as talk, a rarity among men who have had this much success.

The winningest coach in college football is Mount Union's Larry Kehres, whose team plays for the Division III national title today at noon against St. John's of Minnesota in Salem, Va.

If Mount can win, Kehres will have scaled yet another coaching mountain, giving him five Division III national titles.

No other school or coach has ever won that many.

Just as no coach has a higher winning percentage (.897) than Kehres.

But the winningest coach in college football doesn't want to talk about that. Instead, he is proud of what he heard from some players on the other side of the field after his team crushed Widener 70-30 last week.

"They said if they were going to lose, they were glad it was to a class program like Mount," Kehres said. "That meant a lot to me, especially after what had to be a real tough game for them."

Kehres is a tall man who stands ramrod straight. He seldom screams, and his face is almost Rushmore-like, seldom changing.

"Coach is the same most of the time," star receiver Adam Marino said. "Our practices are more intense than our games, but it's not because Coach is yelling at us. It's just the atmosphere here."

That mood is created by Kehres. Walk with him during practice, and you'll hear him tell a third-string center, "You need to move your left leg about six inches forward."

Players insist, "Coach sees everything."

And if he doesn't like something, he mentions it. Rarely does he bellow; just a few sharp words deliver the point.

Kehres also is obsessive about the field. Before the game, he patrols the area, picking up small pieces of paper that have blown onto the grass.

"You should see him in practice," Marino said. "He walks around digging out rocks with his keys. He wants everything to be perfect."

The winningest coach in college football is a guy who makes sure his father and mother are at every home game, sitting in a van at the end of the field. Kehres' father is a stroke victim, and the winningest coach in college football doesn't forget what it means to be a son.

He is so respected that Akron coach Lee Owens and former Carolina Panthers coach Dom Capers have attended his practices to study his intricate passing game. Yet he also wasn't afraid to grab a shovel and help the grounds crew clear the field when a surprise snowstorm buried the Alliance campus last year.

"What I appreciate about Larry Kehres is that he doesn't act like he knows everything," Cuyahoga Falls coach Don Ross said. "He is one of those guys who really wants to hear what you have to say, even if you're just a high school coach like me. A lot of college coaches, they're just waiting for you to stop talking so they can start."

The winningest coach in college football passed up a chance to coach at Kent State a few years ago. He interviewed at Princeton at the end of last season, but he decided that wasn't right.

The winningest coach in college football is a homebody, his office no more than a 50-yard pass from the dorm where he stayed while an underclassman at Mount. He lives but a brisk walk from the campus.

"I really think Coach is a genius," Marino said. "Everything our receivers do is for a purpose, from where we stand to how we run our patterns. I watch tapes of other teams, and I see their receivers just don't do the same things we do.

"I don't think they're as well-coached as us."

Certainly something is being done right, because Marino has tied a school record with 102 catches this season. Mount's passing attack is the best in small-college football, with quarterback Gary Smeck throwing 37 TDs compared with only five interceptions.

Kehres has won those four national titles with three different quarterbacks, including Smeck.

The head coach also serves as the offensive coordinator. He is a former Mount quarterback, so he is very demanding on those who throw the passes.

And those who catch them.

"I doubt any team in the country practices the passing game more than we do," Marino said. "We'll catch 100 balls each practice."

Yet, the winningest coach in college football is flexible. In this, his 15th season, Kehres still loves the pass, but he altered his offense so that Chuck Moore has rushed for 1,501 yards and Dan Pugh 953, creating the best running game in school history.

There is something special about Mount Union's football program.

This is a team that has an 89-1 regular-season record in the last nine years, a team with four national titles since 1993, a team that has owned the Ohio Athletic Conference.

"You come here and you just expect to win, to play for a national title," Moore said.

Kehres is proud of his team's nine consecutive regular-season Ohio Conference titles, something that is taken for granted by most Mount fans.

But think about this: Mount has won its last 64 regular-season games.

"That's pretty hard to do," admitted Kehres.

So true, because you'd think the team would have a bad week somewhere along the line, a week when the weather was lousy, the players overconfident and the opposition overachieving.

Sooner or later, they'd be upset.

Yet, Mount has not lost a regular-season game since October 15, 1994.

Yes, it was defeated by Rowan in the semifinals of last year's playoffs, but Rowan, with its Division I transfers, clearly had the superior talent.

While Mount is dominating, it placed only one player (Marino) on the Division III coaches' All-America team.

The winningest coach in college football does just that—wins. He does it with players who are future teachers, lawyers, doctors and accountants. He does it with grace, as he will not tolerate any trash talk or taunting.

Best of all, the winningest coach in college football doesn't just win, he wins the right way.

12/16/2000

It took guts, but Tressel was the right hire

Did you think Ohio State would do it?

Did you think Athletic Director Andy Geiger would do the obvious, hire the guy in Ohio best-suited to be the Buckeyes' next football coach?

Did you think Geiger would name Jim Tressel to replace John Cooper?

I didn't.

But Geiger will make that official at today's 4 p.m. press conference. For that, Buckeyes fans should applaud. Not just for Tressel, but also for the man who brought him to Columbus.

It wasn't easy for Geiger to pick Tressel. The temptation was to find a "national name," someone such as Oakland Raiders coach Jon Gruden.

Or to pick Glen Mason, a known commodity with Division I experience at everywhere from Kent State to Kansas to Minnesota.

Or to break the bank for a phenom such as Oregon's Mike Bellotti, who is one of the young, hot items in college coaching.

But Geiger went with Tressel, who has spent the past 15 years of his life in Youngstown, waiting for a chance to coach the Buckeyes.

Area football fans appreciate what Tressel did in Penguin-land, especially the four Division I-AA national titles (1991, '93, '94, '97). He made two other appearances in the final. So six times in 15 years, he played for a national title. His record is a glimmering 135-57-2, not bad after a 2-9 start.

But Geiger could have dismissed Tressel with: "Jim was coaching at Division I-AA. Ohio State is a completely different ballgame."

He could have mentioned some Division I-AA coaches who jumped to Division I-A and fell on their faces . . . taking their ADs with them.

Had he hired Mason, few would have second-guessed him.

And should Tressel fail, some will say, "How can you give a great job like Ohio State to some guy from Youngstown?"

Geiger would take as much heat as his coach.

But Geiger understands that the next Buckeyes coach has to put Ohio back into the biggest college football program in the state. He has to know the high school coaches, he has to make the state his recruiting base.

He has to be respected.

Cooper was never quite able to achieve that.

He was viewed as an outsider from the moment he was hired off the campus of Arizona State in 1987, and despite having the winningest record in the Big Ten in the 1990s, his teams didn't win bowl games, didn't beat Michigan and seldom walked down the aisle with diplomas.

There never seemed to be much affection for Cooper, be it from the fans or his players.

That has to stop, which is why the 48-year-old Tressel emerged with the job. Tressel is not especially colorful. He certainly isn't after money, or he would have left Youngstown State long ago for a Division I job. He made about $110,000 at Youngstown as both football coach and athletic director.

Nice money, but mere change rattling in your pocket, compared to what most coaches earn in Division I.

But Tressel didn't want to leave Ohio. He felt loyal to Youngstown. If Ohio State had passed him by, he might never have left. He's that kind of guy—exactly what Ohio State needs.

Tressel has a chance to be a great hire, to be the next Frank Beamer.

Beamer is the guy who made Virginia Tech a national power. His graduation rate is surprisingly high, near 50 percent, in an age where Ohio State checked in at 28 percent in the last NCAA survey.

Where did Beamer coach before Virginia Tech?

How about Murray State, a Division I-AA school?

Good coaches can win at every level, especially if they understand players, know how to recruit and enjoy dealing with the public.

Tressel brings all those attributes to Columbus. He also is a former assistant at OSU, Akron and Syracuse, meaning he has been up close and personal with major college football.

Around the country, Tressel's hiring might be greeted with a yawn, even by some of Geiger's fellow ADs.

But in Ohio, we know he did the right thing, and how often can you say that when it comes to big-time sports?

1/18/2001

Coach 'Smitty'

IT MAY HAVE BEEN his last practice of the high school season, but Steve Smith wasn't thinking about that. The Orrville High basketball coach has a team with a 1-6 record that plays at Lexington High tonight.

"Guys, PLEASE!" said Smith, a raspy voice coming from a scarlet face.

This 56-year-old man paused.

Not because he has a lump on his throat. Not because he will start major chemotherapy treatments on Monday, which will sentence him to University Hospitals of Cleveland next week. Not because there is fear whenever anyone hears the word—cancer.

He was upset because his players failed to pass the ball to the proper places on the court.

"I mean, Shaquille O'Neal could be on our team and he'd be lucky to score two points, BECAUSE NO ONE WOULD SEE HIM!" roared Smith. "We'd never throw him the ball!"

Then he held his head and looked as if he was about to cry.

"Guys," he said, his voice calming down. "How many of you want to win one other game this year?"

All the hands went up.

"Good," he said. "That's our goal. We're 1-6 and we want to win one more game in 2002. We can do that, can't we?"

The players yelled they could.

Then Smith turned to a friend on the sidelines and said, "When I had lousy teams before, at least I could say I had my health. Now, I can't even say that."

Then he laughs, a warm, embracing belly laugh without a trace of bitterness.

"That's my dad," said his son, Rocky Smith, who helps as an assistant coach. "Around all of us, he has been the same. He is the toughest guy with the biggest heart that I know."

Smith is expected to coach at tonight's game. He has 509 career victories. He has three state titles. He has won every Ohio high school coaching award worth winning.

But he's never faced anything like this.

"The waiting is the worst part," he said. "I want to start with the treatments. I hear it can be bad, that I might end up needing a feeding tube for a while."

The tumor in Smith's throat is too large for surgery because that could damage his vocal cords or his ability to swallow. So the battle plan is to use aggressive chemotherapy and radiation to shrink the tumor to a point where an operation would be less dangerous.

He is to be in the hospital next week, then home for three weeks, then back to the hospital for another week. Then, it's hoped, he'll have surgery to remove the tumor. In the meantime, the massive doses of chemotherapy and radiation are expected to dry up his saliva and turn his throat raw, making it hard for him to eat and speak.

"That's why I'm gonna keep coaching until I have to stop," he said. "When I'm with the kids in the gym, I don't think about anything else but basketball. Away from it, I ache. My back hurts. I try not to worry, but I do. It's not something I dwell on, but when you hear 'cancer,' you know people die from it."

Back at practice, Smith has a mantra, "PASS-AND-MOVE, PASS-AND-MOVE, what's so hard about that? PASS-AND-MOVE, it ain't brain surgery!"

To some of the new players, the words sting. Those who have been coached by Smith for years sort of smile.

Watching practice was Andre Johnson, who played for Smith in the early 1990s. He attended Virginia Military Institute on a football scholarship, and is now a supply officer in the Army.

"Other than my parents, no one had a bigger influence on my life than Smitty," he said. "He's into tough love. He used to tell me to quit acting like a big baby. I hated hearing it back then, but that stuck with me."

During a break in practice, Smith hugs Johnson. Smith hugs a lot of people—friends, players, coaches, someone whom he just met.

And now, he's feeling all these people hug back.

At his home are more than 100 cards from former students and old friends. A former player, John Hoover, sent him a note about what Smith meant to him, and how Hoover has been working with mentally ill children.

"I haven't heard from him for over 25 years," said Smith. "And he sent me a picture of him and his family. Don't misunderstand. I love to win. I love the three state titles. But hearing how you played a role in their lives—that really is the biggest thing."

Since word of Smith's cancer became public a few weeks ago, nearly every day a former player has stopped at the gym or at his brick house in Orrville. They hug him. They tell Smitty stories, of the coach dragging his middle-aged, potbellied body across the floor, comically hopping around like a dancing bear.

Former Orrville football coach Mo Tipton has appointed himself "director of transportation," telling Smith not to worry about those trips to Cleveland, that Tipton and others will take care of it. Orrville teachers took up a collection and handed him $368 just because they wanted to do *something*.

Texas Tech coach Bob Knight called, touching base with the man who coaches in Knight's hometown. About 30 coaches from other schools have sent notes.

Person after person has called or written or stopped Smith on the street to tell him about their duels with cancer, and how they have emerged scarred, but stronger because of the experience.

"I hate all this attention," he said, but he was smiling, and fighting back tears. "So many people are so good to me."

Orrville team captain Rob Amstutz can't quite believe it.

"Coach brought us together in the dressing room and said he had cancer," he said. "It was a shock. We had no clue. We all just sat there, and no one knew what to say."

So they went to practice.

"The only difference I notice is he's even more fired up than normal," said Amstutz. "He picks on you, but then he throws his arms around you and says he really cares about you. I know that he's made me a much better player than most coaches could."

Amstutz looked at the other end of the Orrville gym at a sign reading WE LOVE U SMITTY.

"We do love our coach," he said.

And Donna Smith loves her husband of 35 years.

When Smith noticed the lump in his throat, his first assumption was a swollen gland. But then an examination revealed a lump, and the doctor didn't like how it looked. There was a biopsy, and cancer was the verdict.

"I just never thought it would happen," said Donna Smith. "It was like a kick in the stomach when we got the news. You can't talk. You can't think. You can't feel. I remember we walked out of the doctor's office, and when we got to the parking lot, all we could do was put our arms around each other and hold each other."

Donna Smith said she has spent "too much time" checking the Internet for information about throat cancer. She says she has been more distracted by it than her husband has.

"But it has brought us even closer together," she said.

They spent New Year's Eve at home, watching movies. First, it was *Legally Blonde*, then *American Graffiti*. "We wanted something funny and mindless," she said.

On New Year's Day, they started with a breakfast of sauerkraut, potatoes, pork and black-eyed peas. "That comes from Smitty's mom," she said. "Supposedly, if you start the year by eating black-eyed peas, then you'll always have money in your pocket."

Assistant coach Ken Landis will take over while Smith recovers. "For all of us, it's just hard to believe this is happening to Smitty," Landis said.

Or as son Rocky Smith said, "My dad is such a strong person, and he always preached toughness to his teams and to me. I think he's keeping a lot of the emotion inside."

Smith has coached Orrville for 25 years. He is a Vietnam veteran, a former steelworker who didn't earn his college degree and start coaching until he was 27. He teaches Occupational Work Education, dealing with kids who have academic and/or personal problems that have caused them to struggle in school.

Part of him has always felt as if he had to play catch-up for the lost years. He has always had soft spots for kids who drive other teachers to despair, kids who need a male role model in their lives, but whose first instinct is to fight authority.

That's because Smith was one of those kids.

"But one thing I've always had has been my health," he said. "The last time I spent a night in the hospital was 1963, when I had knee surgery. It's funny, but I knew it was cancer the minute they talked about the lump."

Did he wonder why it happened? "Not once," he said. "Rather than, 'Why me?' I've said, 'Why not me?' I've had a few close friends die of cancer. You just don't know. In the end, we're all in the Lord's hands.

I've always believed God has a plan for your life, so I guess I have to wait to see what this one is."

1/4/2002

The Move

Browns brass deserves to be ripped

THE BROWNS ARE TRYING to tell us that Bernie Kosar has slipped so far that they are better off with a quarterback who hasn't taken a snap all season.

Or else they are saying they would rather have a waiver-wire refugee such as 39-year-old Steve DeBerg than a 29-year-old Kosar.

In the shocking announcement of Kosar's release on Monday, the Browns are saying that Kosar doesn't belong in the NFL, even with a team that is desperate for a quarterback.

Just who are they kidding?

Does anyone believe that this was a "pure football" decision?

Does anyone believe that 100 percent of career-backup Todd Philcox is better than even 70 percent of Kosar?

And yes, the Browns plan to start Philcox in Seattle on Sunday, the same Todd Philcox who actually was cut by the Browns toward the end of training camp, then re-signed about a week later.

Philcox is only two years younger than Kosar, yet this will be just his second career start.

This is how a team that is 5-3 is supposed to make the playoffs?

Coach Bill Belichick and Owner Art Modell apparently think so. And they also must believe that the Browns will never win another game with Kosar, or else why kick him out now? Especially with Vinny Testaverde's broken wing still on the mend.

Why not just come out and tell the truth—that Belichick and Kosar couldn't agree on how long the football field is, much less how you are supposed to cover the ground.

That's too bad. No, it's worse than bad. It's just plain dumb.

If Testaverde were healthy . . . if Kosar were embarrassed and bolted to the bench—fine, let him go. He deserves that much.

But release him now?

Why?

Because Kosar returned to the lineup Sunday, for the injured Testaverde, and the Browns lost 29-14?

Yes, Kosar didn't cover himself with glory Sunday, but who did? Last time anyone checked, Kosar wasn't in the defensive secondary. He wasn't on the offensive line, a line that is on pace to set a team record for sacks allowed. Apparently, Kosar wasn't even calling the plays. After the game, he questioned Belichick's conservative play-calling, something he has done for much of the season.

Belichick was sick of hearing it. Modell admitted the quarterback debate has had a "negative impact" on the team, especially on Sunday.

After saying that, Modell then put his arm around Belichick, insisting that his coach has "my unwavering support."

If you have any doubts, remember that Belichick also has a 5-year contract. Ironically, Belichick said that he "didn't want to make Bernie a scapegoat" for what is wrong with the Browns. No need to worry about that. This move will make Kosar a hero, a martyr, more popular as a former quarterback than he was as an All-Star.

Granted, the Bernie Kosar of 1993 is not the Bernie Kosar of the late 1980s. Modell is right when he said, "Bernie has been hurt so much . . . I don't know of any other quarterback who has ever taken more punishment."

Modell then said he had doubts about Kosar dating back to last December, doubts about his physical condition that were shared by the coaching staff.

That was one the reasons for the signing of Testaverde as a free agent.

Fine. If they believed that Kosar took too many hits, that he was gun-shy, that he was trying to survive on two wobbly legs and a lame arm, why did they open the season with him as the quarterback?

Why didn't they just open the season with Testaverde, whom Belichick & Co. always have loved?

Regardless of how you feel about Kosar, that would have been the truly courageous and honorable way to handle the situation. Instead, they waffled, they tried to straddle the thorny quarterback fence and they ended up with an early season controversy due to their own bungling that has cut open this team.

Kosar is one of the most popular players in the history of the franchise. He never won a Super Bowl, but the Browns never came closer than when Kosar was in charge. That is why fans picketed the Browns' training headquarters in Berea Monday, carrying signs such as CUT BELICHICK, KEEP BERNIE.

The publicity over this move will be devastating to the franchise, especially if the Browns fail to make the playoffs.

Even long-time Kosar-bashers will correctly view the mid-season unceremonious canning of Kosar as outrageous and cruel, and the Browns deserve every bit of fan hostility that comes their way.

11/9/1993

The only You in Browns' move is U-Haul

THE BROWNS MOVING to Baltimore has nothing to do with you.

You think because you are the fans, you somehow count.

You think because you wore orange and brown and shivered through those polar December games on the lakefront . . . because you screamed your throat raw and barked like a dog—that you are a part of this team.

You're not.

You think because you buy the tickets and souvenirs that what you say about the Browns matters.

It doesn't.

The Browns may stay in Cleveland, or they may move to Baltimore—but no one is interested in what you say about it.

Owner Art Modell's decision on what to do with his football team has to do with power, politics, money, ego—and even inheritance taxes.

Cleveland Mayor Mike White's efforts to keep the team has to do with his political future. It has to do with his legacy as mayor and his image—but it has nothing to do with you.

White doesn't want the Browns to leave town on his watch. He calls this a "cruel hoax" by Baltimore to steal the Browns and says he will move "heaven and earth" to pass Tuesday's extension of the sin tax and put together a package for Modell.

Well, there better be a lot of cash in the deal.

Part of Baltimore's offer—considered the most lucrative in NFL history—is reportedly a $50 million up-front payment.

Modell not only wants the money now. He often has said he's "not a rich man." He is 70 years old and has a heart condition. He knows he is not immortal, and he wants his son David to take over the team.

Thirty five years ago, Modell bought the Browns for $4 million. What is the team worth now? Maybe $150 million? Perhaps $200 million? When the team passes into his estate, his family would have to sell the team just to pay the inheritance taxes.

The $50 million will help cover that.

By threatening to move to Baltimore, he put a gun to the head of the city of Cleveland. It is working, as White almost went down on bended knee to beg Modell to "read our package, consider our offer ... it is the only moral thing" before he makes any final decision.

If you are a fan, you have every right to ask, "You mean to say that Art Modell's inheritance taxes may determine where the Browns play next year?"

In a word—maybe.

Inheritance taxes, luxury boxes, revenue streams and other sweet-heart deals are all a part of pro sports as we head into the next century.

The fan? He is just there to watch and pay the ever-increasing ticket prices.

How often have you heard a player say: "I love the fans in this city, but I need to look out for my family. It's pure business. Don't take it personally that I have to leave."

This is usually a guy like Alonzo Mourning. He couldn't make his family feel secure on $11 million annually in Charlotte, but $13 million a year in Miami might just be enough—for now.

When a player talks like that, the owners bristle and bring up subjects such as "loyalty" and "owing something to the fans and the sport."

But when the owners want something, suddenly this isn't a game anymore—it's just business.

So Modell stands up and says that even though his team averages 70,000 fans, he has lost "a bundle of money" over the last few years. He has told some people that he needed to secure a bank loan to pay the $5 million bonus for Andre Rison.

Modell insisting that he is taking a financial bath means one of three things:

1. He's not telling the truth.

2. He and his people are lousy managers. His organization is too big, too bulky and too fat and needs to be cut.

3. His accountant should do all of our taxes.

As for the fans, you are stuck in the middle. You are used and abused by owners and players. You have enough grounds to divorce all of them. Instead they toy with your emotions, lie to you and take hostage of your hearts.

Then they wonder why you call up talk shows and vent your anger like rabid dogs. They wonder why you are more demanding than you were 30 or 40 years ago, when franchises and players seldom moved.

They call you hysterical and fickle.

They don't get it—and they never will.

11/5/1995

Owner gone, team gone, hearts stolen

CLEVELAND STADIUM was a gray, cold tomb yesterday.

There was a team wearing the Browns' colors, but it was someone else's team.

There were 57,881 fans wearing orange and brown. They tried to cheer. They tried to be angry. They booed a little bit.

But mostly, they were numb.

Imagine going to the store, then coming home, opening the door—and seeing that crooks had cleaned out all the furniture.

How are you supposed to react to that? How do you feel when someone steals your heart?

You can shake your fists at the heavens. You can drop to your knees in prayer. You can scream into the wind, or shake your head in silence.

But no matter what you do, you know that it doesn't matter. What is done, well, it's done.

That is how most fans felt as they watched the Browns play almost as embarrassingly as their owner has acted, losing 37-10 to those rough-and-tumble Houston Oilers, who now have the same record as the Browns.

Kid quarterback Eric Zeier threw three interceptions and looked a lot like Vinny Testaverde. That is, Vinny on a bad day.

The defense was a disgrace. Coach Bill Belichick wandered up and down the sidelines like a man who couldn't find his car in a parking lot.

And the fans? Some of them carried signs.

One said: MOVE MODELL.

Another: $PINELESS $LUG.

Another: ART, WE DON'T LOVE YOU, MAN!

That may be the case, but the fans still can't have Art Modell's football team. He can take it to Baltimore. He can threaten to take it to Baltimore, to clean every last dime out of those putting up the cash for the stadium project.

Modell can do anything he wants with the Browns—except go to the games. Wonder how Modell feels about that. Yesterday was the first time in 25 years that he could not attend his own game. Wonder if he was surprised by the bomb threats and the concerned security people.

Wonder if he realizes that the fans don't care about what is good for Art's business—because they know they have been good to Art.

If Modell indeed takes up residence in Baltimore, he better not say one discouraging word about the folks who boughts the tickets and paid the freight for him here—and they did it for 35 years.

The Browns averaged 69,947 last season, sixth best in the NFL.

They averaged 71,059—in 1993, the year they cut Kosar.

They average 71,012—in 1990, when they were 3-13.

The Browns—they draw . . . they always did and always will.

If TV ratings mean anything, there is no better pro football market than this one.

Consider that the Indians had tremendous viewership for the World Series—but those ratings were no higher than any given Sunday for a Browns game.

There is nothing more that his customers can do for him. Modell needs to remember that.

Consider that on Saturday, when it became clear that Modell was loading up the moving van, the Browns actually sold 600 more tickets within 24 hours of the game.

It's amazing there weren't 60,000 fans lined up, demanding refunds.

There were 7,868 no-shows yesterday. But it is surprising that anyone showed up at all. How many of us volunteer to go to a funeral?

If there ever is to be a worse day in Cleveland sports, who wants to see it?

This stadium which had seen everyone from Paul Brown to Jim Brown . . . from Frank Ryan to Brian Sipe to Bernie Kosar . . . the old building seemed to hang its head as the team played with utter despair and hopelessness.

Under ordinary circumstances, the fans would have pelted them with snowballs—but there were only a few. There would have been loud, demanding chants that "Bill Must Go."

But there were only a few feeble obscene chants about the owner.

One jerk in the Dawg Pound threw a cherry bomb, which thankfully landed in an empty part of the end zone.

Hey, the players had nothing to do with this. They are just hired hands, taught from the time they first play Pee Wee football to do and go where they are told.

"If Art Modell says we go to Baltimore, then I get on the bus," offensive captain Tony Jones said.

"What am I supposed to do? If you are a player, you go or retire."

But if you are a fan, then what?

You feel betrayed.

11/6/1995

After 35 years, it's 'just business'

THE MAN WHO STOLE the Browns from Cleveland looked like he was about to pass some very bad gas.

Then Art Modell took the microphone and talked about "being in pain."

Then the owner of the "Baltimore Browns" introduced his "Maryland banker."

We can assume the money made Modell feel better.

How else can Modell explain turning his back on the town he called home for 35 years? How else can he rationalize selling out millions of fans who have supported his team?

How else can he find the bluster to dance so far around the truth that it makes it nearly impossible for anyone to take his word about anything again?

Sitting on that podium next to a bunch of political hacks from Maryland and in the shadow of Camden Yards, Modell looked 70 years old going on 90. His face was red and puffy, his voice cracked from fatigue.

He knew he didn't belong there. He knows that Browns have no more business in Baltimore than the Colts do in Indianapolis.

But he "had no choice," he said.

He made a "business decision," he said.

Today, "making a business decision" is a code word for doing what you want—then exonerating yourself from the responsibility of the broken hearts and lives you leave behind.

These "business decisions" are made by guys in expensive suits— faceless guys wearing reflector sunglasses and beepers on their belts. They are the suits behind the governors, mayors and team owners— and these guys may be the most scary of all.

You don't know who they are, your gut just tells you that they are up to no good. These men in suits often make us feel helpless—and the suits were everywhere in Baltimore yesterday afternoon.

Modell arrived at yesterday's press conference in a limousine. He was led up to the podium by the suits, a podium in the parking lot where his new 70,000-seat football stadium will be built.

It will be called "Browns Field."

Try not to gag.

Modell watched a governor of Maryland, a suit named Parris N. Glendening, wave a 30-year lease, a legal kidnapping of the Browns to Baltimore. Modell knew that 28-page document meant he could no longer insist, "I'm not a rich man," yet he didn't look happy.

Modell listened as the good governor sounded like an absolute twit when he compared this day to Cal Ripken's Ironman streak.

Cal Ripken should sue for libel, his name being dragged into the middle of this field of schemes. Ripken is about loyalty, hard work and staying through the hard times.

This was about an owner who cut and ran, and about a city that stole another's team. Yes, the city knew it was wrong, but it had been wronged before by the Colts scampering to Indianapolis . . . so somehow, that makes all of this OK.

It was nothing personal, just a "business decision."

Then this great statesman from Maryland screamed, "It's a great day to be governor" and introduced Model as "Baltimore's newest resident."

The writers from Northern Ohio had a pool going, picking how long it would take for Modell to invoke the name of the old Colts quarterback Johnn Unitas.

The answer was two minutes.

Then Modell said something strange: "I won't steal the Al Davis line about a commitment to excellence."

No, instead he borrowed a page from Davis' business playbook: He took the money and ran.

After a while, you just hate all these guys—the governor, the mayor, Modell, the suits and the 100 or so Baltimore fans who were chanting "Art . . . Art . . . Art!"

You look at Modell and think about how he attacked Dallas owner Jerry Jones and the other "new breed" of owners who are making their own "business decisions" that may not necessarily be in the best interests of the NFL.

Then Modell does this.

At least Jones was upfront about his deals with Pepsi and Nike, and dared the NFL to stop him.

Meanwhile, Modell actually signed away the Browns back on Oct. 27, and he did it under the cover of darkness in a corner of the Baltimore-Washington Airport. The governor talked about meeting Modell on a private jet, then joked about secret knocks and passwords.

Than he laughed about the wild and desperate media speculation—while Modell sat behind the governor and stared at his shoes as he forced a smile.

What great fun it was, stealing a team on the sly.

Then it was revealed that Modell planned to wait until the end of the season to soak the last dollars out of Browns fans before letting them in on the deal—only there were too many leaks.

So he had to come clean—or whatever this was—on this sunny Monday. Is this how one of the NFL's "great" owners makes "business decisions?" Is this what the NFL is all about?

Before the Browns finally play a game in Baltimore, there will be charges and countercharges—suits and more lawsuits.

It won't matter. The Browns are gone.

Then we'll find ourselves in the same position as Baltimore. And one day, the suits and rich guys will show up at some parking lot in downtown Cleveland and out of the limousines will come someone such as Cincinnati Bengals owner Mike Brown or some other guy looking for a fast buck and a better stadium.

Yes, we'll have another football team. But in our hearts, we know it won't be the same.

11/7/1995

We're paying for Modell's army of debts

ART MODELL used to joke that he was a lousy businessman.

He wasn't kidding.

So he sold out Cleveland and the Browns' fans to pay the bills.

Checking around, I've heard that Modell is more than $28 million in debt.

That is why he grabbed the sweetheart deal from Baltimore—a deal that could be worth $75 million in "moving expenses," along with a rent-free, $200-million stadium from which he also would receive all concession, parking and loge revenues.

But I kept asking myself, "How was Modell $28 million in the red while running a franchise that draws more than 70,000 fans a game?"

Or how about this?

Modell's credit was so shaky, he went to five banks before he found one willing to lend him the $5 million needed to pay Andre Rison's signing bonus.

Someone on the inside told me this and more, painting a bleak mosaic of Modell's financial landscape. In essence, Modell was leveraged to the eyeballs when he bought the team back in 1961, and he never really climbed out.

Instead, he used goodwill toward the Browns' franchise and the huge crowds it attracted as collateral to keep borrowing money, be it to pay off a fired coach (Sam Rutigliano) or a wasted draft pick (Mike Junkin).

"Imagine a house with three mortgages on it," I was told. "That is the Browns now."

Modell fell deep into this sinkhole in 1974, when he took over control of the Stadium for $10 million. He says he has poured more than $67 million into that 80,000-seat pit by the lake—and maybe he has.

And the Gateway complex, with its luxury suites, has hurt his loge sales.

But the Browns' record and controversial personnel moves in the 1990s haven't helped much, either. For whatever reason, 24 of the 102 loges (at $35,000 to $55,000 each) were not sold for 1995, despite the Browns coming off a playoff season.

At his press conference yesterday, Modell blamed escalating player salaries, especially the outrageous signing bonuses given to free agents to circumvent the salary cap.

Of course, the salary cap was supposed to contain all this. But Modell couldn't control himself. He just spent and spent in his lust to build a winner.

He also blindly allowed Coach Bill Belichick to hire an embarrassing number of assistants, scouts and other hangers-on—all in the hope that this coach would be Modell's own Paul Brown, that Belichick could deliver Modell a Super Bowl that would make Cleveland love him.

More than anything, Modell wanted to be loved by Cleveland. He longed to be seen as a "good guy."

His complex in Berea has an incredible number of front-office types doing Lord Knows What for their money. Some of them work there simply because Art likes them and gave them jobs.

Speaking of the training camp compound, Modell supposedly owes about $2 million to Berea for that.

With Modell, the money came in and the money went out—and interest payment piled upon interest payment as the bank bills grew.

Suddenly, Modell was 70 years old, and realized that if he dies, his family couldn't afford to keep the football team. The weight of the debt and inheritance taxes would force his family to sell.

Modell also refused to consider selling the team to someone who might have kept it in Cleveland. As much as life itself, Modell wants to hang onto the Browns and then turn them over to his son, David.

Rather than leave football, he took football out of town.

Modell's revelations at his press conference in Dallas also demonstrated his lack of business savvy.

He allowed himself to be saddled with that albatross of a stadium. When Gateway began, he was asleep at the switch, trying to convince the Indians to join him at a renovated Stadium when Tribe owner Dick Jacobs had no interest whatsoever in that project.

And he hardly said a word when the Gateway folks lured Gordon Gund and the Cavaliers from Richfield to downtown Cleveland.

Modell is right. He was pushed aside and not treated with the same respect as Jacobs or Gund.

But the sad truth is that he didn't play the corporate, political or public-relations games as well as they did.

Modell should have had this kind of press conference a year ago. He should have taken his case to the public, making clear that the sin tax and the other parts of the crazy-quilt financial package would not pay for a new or renovated stadium.

He could have shown pictures of everything from the Rock and Roll Hall of Fame to the Science Museum to Gateway, along with the price tag for each.

Then he could have shown a photo of that dump on Lake Erie where he is sentenced to play football.

He should have told the fans and government leaders: "It is my turn, and we need a real stadium deal to pay the bills.

"If not, I'm outta here in a year."

If nothing else, he would have scored points for candor.

Instead, he imposed a moratorium on the stadium discussion—all the while talking to Baltimore behind the backs of his fans.

"I didn't want to go public with all my demands, because I didn't want to look like an extortionist," he said yesterday.

Instead, he looks like a traitor. A man who can't even come home to the town where he has lived for 35 years.

11/8/1995

Benedict Art

I STILL DON'T KNOW how Art Modell did it.

OK, I know how.

I know about the secret meetings, the limousines, the private jets, the big money waiting in Baltimore and the huge debts left behind in Cleveland.

But I still don't know how he did it. How does a man spend 35 years in a city, then tear its heart out?

How does a man, at the age of 70, leave this as his legacy? Why would he want to be known as the man who stole the Browns from Cleveland?

Modell and his wife are on countless boards of charitable organizations, yet he knows he can't go home again. He is selling his home in Waite Hill. He is making his Florida home a permanent residence and moving to Baltimore for the season.

In many ways, he is heading into a self-imposed exile.

Modell is up for the Pro Football Hall of Fame in a year in which he pulled a stunt straight from the Hall of Shame.

Even some of the nitwits who owned the Indians over the years never sunk this low.

Many went just as bust as Modell did, but they bailed out by cashing out. They sold the team to someone who would keep the Tribe in Cleveland.

They had stronger cases to move than Modell. The Stadium was an unmitigated disaster for the Indians, and they will tell you that Modell was not the ideal landlord.

But the owners made sure that the Tribe stayed here, even though better deals were to be had elsewhere.

When Steve O'Neill died in August 1983, the Indians were owned by his estate. Put in charge of finding a new owner was O'Neill's nephew, Pat.

He had one death-bed order from his uncle: Find an owner for the team who would be good for baseball and good for Cleveland.

It took three years, but Pat O'Neill finally struck a deal with the Jacobs brothers, and Dick Jacobs then muscled the civic bosses into building him a stadium.

In the end, guys such as Gabe Paul (who ran the Tribe for 21 years) certainly took care of themselves, but they also assumed some civic responsibility.

Now retired in Tampa, Gabe Paul can come back to Cleveland. He can proudly say, "I fought to keep the Indians here." Not everyone might believe him, but the team remains in town and Paul had something to do with that.

History will treat Paul kindly because of the success of the franchise after he left.

But Modell?

He hereafter will be the Benedict Arnold of Cleveland sports. He knows that. He is not a buffoon.

There are legions who will stand up and swear that Modell is a good person—and there are many examples that he is exactly that.

But few in Cleveland will believe it. Not after Baltimore.

Modell is an old 70, not in the best of health. He has a heart condition and often seems just plain worn down. Why did he want to put himself through the pressure and agony of this kind of deal?

Given that he's $28 million in debt and believes he can no longer "compete" in Cleveland despite being supported by 70,000 fans, the honorable decision would have been to sell out.

Certainly, he would not have had to look for long for someone willing to buy the Browns and keep them in town.

But he wanted to keep the team in his family, especially for his son, David. No matter how he spins it, he comes off as petty and selfish.

"Baltimore Browns may sound good to some people, but it clanks in my ears," Cincinnati Bengals owner Mike Brown said. After all, the Browns are named for his father, Paul Brown.

That is how most everyone in the NFL seems to feel.

Modell had the audacity to say, "I would lead the drive for a team in Cleveland if the city, county and state make it attractive for a team to be there."

Art, there has been a team in Cleveland—and you could have been the motor of the movement for a new stadium.

But you turned your back on what you considered your hometown—and nothing you ever do or say can change that.

11/9/1995

Browns fans still love this team

IT STARTED AS A PROTEST, then a football game broke out.

That is what it was like at the Stadium yesterday.

Browns fans couldn't stay home. They couldn't just stand outside and carry signs. They couldn't pretend they had something better to do on this Sunday afternoon.

They had to go in. The Pittsburgh Steelers were in town. And once they were inside the Stadium, they tried to cheer for the Steelers. Who could blame them?

The owner is considered a traitor.

The coach makes their skin crawl.

The star receiver should have his mouth stuffed with rancid crab cakes.

Their team was leaving, breaking their hearts and taking a piece of their past to Baltimore.

But they couldn't do it. They couldn't be Steeler fans, not even for one afternoon. That was the message from yesterday's 20-17 loss to Pittsburgh.

OK, Andre Rison was booed every time he caught a pass.

"If they want to boo me, that's fine," he said. "It started when I came on to the field for the warmup . . . But you know what? This ain't home for me. The fans can boo me for the next 12 weeks for all I care."

All Rison does every week is show the world what happens when you give a lunkhead $17 million and stick a microphone in front of his face.

"If Art Modell says go play in Alaska, then I'll go play in Alaska," Rison said. "That's all I'm saying."

That's enough already.

As for the rest of the Browns' players, the fans were on their side. They stuck with Vinny Testaverde, who started the game as if he were a guy in a beer commercial.

You know the guy, the bozo who is watching sports on TV one moment, then he's out there on the field the next—and bewildered by it all.

Testaverde's first pass—the first Browns play of the game!—was a ridiculous interception. On their next possession, Leroy Hoard fumbled on the first play.

The Browns spotted the Steelers 10 quick points, but the fans didn't abandon them. Even Modell was ignored as there were only a few "Modell [Trucks]," chants, and those came late in the second quarter.

By the middle of the third period when the Browns had cut the Steeler lead to 17-10, they were screaming, "Pittsburgh [Trucks]."

Browns fans can't help themselves. They love this team.

That is why there were 67,269 of them on this gray, dreary afternoon on the Lakefront. That is why they packed this old, sagging stadium to see a team with a 4-7 record, a team that had lost 6-of-7.

No matter what Modell says about not being able to make money here, this is a football town like no other football town. This is a team where most of the players have been insulting the fans . . . fans who have done nothing but support them with their hard-earned dollars . . . and yet these same fans keep coming back, waiting for the lads in orange and white to do something—and when the Browns score, they stand and stomp and scream.

Through thick, thin and treachery, they still love this team.

More than anyone else, Earnest Byner sensed this.

If any of these guys is a true Brown, it's Byner. He was here for The Drive and The Fumble. Heck, he is The Fumble.

Byner may have cost them a Super Bowl trip, but at least he was a member of a team good enough to think about a Super Bowl.

Byner is like these fans and this town.

You can kick him in the teeth. You can write him off. But Byner was there when this team owned the city, a team that so grabbed the emotions of the fans that it reduced the Indians and Cavs to footnotes on the sports page.

Byner was there with Bernie and Mack and Brennan and the defense that gave birth to the Dawg Pound.

It is worth remembering that Byner is 33 years old. He was cast off by the Washington Redskins two years ago, and now he has emerged as the Browns best offensive player—and whoever would have believed that?

Byner is first on the team in receiving, second in rushing and he even plays on the punt-coverage team, trying to tackle people. Yesterday, he was on his hands and knees, eating dirt and crawling for extra yards.

It would have been nice to know what Byner thought about yesterday's game, but he left the dressing room early. What has happened to the Browns probably hurts him just as much as it does you.

To Browns fans, that is all that really matters.

11/27/1995

Signs of deceit, arrogance, hypocrisy

THE SIGN READ: ART, THANKS FOR 34 EXCITING YEARS.

It was enough to make you gag.

That sign at the Browns' final home game yesterday was posted by the mercenaries in the team's front office.

So was this one: THANKS FOR THE MEMORIES, ART.

Who are they kidding?

Both professionally painted signs were on the tarp, where the fans couldn't touch them. They are the signs of the times for the Browns— signs of the deceit, arrogance and hypocrisy that has led to the hijacking of the NFL's most beloved franchise to Baltimore.

The signs came a day after Al Lerner went public saying that Cleveland is a great football town and is entitled to a team. This civic titan even said that he'd work to bring a team to Cleveland.

Lerner is a minority owner of the Browns, a guy with strong Maryland ties.

It was on his private jet the deal was signed delivering the Browns to Baltimore. He is Modell's best friend, one of the 100 richest men in the country, according to several financial magazines.

If Lerner wanted to keep the Browns in Cleveland, all he had to do was cut a deal with Modell.

Instead, he introduced Modell to a Maryland banker and a governor who could be the Ted Baxter of the 1990s.

Now Lerner says that Cleveland deserves pro football, but not the Browns.

You couldn't help but think about the utter gall it takes to say something like that while watching the Browns beat Cincinnati 26-10.

This was the kind of Stadium afternoon that was once known as "Modell Weather," a sunny, dry December day that meant even a bigger throng and more bucks for the Browns' owner. Now Modell Weather means a December day when the fans start tearing up the chairs and throwing them on the field.

The amazing thing is that there were 55,875 fans at the Stadium. Think about this. The Browns drew more than 55,000 (not counting 10,000 no-shows) for a lame-duck team that stabbed them in the back.

Compare that with the Bengals, who had only one home crowd of more than 55,000 this season—and, you guessed it, that was when the Browns played in Cincinnati.

Lerner is right. The Browns' fans deserve a team. This team. In fact, the fans are more than the Browns deserve.

But Lerner has a different view.

"What I'm doing is talking to the league because I think it's a league problem," he told the Plain Dealer.

Say what? It's whose problem? Did the NFL move the Browns? Are we supposed to believe that Modell is some kind of innocent victim, that he just went along to Maryland for the ride, then someone put a gun to his head and forced him to betray the folks who have paid his bills for 35 years?

Statements like that are as outlandish as the phony signs the Browns' marketing nitwits posted on the field. But what else would you expect—the Browns' marketing wizard is none other than David Modell, Art's son.

As you looked at those signs, you realized that the Browns just couldn't help rubbing the fans' noses in it one more time. They couldn't let what has become the longest funeral in the history of sports come to a merciful end.

They tried to make Modell and the TV audience (the signs were at the perfect angle to be picked up by the NBC cameras) believe that some fans actually appreciate what he has done for the city.

Don't you just hate these guys?

The Browns played one of their best games of the season.

So what? They're still outta here. The front office still has no respect for you, despite the self-serving Thank You message on the scoreboard at the end of the game.

The fans saw that and booed, God bless 'em.

They also booed Andre Rison every time he came near the ball. Rison said he doesn't understand why the local folks would be upset with him. Then the lunkhead said, "Next year, I'll get cheers. I don't think they have anything against me in Baltimore."

Give 'em time, Andre, give 'em time.

It was a nice gesture when many of the Browns' players rushed to the Dawg Pound after the game, pressing the flesh with the paying customers.

But did you happen to notice who led the charge?

None other Dana Hall, the same Dana Hall who last month said, "I won't miss 'em. They're not real fans."

Thankfully, class acts such as Vinny Testaverde, Earnest Byner, Rob Burnett and Tony Jones all had big games—and then shook hands with countless fans afterward. They appreciate you, they really do.

But you know who signed more autographs than anyone?

It was Big Dawg—the ugly, blubbery mascot in the bleachers. It was a spontaneous and sincere gesture, the Browns' fans sort of celebrating themselves.

That's good, because no one else cares about them—as the front office proved once again yesterday.

12/18/1995

NFL buries its head along with Browns

THE FUNERAL IS FINALLY OVER, the last rites administered as the Browns lost to a team wearing teal.

The Browns were buried on Christmas Eve in Jacksonville, which is appropriate as the NFL believes the future of the league is in Sun Belt cities such as this.

The Jacksonville Jags (as their fans call them) play in the old Gator

Bowl, which received a $139 million facelift so it would meet NFL standards.

NFL standards mean that there are 80 luxury suites that sell for $40,000–$100,000 annually. There are 11,000 club seats selling for $162.50 each. There are so many things that bring in so much money to the folks who own this franchise that it's obscene.

NFL Life is supposed to be good down here in expansion land just south of the Georgia line.

I hate it.

I know this is Christmas morning, but watching the Browns franchise die in Jacksonville—of all places—just didn't fill me with holiday cheer. Especially when I saw this sign at the Gator Bowl:

OUT WITH THE OLD

IN WITH THE NEW

GOODBYE, CLEVELAND

Merry Christmas to you, too, Jacksonville.

Yes, there were a lot of signs supporting the Browns, probably from Ohio transplants. Certainly not everyone in Jacksonville wants the Browns to go the way of the T-formation.

But how can any fan say that? Don't they know their team may be next?

The message of the Browns' move is that no team is safe. Most of these owners have the loyalty of a starving grizzly bear—yes, they'll eat their own young if they don't like their bottom line.

I thought about that as I watched Coach Bill Belichick's post-game press conference.

This is the end of his tenure in Cleveland, and he just put a 5-11 record in the books. Add up the Belichick era, and you have the most unpopular coach in the history of this franchise, a guy with one winning record in five years.

The press conference probably was Belichick's last opportunity to speak to the Browns fans.

If he is fired, it will happen in Baltimore. If some miracle occurs and Owner Art Modell brings him back for more, that will be in Baltimore, too.

What did Belichick have to say for his five years?

Not much of anything.

He said losing to Jacksonville [24-21] was "disappointing." He said a 5-11 record was "disappointing." He said he wasn't going to complain about the key pass interference call that set up Jacksonville's winning drive—then he complained about it.

After 45 seconds, he was sort of looking back over his shoulder, wanting to get out of the room. He was asked a few more innocuous questions, and acted as if someone was driving a steak knife through his skull.

You wanted to grab him by the shoulders and shake him a couple of times. You wanted to scream, "Bill, say what you feel. Are you glad it's over? Do you hate everyone in Cleveland? Do you think your owner pulled the rug out from under your season? Do you think you messed up?"

Whatever it is, you wanted the guy to say something.

He could have said that part of the 5-11 record was his fault . . . or that he appreciated coaching Earnest Byner . . . or that he'll miss those Sundays on the Lakefront.

There was a lot Belichick could have said to at least make you think that he had more than ice water running through his veins. But after two minutes and a couple of cryptic words, he was gone.

That is what is wrong with the NFL today: Where is the heart?

It's why Belichick never could understand Cleveland's love affair with Bernie Kosar and the other veteran players he ran out of town.

He saw them as old guys. He saw "diminishing skills." He saw cold numbers on a piece of paper revealing the ravages of age to a player's body.

In many cases he was right. Many of the veterans' best days were yesterday. But he didn't have to kick them out in the street as if he were a slum landlord and they were a bunch of 75-year-old widows who were three months behind on the rent.

Then he treated the fans as if they were idiots, telling them that Todd Philcox was better than Bernie Kosar—and wondering why the fans were mad about it.

He couldn't understand why the fans cared so much about the players he knew could no longer help the team—forgetting that an emotional attachment to the players is why many fans buy tickets.

Heck, only Bill Belichick could make Vinny Testaverde a hero in Cleveland. He did it by unfairly benching the guy who replaced Kosar—and never really honestly explaining that move, either.

Whenever the fans mentioned missing their favorite players, they were given stern lectures about free agency and the salary cap. They were given mercenaries such as Andre Rison. They watched the

Browns play their final game in a stadium where seats intentionally match the home team uniforms—as if the league were one big marketing scheme.

This is how it ends for one of the league's premier franchises?

At least that's how it did for the team we once knew as the Cleveland Browns.

12/25/1995

Modell doesn't belong in Hall of Fame

ART MODELL DOES NOT BELONG in the Pro Football Hall of Fame.

I'm pretty intolerant on this issue because for most of his career, Modell's primary job was owner of the Cleveland Browns.

And he moved the franchise, betraying his fans.

Part of being a "great owner" is having a moral responsibility to your customers. Owning a pro sports team is different from most other businesses. The reason is, most pro franchises play in taxpayer-financed facilities, often rent-free or at a deep discount.

Yes, some businesses might receive tax breaks, but you don't see the city of Cleveland rushing to rescue LTV Steel by building them some new mills and ensuring that LTV's products get sold for a fair price.

But some cities do that for pro teams. Construct them castles, and even guarantee that a certain number of tickets will be sold.

Art Modell acted like he built the old Cleveland Stadium. He did not. He acted like he owned it. He did not. He did pour a fair amount of money into it, but it still was a bargain.

And Modell was well-supported.

In 1994, the year before Modell announced the move, the Browns averaged slightly fewer than 70,000 fans.

But Modell said he was losing money.

From 1990–93, the Browns' record was 23–41, yet they averaged nearly 71,000 fans. He hired a very unpopular coach, who gave the fans mediocre teams to watch—and the fans kept buying tickets.

But Modell said he was losing money.

In 1995, when the move to Baltimore was announced at midseason, the Browns still averaged 65,000 fans to watch a lame-duck franchise!

But Modell said he was losing money.

The Browns play in the NFL, where the huge pie of TV money is evenly divided, not like baseball. The league has a workable salary cap. Yes, the stadium didn't generate cash like newly built facilities, but just decent financial management of the revenue from those crowds of 70,000 theoretically would have made the franchise profitable.

But Modell said he was losing money.

Even after he took the team to Baltimore in a spanking-new, rent-free stadium, he had to take out a mega-loan, and eventually bring on a new investor, who will take over the team in 2004.

Modell still said he was losing money.

Art Modell moved the Browns because he was an inept business-man. He also was very jealous, because the Indians and Cavs received new facilities, and he did not.

Modell said he "owed" it to his family to go to Baltimore and cut a better deal than he had in Cleveland. But where was his responsibility to the people who supported him for 35 years?

An obvious answer to Modell's problem would have been to sell the team to his former best friend, Al Lerner, who now owns the expansion Browns. Lerner had both the cash and the political clout to get a new stadium built and then run the Browns the proper way.

Hey, Modell still could have been owner-emeritus, keeping a small piece of the team and still being in the spotlight.

But he wanted the Browns all for himself. He wanted someone else to pay for his financial mistakes. He wanted son David Modell to run the team when he is gone.

Yes, Modell did a lot to help the NFL in its television contracts, and he certainly helped in the area of public relations—at least until he moved the Browns.

And yes, Al Davis is in the Hall of Fame, and he kept moving his Raiders between Oakland and Southern California. But that just shows how the buddy system works, and how it cuts out the best in-terests of the fans by honoring a guy who continually was out for the best deal, period.

A man has a right to run his business that way, but does he deserved to be enshrined in the Hall of Fame for it?

Not in the case of Art Modell, no matter how many Super Bowls his Ravens might win.

1/27/2002

The Return

It's time to make more memories

THE NEW CLEVELAND BROWNS STADIUM is more than 73,200 seats, 70 bathrooms or 640 speakers.

It's more than a price tag approaching $300 million, more than the 11 miles of pipe installed by the plumbers. And it's certainly more than the 10,000 square feet of Taj Mahal locker rooms, which the fans will never see.

The new stadium is a place to make memories, and not just memories of things on the field.

Browns fans will never forget Red Right 88 or Joe "Turkey" Jones slamming Terry Bradshaw head-first into the turf. Some fans will treasure the image of Bernie Kosar looking more like a stork than a quarterback, sort of winging the ball downfield—yet completing one clutch pass after another.

Older fans will tell you about Jim Brown carrying the football like a loaf of bread, holding it out there in one hand—daring anyone to even try to take it away from him.

Some still remember Paul Brown on the sidelines, standing ramrod straight, always wearing a hat, always under control and never seeming to blink.

The players, the coaches, the games.

Yes, they are a part of it.

But the new Browns and the new stadium will be so much more than that. It will be a piece of their lives.

That is why so many of them stayed at the old stadium after the last game of December 17, 1995.

A game against the Cincinnati Bengals, of all teams, the Bengals who were founded by Paul Brown—the same Paul Brown who built the Browns. Somewhere, Paul Brown was either rolling over in his grave in disgust, or glaring down from the heavens above to say, "I warned you about Art Modell."

There were 55,875 fans at that game, an astounding number to attend the wake of a team that had never been to a Super Bowl, a team that hadn't won an NFL title since 1964, a team that was turning its back on the paying customers.

Yes, they were there for the Browns, for one last peek at those pure, plain orange helmets before the team bolted for Baltimore.

They also were there for a few of the players they liked: Earnest Byner, Tony Jones, Matt Stover and, yes, Vinny Testaverde, who showed so much grace during those trying last days.

But this was not a team you could love, not with Andre Rison, Bill Belichick and Art Modell around.

This was really about the fans, about memories, about what the old stadium meant to them.

That was why some fans brought tool belts with them, so they could pull out the hammers, screwdrivers, wrenches—even hacksaws!—to rip out their favorite seat and take the chair home with them.

It's why some fans sat in the Dawg Pound and cried.

Yes, they cried.

Big tough guys with sandpaper hands and a gut full of Old Panther Juice, bawling their eyes out.

Kindly older ladies who knitted their own Browns sweaters, well, they cried, too.

They cried because a part of them was leaving with the team. A part of them was headed to the bottom of Lake Erie, where the demolished stadium was to land.

And the new stadium will be a part of this generation of Browns fans.

Long after Chris Palmer, Tim Couch and Carmen Policy are nothing more than new chapters of Browns history, the new stadium will live in memory.

It will be where some children see their first Browns game, and it will be where some senior citizens see their last.

It will be more than the state-of-the-art scoreboards, more than the soft drinks, hot dogs and beer.

It will be where some met their husbands and wives. Don't think so? Several old Dawg Pound barkers wrote letters telling stories of romance breaking out among the milk bones.

The new stadium will be where a father will take his son during a weekend when the young man came home from college. And maybe this father and son had been growing apart as they grew older, as often happens with fathers and sons, or mothers and daughters.

And more than likely, this stadium will bring them a little closer together, at least for one Sunday afternoon.

The new stadium has everything from PSL to luxury suites to a concession stand for every 200 fans, but that isn't what most fans will remember.

The new stadium will be for the fans, who will be making new friends and healing old wounds—and there's much to be said for that.

8/15/1999

Belichick Era root of expansion woe

WHEN BILL BELICHICK comes back to town this week, old wounds will be opened, unanswerable questions will be asked again.

If Art Modell hadn't hired Bill Belichick, would the old Browns have moved to Baltimore?

No one knows.

But the Belichick Era was the beginning of the end for the old Browns.

It led to three years with no NFL, to Browns fans now being sentenced to NFL purgatory with an injury-decimated expansion team that is 4-22 with no hope of another victory this season unless they can ambush Coach Bill's New England Patriots on Sunday.

Should you blame Belichick for this?

Obviously, Modell was the main culprit. He didn't have to move the team. He could have sold to someone like his former best friend, Al Lerner, who would have kept it here. Lerner obviously was wiser and shrewder than Modell when it came to convincing the city fathers to build a new stadium.

But in 1991 when Modell stood next to Belichick and announced that this scowling young man was "my last coach," the Browns were doomed. No coach in the history of Cleveland sports ever turned off the fans as Belichick did from 1991–95.

Think about 1994 when the Browns were on their way to an 11-5 season and a playoff berth. It should have been a time when fans came together. Instead, so many of them said, "It kills me, but I hope they lose so they get a new coach."

Can you believe it?

If you remember the Belichick Era, you do.

To this day, you can't help but wonder what Belichick and Modell discussed on the day that the decision was made to hire him as coach.

Yes, Belichick came to town as a Bill Parcells disciple. And yes, he had a couple of Super Bowl rings on his fingers. But he was a defensive coordinator and never had been a head coach at any level, period.

He was known for his brilliance in the film room and with Xs and Os, but even his friends conceded that he was "shy" around people. That's not a quality you want in a head coach.

His critics said it was more like arrogance, that he had trouble connecting to people because he didn't respect most of them and had little patience when it came to trying to get to know someone whom he considered to be unworthy of his time.

Others said he felt some inferiority because he never played football at a higher level than being a small-college center at Wesleyan University.

Either way, these were problems for this man who seemed to go into such agony when he had to do something as basic as make eye contact and small talk with a stranger.

Modell was fond of saying Paul Brown had a sarcastic streak, but there were many sides to Paul Brown. He could be charming. He knew how to handle the media. He was popular with fans. He coached at Ohio State and Massillon. He understood the football culture in Northeast Ohio.

And most of all, he respected the fans and the tradition of the team that he built.

How Belichick ever even ended up in the same sentence with Paul Brown is enough to turn the stomach of any Browns fan.

Belichick never was able to grasp the basic idea that Browns fans loved their players and are loyal to them.

In many cases, the judgments about the team that he inherited were correct. Many of the stars from the good teams of the late 1980s were aging. The roster had to be turned over.

But the players didn't have to be rudely booted out and told not to let the door smack them in the rear end. Belichick couldn't manage to say something nice about the players who had meant so much to this franchise.

He hit bottom with the fans in 1993 with the decision to cut Bernie Kosar and mumble that infamous phrase "diminishing skills" into the microphone as an explanation.

And that move wasn't made because Vinny Testaverde was ready to take over as the starter. Rather, Testaverde was out for several weeks with a shoulder injury, and poor Todd Philcox was the only quarterback whose arm was not in a sling.

Then, the Browns had the audacity to tell the fans that Philcox was better than Kosar, which the paying customers knew was a blatant lie. The Browns, especially Belichick, couldn't understand why fans were outraged. And why they never forgave him, not that Belichick ever conceded the mistake.

Through it all, Modell bit through his lower lip and stood "shoulder-to-shoulder with my coach."

Suddenly, Modell threw himself into a bunker with perhaps the most hated man in Cleveland. In the middle of this angry public cauldron, Modell was trying to convince the politicians to build him a new stadium.

Talk about lousy timing.

Being coach of the Browns demands so much more than understanding football.

Chris Palmer also is an apostle of Bill Parcells. Like Belichick, his roots are from the East Coast. But Palmer has been a head coach in high school and college. He knows what the Browns mean to Cleveland, and one of the first books that he read after taking the job was Paul Brown's autobiography.

Palmer realizes a big part of his job is explaining the obvious to the media, because that's how the fans get their information. He also comes across as a genuine guy who is dedicated to his job and cares about the people in the stands.

Does that mean Palmer will be a great football coach?

Who knows?

But it does buy him some time with the fans. He doesn't embarrass the front office with his conduct in news conferences or his foul language, as Belichick sometimes did.

The amazing thing is New England became so enamored with Belichick that it worked a deal with the New York Jets just to hire the guy who had only one winning record in five seasons with the Browns.

A coach can act like an insensitive jerk if he wins, but Belichick never was able to make a lasting impact with the Browns.

He always has said the team moving to Baltimore undercut his work, but the 1995 Browns were 4-4 when the move was announced, having lost 3-of-4 games and Testaverde having been benched as the starting quarterback in favor of Eric Zeier.

Maybe the wheels weren't falling off, but the bolts were coming loose.

He eventually became a hot coaching property again, but now, his team brings a 2-7 record to town, so it's obvious that much of what plagued Belichick before remains.

You can say the Browns are better off in the long run with the Belichick/Modell fiasco causing the team to leave, bringing in a new era with Lerner and an expansion team.

That might be correct.

But the pain of this expansion era can be traced to the man who was supposed to be Modell's last coach, the man who never was able to learn what it means to be the coach of the Cleveland Browns.

11/7/2000

Ravens are a slap in the face

THERE SHOULD BE A LAW.

What else can you say when watching Ozzie Newsome hand an award to Earnest Byner.

In Baltimore.

It's supposedly to honor Byner's distinguished career with the Ravens, which spanned exactly two years. Yet, he's in Baltimore's Ring of Honor.

Go figure.

And all of this was happening while the team that used to be the Browns was pummeling the new Browns. And the team that used to be the Browns is a legitimate Super Bowl contender, only it now plays in Baltimore.

Called the Ravens.

Put together by Newsome, who used to be Mr. Cleveland Brown.

Final score: Baltimore 44, Browns 7.

Try not to lose your breakfast as you read this.

But what are Newsome and Byner doing in Baltimore, working for the Ravens? And what next, Bernie Kosar in purple and black?

This is not to call Byner and Newsome traitors. They are just trying to survive in a world where a team can draw 70,000 fans, yet the owner can spend himself into oblivion and then set up shop in Baltimore.

As Baltimore defensive end Rob Burnett said, "I loved playing in Cleveland. Those fans knew every player. I remember a game in my rookie year when we were 3-13 and it was still a sellout—80,000 people still showed up. For a team with that record."

And that team still moved to Baltimore, taking Burnett with it.

Or how about this?

During yesterday's game, John Unitas was on the Baltimore sidelines. Great player in Baltimore, right?

Only the team where Unitas was a Hall of Famer now plays in Indianapolis.

Don't even try to figure that one out.

If you're a Browns fan, none of this makes any sense. You want to like these Browns, to draw them close to your heart.

But how can you?

They are so young, so old, so injured, so overmatched. They're not just an expansion team, they are a shell of a lousy expansion team.

As one Browns' operative said at the end of yesterday's fiasco: "I just hope we have 22 guys left standing by the end of the year."

There is no need to mention the lame and broken players. A million trees would have to be killed just to print the paper for all the names. Just know that guys are now playing for the Browns who didn't even start for some of their college teams.

But Baltimore showed how far the new Browns are from . . . from what? . . . mediocrity?

As Browns coach Chris Palmer said, "We just got beat up, they manhandled us."

It was pathetic.

Facing perhaps the NFL's premier defense, the Browns ambushed them for a quick seven points, Palmer employing a no-huddle offense. Receiver Kevin Johnson breaking a few tackles and sprinting for 67 yards. That set up 4-yard TD run by Travis Prentice.

"For us, that was a slap in the face," Baltimore coach Brian Billick said.

For the Browns, it was the start of a spanking.

After that, they couldn't pass, run, block or tackle.

This is pathetic.

As a Browns fan, how are you handling this?

Here are the old Browns in Baltimore with a 9-4 record. They are coached by Brian Billick, who, no matter what the new Browns claim, turned down a chance to coach in Cleveland to take the Baltimore job.

Don't think he's second-guessing himself this morning, do you?

And if you had a strong enough stomach to watch some of yesterday's game, you had to wonder what would have happened if the Browns had stayed in town, if Art Modell had sold to Al Lerner, and if Newsome was allowed to go to work with Lerner's MBNA bankroll behind him.

Look at what Newsome has done while saddled with Modell's skimpy budget and slip-shod finances.

And then look at the current Browns.

Billick is one of the few to have sized up this situation clearly.

He saw that Newsome was drafting excellent players, and that Baltimore was armed with a state-of-the art stadium, rent free. He sensed Modell eventually would have to find another investor, and there would be money for some free agents.

He also had to sense the Browns were a long way from legitimacy, much farther than the front office or fans realized.

And for Browns fans, that may be the hardest lesson of all.

11/27/2000

Cleveland issues beating

BUTCH DAVIS RUSHING across the field, fist raised, fans cheering, wind whipping, sheets of rain pelting Cleveland Stadium.

Tim Couch carrying the football as if it's his firstborn child.

Drenched fans who were complete strangers at the start of the afternoon slapping palms like old friends.

So this is what it feels like to beat the Super Bowl champions.

This was the day when Browns football really returned, the day when some old debts were paid, when some new tradition was made.

Browns 24, Baltimore 14.

It was a day when the Browns went shoulder to shoulder, bruise to bruise, block to block with what's supposed to be the meanest, nastiest, most arrogant team in the NFL.

And they never flinched.

"Every play was a fight," said Browns defensive back Daylon Mc-
Cutcheon. "It was like a boxing match. They hit us with an uppercut,
we give them an uppercut back. They talk to us, we talk to them. They
push, we push back."

In the end, the Browns didn't just beat the Ravens, they beat 'em up.
Or as Davis said, "Our defense was just relentless. It was suffocat-
ing. They spilled their guts all over the field."

Not a pleasant image, but football guys love that kind of talk because it's the ultimate compliment. It means every step, every hit,
every play was contested. Helmets cracked. Pads crunched. Bodies
banged.

"We turned up the heat," said Davis. "We got quarterback sacks. We
batted balls down. We forced bad throws. The defense made the commitment not to lose this game."

And the Ravens felt it, as their purple and black colors probably re-
flect the condition of some of their bodies this morning.

Baltimore running back Terry Allen limped off the field with a
pulled calf muscle, down for the day in the first quarter.

Baltimore quarterback Elvis Grbac staggered with a bruised chest,
finished in the third quarter thanks to a slam-sack by Jamir Miller that
led to a fumble.

Baltimore backup quarterback Randall Cunningham lay flat on his
back, rain in his eyes, feeling all of his 38 years as he was sacked. There
was Cunningham, staring at the sky, searching for a normal breath,
probably thinking, "I'm getting too old for this."

Baltimore in retreat.

Baltimore backing off.

Baltimore, the team that Art Modell stole from Cleveland, sent
back home, humbled and hurting.

In the middle of all this is Davis, the new Browns coach who has
made this team believe when it seemed there was no room for anything but doubt.

Four wins in six games? For a team that won only five games in the
first two years? A team that played much of the day without two key
offensive linemen? A team that was picked for last place by virtually
everyone?

This team that has a better record (4-2) than the Super Bowl
champs (3-3)? This team is a playoff contender?

Why not?

On days like this, anything seems possible.

And it was a great day to be a Browns fans. Or a Browns coach. Or a Browns player.

After the game, Davis dashed into the stadium tunnel. He spotted linebacker Dwayne Rudd. The coach gave perhaps the Browns' most underrated defender one big, beautiful bear hug—an embrace for a man who Davis said "was brilliant, he blew things up out there [with his tackles]."

Then Davis saw his wife, Tammy. He rushed to her, picked her right off the ground, gave her a big hug and kiss.

A half hour after the game, Davis was in the clubhouse still shaking hands. He even delivered a kiss to the shaved head of defensive back Corey Fuller.

Davis has made Browns football fun again. He has brought a sense of urgency, a dose of high-octane optimism, a dash of downright zeal to a franchise that had been lower than Charlie Brown failing to kick the football for about the millionth time.

If you're a Browns fans, wasn't this the game you've been waiting for?

It had to sting seeing Art Modell with that Super Bowl trophy, with the team of your youth in Baltimore. And the first four times the Browns played the Modells, they lost by a combined score of 114-26.

In some of those games, the Browns were like the wimp on the beach who spots a bully and says, "Go ahead, just kick sand in my face."

Last year, the Browns thought Baltimore ran up the score in that 44-7 debacle. But the Browns scored on their first possession in that game, then lay down and went into a football coma.

Davis vowed that would never happen this season.

That's why alarm bells gonged after last week's 24-14 loss at Cincinnati, where the Browns were outhustled in addition to being outplayed.

Last Monday, Davis was angry, wired, determined. With his jaw out, he was challenging his players to regain their passion. He was insisting to the media and fans that the Browns were ready for Baltimore, ready for anyone. He was serving notice: The past was buried. This is a new Browns team.

And it sure was yesterday: From Tim Couch throwing key TD passes, to gutsy calls by the coaching staff, to the determined defense.

"Right now, we are a little battered, a little beat-up, a little bruised," Davis said.

But feeling no pain.

10/22/2001

Browns, Davis never lost faith

JUST WHEN YOU THINK the tank is empty, here come the Browns—again.

The Browns who came to Tennessee with 19 players who weren't even on the roster at the beginning of September. The Browns who lead the league in injuries. The Browns who had lost their past four games, whose quarterback was in a slump and whose playoff dreams had been broken.

These Browns were down 14 points early in the fourth quarter against the Titans. These Browns, whose best offensive lineman (Ross Verba) was too sick to play. These Browns, whose defense just seemed too tired after carrying this team for so long.

These Browns appeared to be finished.

Or at least, that was true of the old Browns, the Browns who were 5-27 in their first two expansion years.

But these are the new Browns, the Browns of Butch Davis, the world's most positive man.

These Browns beat Tennessee, 41-38, by scoring 17 points in the final 9:21 of the game. That's 17 clutch, fourth-quarter points from a team that hadn't scored 17 points in any of its last four games.

These Browns are different.

These Browns are coached by a man who told kicker Phil Dawson, "We're gonna have the wind at our back in the fourth quarter so you can win the game with a 44-yard field goal."

Davis spoke it, and it happened.

Said it at halftime, when there was no way to know, to even guess.

And he said 44 yards, not 40 or 45 yards.

And Dawson heard that, nodded, and thought, "Sounds good to me."

So here it was, 55 seconds left in the game. Score tied, 38-38.

On to the field comes Phil Dawson, the smallest Brown, who is very generously listed at 5-foot-11 and 190 pounds.

Little Phil Dawson jogged on to the field, the game resting on his toe, the ball to be set up at the 34-yard line.

With the uprights 10 yards deep in the end zone, that made it a 44-yarder.

Just as Davis said.

With the wind at his back

Just as Davis said.

And then Big Money, Gerard Warren, perhaps the largest Brown, came over and said, "After you make it, just polish your shoe."

Dawson nodded.

"All I could think was I owed it to the guys to make it, after all they did for three hours. They played their hearts out," he said.

Then Dawson talked about Ryan Kuehl, who "made a great" long snap. And he praised Chris Gardocki, "who is a super holder." He made it sound like they did all the work.

But Phil, someone put a perfect foot to the ball. Someone made sure it went end-over-end until it split those uprights, with plenty of room to spare.

Someone made a very, very huge kick.

None other than the littlest Brown, Phil Dawson, who then took Big Money's advice, and wiped his shoe in celebration.

It was only then that he remembered Davis' words, the halftime prediction of the 44-yard field goal to win the game.

"When he says stuff like that, it's kind of scary and makes me think that I should [hire Davis] to be my stockbroker," Dawson said.

Here is what makes Davis special.

During the preseason, Dawson missed a couple of field goals. There were rumblings that the Browns should bring in another kicker. Davis insisted, "Phil Dawson is my kicker, and just you watch, he's gonna go on one of those streaks where he makes 10 in a row."

That 44-yarder yesterday?

That was No. 15 in a row!

That was why Dawson said, "When a coach has that kind of confidence in you, it's contagious, and when he goes public like he did, it turns down the heat and it makes you want to prove him right."

Tim Couch said much the same thing.

The most criticized Brown of late took the team on his shoulders and carried it to its biggest offensive day since the end of the 1993 season. He did it by completing 20-of-27 passes, including three for touchdowns. He threw to eight receivers. He rarely made a bad decision and seemed totally in control.

This is the Tim Couch who was the first draft choice of the new Browns in 1999. It's the Tim Couch of whom Davis says, "He can take this franchise to a place it's never been before." It's the same Tim

Couch who had 13 interceptions and only three touchdown passes in his past six games.

This Tim Couch was backed by Davis last week, as the coach insisted that he's the quarterback of the present and future, a great one in the making.

"I never lost confidence in myself, but when I heard the coaches and my teammates supporting me, that means a lot," he said.

Davis loves to talk about his players "leaving their hearts and guts all over the field." He talks about "fighting to the bitter end." He talks about pride and demands a tremendous effort.

And he has a team whose record is 7-8, a team that could easily have fallen flat with all the injuries and road games at the end of the season. Under these circumstances, it's tempting not to care.

Instead, the Browns are acting like it's the start of the season, like they still believe in themselves and their coach.

And they showed it again yesterday.

12/31/2001

Underappreciated Palmer isn't bitter

MOST BROWNS FANS never will fully appreciate Chris Palmer.

They'll just take a quick glance in the rear-view mirror and see two dismal Browns seasons. They'll spot a 5-27 record. They'll remember something about a lot of injuries, and a lot of games that seemed to be over by the middle of the third quarter.

And Palmer?

They'll just compare him with the current coach, Butch Davis, and Palmer will lose every time.

But that's really not fair.

Palmer is back where it began for him and the new Browns, at Canton for tonight's Hall of Fame Game. He's the offensive coordinator of the expansion Houston Texans, who take on the New York Giants at Fawcett Stadium.

It was on this same field on Aug. 9, 1999, that Palmer coached the first game of the current version of the Browns. He had been hired only seven months earlier. It was a warm and fuzzy football evening in Canton; the crowd roared at the sight of orange helmets. They cheered Tim Couch when he came off the bench and led the team to a 20-17 victory over Dallas.

It was just an exhibition game, and in the big scheme, it meant nothing.

But pro football was back, and Browns fans started to heal from the betrayal they experienced when Art Modell hijacked their favorite team to Baltimore after the 1995 season.

Three years with no football, then a Browns team that had been tossed together in nine months.

"I compare that to what we have here in Houston," said Palmer. "I've been with the organization for 18 months, and the team has been in operation for nearly two years. That is a huge advantage over what we faced in Cleveland."

When Palmer was hired, he had no secretary, no players, no assistant coaches. His first duty was to go through every NFL media guide, trying to find any experienced coaches who were out of work. It was tough, because this was January, and most teams had their staffs in place.

Palmer also said the 1999 expansion draft didn't give the Browns the same quality of players as was available to Houston this year.

"You didn't see anyone like Tony Boselli or Ryan Young available," he said. "More teams had salary cap [issues] and that helped us get more than the Browns could back in 1999."

Palmer spent the past season helping Texans' head coach Dom Capers scout pro and college players. They know the type of system they'd like to play, and they can find the athletes to match.

With the Browns, Palmer was just trying to survive. He worked incredible hours, often from 6 A.M. to midnight. He also was available to the media and had a presence in the community.

With every drop of blood in his veins, he tried to make it work for the Browns.

Palmer isn't bitter about his firing, other than he thought it was unfair to have to wait about a month after the 2000 season before he was given the pink slip that everyone knew was coming.

"That could have been handled better," he said. "I was hung out to dry with all the rumors swirling around [about the courting of Davis]."

Palmer remains the same classy man whose character earned the respect of most Browns fans, even if they didn't like his coaching. He thought back to that Hall of Fame Game, and wished he had done something differently.

"I just should have named Tim Couch the starter and stuck with him," he said. "We all knew Tim was going to start, and we may as well have just begun the process right then."

Palmer said he recently had a long conversation with TV analyst John Madden about this. Houston is committed to starting rookie quarterback David Carr from Day 1.

"John said it doesn't matter if you start your first game, or if you wait three years, every quarterback goes through the same things," Palmer said. "I agree with that, which is why I was glad I turned to Couch when I did, but I should have done it even earlier."

Palmer put the ball in Couch's hands after the first game of the season, a 43-0 spanking by Pittsburgh. The front office was against it, as were many members of the media. They believed that the Browns were better off with veteran Ty Detmer starting, with the plan to ease Couch in later on.

"I know I did the right things with Couch, with Kevin Johnson, with Daylon McCutcheon and some of the other young guys by starting them," he said. "I was glad to see Butch continue to break in more young players. In football, you just can't get it done overnight."

Something else will make the transition to the NFL smoother for the new Houston team than it was for the Browns.

"We will be compared with the Browns because they are the last expansion team," Palmer said. "But in Cleveland, we were compared to Carolina and Jacksonville."

Both of those teams made the playoffs in their second seasons.

"But most fans don't know Carolina has had only one winning record," Palmer said.

Palmer loved his two years with the Browns.

"The people are special and they made me feel like one of them," he said. "It's a blue-collar town that loves football and the Browns. I made so many good friends in the community, at church, everywhere. My wife still visits friends from Cleveland. Very few places have a passion for their team like Browns fans."

Palmer is pulling for the Browns to play well, to build on their 7-9 season in 2001.

"The fans there are terrific and so loyal," he said. "I want them to have a team they can really enjoy."

8/5/2002

The Front Office

Joe Tait finds his life's calling on radio

JOE TAIT GREETS YOU in a red sweat suit, and red is not his color. It makes him look like the world's largest tomato.

The Cavs broadcaster is at his Medina County home—12 acres, three cats, two dogs—with a baseball cap that says "Burlington Route" on his head.

The cap is for the Burlington & Northern Railway.

This is not to say that Tait is obsessed with trains, but the phone in his study doesn't ring—it whistles like a train.

In high school, he dressed in early Casey Jones.

"It was a railroad uniform," he says proudly.

But today, Tait is bearing down on his 59th birthday. He is in his 40th year of broadcasting, and, on Thursday, will be honored at halftime as he calls his 2,000th Cavaliers game.

"Very few guys do radio anymore. They are on the radio, but they do television. They are too busy analyzing, telling you why they are smarter than the coach. They don't paint a total word picture. If you paint that picture, the listener can figure out for himself when the coach is a dunce." —Joe Tait

He leans back in a chair in his comfortable living room. He mentions towns that make you want to call Rand McNally. He talks of Monmouth, Illinois, and Frankfort, Indiana He brings up Decatur, Rockford and Bloomington-Normal—all in Illinois.

A young Tait passed through all these towns—and more.

"When I worked in Rockford, I played music in the morning and did the sports at night," he says.

In fact, he was "Joe Tait, the Morning Mayor of Rockford."

"I served two terms," he says. "I worked there twice."

He delivered punchy lines such as, "Here's Joe Tait . . . turning the tables on you." Then he played a song and read a commercial for farm implements.

He was fired in Frankfort.

"I was there for six months and they had 46 staff changes," he says. "I'm not kidding, 46. On Christmas Eve, the station manager called me into his office. He said that since I was the only one left from six months ago, I must be the reason [the others left]. Then he fired me. I went over the desk and grabbed him. I was about to bash his brains against the radiator when I finally came to my senses."

Tait knew there always was another small Midwestern town that needed a "Morning Mayor" or "Jolly Joe Tait," as he was called in Decatur. For 14 years, Tait moved from one small station to another, seldom staying more than three years. By 1970, he was in Terre Haute, Indiana. He was station manager and also did pregame and postgame shows for the Indiana Pacers in their old ABA days.

"I was 33 years old," he says. "I figured I'd be spending the rest of my life doing local sports and managing small stations in the Midwest. The last thing I ever dreamed was I'd be doing 2,000 NBA games."

"If you can do a good job broadcasting high school and small-college sports, the NBA will be a piece of cake. Half the time, the high schools have no rosters for you, no information—you have to work twice as hard. They make it much easier for you in the NBA." —Joe Tait

His first job was in Monmouth, Illinois, where he was the voice of the Monmouth College Fighting Scots. One of the Scots' rivals was a Coe College team coached by a young fellow named Bill Fitch.

"I saw a note in the Terre Haute newspaper that Bill had been hired as the Cavs' first coach," Tait says. "I wrote him a note wishing him luck with his new job, and added a P.S. that read, 'If you want me to do for the Cavs what I did for the Monmouth Fighting Scots [a 66-0 football loss to Coe], give me a call . . . Ha, Ha, Ha.' I never expected to hear from him."

Fitch was more than the Cavs' coach. He also was the general manager. Along with owner Nick Mileti, he ran the organization. The expansion team opened with seven road games (the NBA was so kind to newcomers back then), and Mileti's assistant, Bob Brown, was doubling as the radio voice. The team was so financially strapped, it had yet to hire a full-time broadcaster.

"Mileti said they needed someone young, enthusiastic and, most of all, cheap," Tait says. "Fitch thought of me."

Tait was sitting at WBOW, 1230 on your AM dial. The station's motto was, "Family Radio for the Greater Wabash Valley, 24 hours a day!" In his scrapbook, Tait has a picture of a small glass building that was WBOW with the sign: THE FIRST RADIO STATION IN WABASH VALLEY.

It was there that Fitch found Tait and invited him to Cleveland for a tryout—one home game.

"They put me up at the old Midtown Hotel, which was across from the old Cleveland Arena on Euclid Avenue," Tait says, shaking his head. "In the lobby, I saw Alex Hannum and John Block. Hannum was coaching the San Diego Rockets, Block was a forward on the team and already dressed in his uniform. I walked over to the arena with those guys, and it hit me that I was in the NBA."

But the bottom of the NBA.

"I later found out that all the visiting teams dressed at the hotel, because the visitor's dressing room was nothing more than a squalid pit," Tait says, shaking his head again. "I wasn't very nervous. I always knew I was a good broadcaster, and I figured I could always go back to Terra Haute if it didn't work out."

The next day, Mileti gushed about Tait's work and offered him $100 a game. It was a 50 percent pay cut from Terre Haute, but Tait knew it could be his only crack at the big time.

"I called the station in Terre Haute to quit," he says. "They said that was a good idea, because the station had new owners and I was going to be out of a job."

"It took me seven years to finally admit that sometimes the officials actually made calls that favored the Cavs."   Joe Tait

His den has more train books and pictures than sports material. His family was populated by railroad people, and, in another life, he could see himself riding the rails.

"It is my Walter Mitty dream," he says. "But I know it would never happen. I love radio too much."

The top shelf of his closet is clogged with scrapbooks. He hasn't looked at them in years, but now stares at the yellow, brittle news clips. There also are old NBA plane tickets and box scores.

"The first few years, I was with Fitch day and night," he says. "We ate together after games and then had breakfast in the mornings. I went to practice with him. I watched game films with him."

Along with assistant coach Jimmy Rodgers, Tait and Fitch played a game—created by the coach—called "Cut the Cavs." Each man made a list of the players, from worst to best, and then had to defend their choices—first cut to last.

Tait thinks back to when he was a young broadcaster.

"I recently heard a tape of me from those early years where Walt Frazier went after [official] Darell Garretson," he recalls. "And I'm saying: 'Go ahead, Darell, give him a T. Ah, Darell Garretson wouldn't give Walt Frazier a technical foul in Madison Square Garden if Frazier had pulled out a machine gun and pointed it at him.'"

When the Cavs won some of those early games, Tait sometimes just screamed. "I was so wrapped up in it, because I saw the games through Fitch's eyes," he says.

"Remember, we started that first season with 15 straight losses. We were drawing 2,000 at home. We had a dance team, but a couple of them were arrested for being ladies of the evening. I kept hearing from people around the league that the Cavs were running out of money and would fold."

So Tait pulled for the team as if his livelihood was at stake. It was.

"Every broadcaster who survives for a long time in one place usually has one team that put him over the top with the public. For Gib Shanley, it was the 1964 Browns. For Tom Hamilton, it was last year's Indians. For me, it was 'The Miracle of Richfield.'"
— Joe Tait

He continues to look through his scrapbooks.

There is a $12 hotel bill from the Washington Plaza in Seattle. That was 12 bucks for a room in 1970. . . . There is a $6 ticket for a game at the old Boston Garden in 1972. . . . A box score from a game in which Elvin Hayes scorched the Cavs for 40 points.

"The Big E had four consecutive games against us where he scored exactly 40 points, no more, no less," Tait says. "Look at this box score. Lew Alcindor had 53 points for the old Milwaukee Bucks. We lost 110-108. I kept it because he was booed at the foul line, and Kareem [Alcindor] put both hands over his head and gave the crowd two fingers."

That was Nov. 4, 1970. The crowd at the old arena was 3,575.

He sees a postcard of the arena in Las Cruces, New Mexico, where the Cavs played a game against the old Cincinnati Royals.

"There was a chicken-eating contest at a local restaurant there," he recalls. "I won by eating 21 pieces. Then I topped it off with a piece of chocolate cream pie."

Over the years, Tait's weight has fluctuated like the stock market. He has been in the low 200s, and as high as 300 pounds. He is at the high end now.

"I have gained and lost a family of six," he says.

In those early years with the Cavs, Tait supplemented his income by doing talk radio on WERE. He also did minor-league hockey games and was the public-address announcer for stock-car races at Cloverleaf Speedway. And he spent 17 years doing Indians games.

"When 'The Miracle of Richfield' hit [the 1975–76 playoffs], everyone was listening because there was little TV back then," Tait says. "It was a true happening. Today's marketing nitwits could not dream it up."

Tait's voice was the soundtrack.

"I still love doing high school sports. It's real. There are no dance teams. There is no scoreboard telling the fans when to cheer. For two bucks, you can get into a game and scream your lungs out. It's the purest form of sports, the sports I grew up with."
— Joe Tait

Telling the chicken-eating contest story makes Tait hungry, so he heads off to one of his favorite spots: the Starvin' Marvin truck stop near Lodi. With the red sweat suit and Burlington cap, Tait fits in with the guys who just climbed off the big rigs, guys who have to be in Omaha by the next morning.

Tait is recognized as the best broadcaster in the area, and has a drawer full of awards to prove it. He has been romanced by CBS and spent a year doing their college basketball Game of the Week.

"Hated it," he says. "All these guys in suits who sit in offices in New York. Too much politics. Too much management."

Tait's lunch arrives, a cheese omelet the size of Nebraska. There is a reason he picked this place.

"I have no desire to be Keith Jackson or Dick Enberg," he says. "I can do what they do, but there is a price you have to pay at the network level. The Cavs pay me very well. I can live out here in the country. The fans are super to me."

Tait is one of the few solo acts left on NBA radio. He doesn't want a color man. He acts as though he was back doing the Frankfort High Hot Dogs.

Few fans know that Tait has called eight high school games this season, in places such as Lima, New Philadelphia and Ashtabula. He has done them for free—or at least for food.

He'll accept a meal at the local hangout on Main Street.

Tait remembers his roots. He helps his wife, Jean, muck stalls for their three race horses. He is more likely to return a call from a kid at a small radio station who wants an interview than some fellow from New York.

"When the Cavs moved to Gund Arena, I was having real problems with the new NBA," he says. "I didn't like the people sitting by me in the rich seats who didn't know if the ball was blown up or stuffed. I didn't like the sledgehammer approach the P.A. man used to get the fans into it. It was starting to affect my work."

Then one morning last year, Tait was having coffee at the Lafayette Market.

"There I was in bustling Lafayette center, talking to the girl who sells the lotto tickets, and a fan sat down next to me," he recalls. "The guy was a farmer, and said he used to go down to the old Coliseum and yell for the Cavs. He said that he couldn't afford to go to the games anymore."

Tait figured a complaint was coming.

But the farmer told him: "Joe, I still watch all the games that I can on TV. I turn down the sound and listen to you. A lot of us out here do that. We still love the Cavs, and we love listening to you. You are our link to the team. You are watching the games for us, telling us about it."

Tait looks up from his half-eaten omelet as he tells the story.

"Then it hit me," he says. "I was thinking about the wrong people. I don't do the games for the guys in the loges. I do the games for the people who are like that farmer, the people who love the team and the game as much as I do. That is what keeps me going now."

3/10/1996

For Gund, it's about the people

IMAGINE OWNING A BASKETBALL TEAM, but never being able to see it play.

Then why own it? Why pay the bills? Why try to balance the egos and the budget? Why not just put your money into mutual funds?

"Because you don't have relationships with the people that way," Gordon Gund said.

Gund has owned the Cavs since 1983. He also is blind, having lost his sight 26 years ago to a disease called retinitis pigmentosa.

So he owns the Cavs, but has never seen Terrell Brandon or Mike Fratello. Yet he can give you remarkably accurate descriptions of how they look.

His friends and business associates tell Gund how these people appear. Gund has a remarkable memory and an even more amazing capacity for refusing to feel sorry for himself.

OK, he can't see. But he can still own the team. He can still sit in the meetings with General Manager Wayne Embry and Coach Mike Fratello.

"What I can do is listen and ask questions," he said. "Maybe that is one advantage to not being able to see. You are forced to listen more. You must ask good questions to get the information you need."

Gund talks about sitting in a basketball arena and "feeling the game." He means the emotion in the crowd. He even means the tone of Joe Tait's voice, as the Cavs' radio play-by-play man serves as Gund's eyes during the game.

It is the same in meetings.

He'll tell you he can "feel" when there is strain in a room, or when the principal people are in strong agreement.

"As a team owner, one of my main jobs is to keep the general manager and the coaches talking to each other and staying on the same page," he said. "That isn't always easy. A general manager's job is to look at things long range. The coach wants to win every game. He tends to think only about the next game."

That can create conflict. Some of it creative, some destructive.

"I listen to both sides," he said. "I ask questions. I don't say we should draft this player or trade that guy. I don't tell the coach who to play. Even if I had my sight, I would not do that. But I can help everyone see things more clearly by asking the right questions."

Imagine owning a basketball team and not being able to see.

You sit in meetings. You hear your coach and your general manager talking about drafting this player, trading for that one. There are millions and millions of dollars on the line—your dollars.

"This is such an uncertain business," Gund said. "You can do all the scouting and have all the reports, and maybe the player doesn't pan out as you hoped."

Danny Ferry?

"I like Danny very much," Gund said. "I believe he is getting the most out of his ability. I think he has developed nicely."

But didn't the Cavs believe he was a star? If not, why make the Ron Harper deal and commit more than $30 million to him?

"All indications were that Danny would be a star," Gund said. "To this day we don't know what effect him playing a year in Italy had on his career. Or what did Danny having a knee problem in his first year with us do to his career? That is what I mean about the uncertainties. And it works the other way."

For example, Mark Price?

"Exactly," Gund said. "We had good reports on Mark [in the 1986 draft]. But no one said he'd be a lottery pick. We wanted him very much. While Wayne Embry was not officially general manager, he was pretty much in place at the time. We knew the players Wayne wanted, and he wanted Price."

So the Cavs traded for a second-round pick from Dallas and obtained Price.

"Some people thought he was too slow to play in the NBA," Gund said. "Others said he would be a useful player. Not one person said Mark would become the great player that he did for us. Before we drafted Brad Daugherty, we had some people saying we should take Lenny Bias, that Bias was more spectacular, that Brad might not even become a good center. So you never really know."

Doesn't that drive you crazy?

"Sometimes," Gund said, laughing. "But I like that part of it, too. I like the challenge, the uncertainty. This is a business where you are taking some very young and sometimes immature young men. They also are very highly paid with big egos. And what you are trying to do is mold them into a team—I find that fascinating."

Not frustrating?

"Of course it can be that," he said. "I think back [to the early 1990s] when we had some of our best teams, and it seemed we never could stay healthy for very long.

"I don't know if we could have beaten Michael Jordan and the Bulls. Maybe no one could have. But I would have liked to have seen us with a healthy roster for the playoffs so we'd known for sure."

Wouldn't it be nice to at least see Ferry, Daugherty or any of these other players before you commit a king's ransom to them?

"Not really," Gund said. "Because that wouldn't change our decision. I would go with the advice of my basketball men. Simply by seeing them in a three-piece suit—or even seeing them play—that wouldn't change our course of action. I'm not going to overrule my coach and general manager on whom to draft or something like that."

Gund paused.

"You know what I'd like to be able to see?" he said.

"I'd just like to see a game. Just like a fan. I'd like to see the team play. I'd like to see the arena. I'd just like to sit back and enjoy the sight of it all."

When Gund bought the team back in 1983, most experts believed he'd keep it for four-to-five years, bring some stability and financial health—and then sell it.

He owns a company called "Gund Investments," and part of what he does is buy suffering companies and heal them. Some he keeps, some he sells.

When Gund bought the Cavs, he was not a basketball fan. He was a hockey man. Even though he was blind, he'd go on the ice . . . on skates . . . and play goaltender as his young sons shot pucks at him.

But basketball?

He played a little in the driveway, but that was it.

Yet, he has become one of the mainstays among NBA owners. Last fall, he was elected by his fellow owners as chairman of the NBA's Board of Governors, a prestigious position. He works closely with NBA Commissioner David Stern on everything from labor-management issues to helping the financially struggling franchises.

Gund has a reputation among NBA owners for being honest and a good listener. He doesn't jump to conclusions. He is patient. But when he does act, he can be decisive as with the 1986 draft that yielded Daugherty, Harper and Price. Or the Ferry trade, or matching John Williams' $26-million offer sheet from Miami.

"My only regret with the Cavs is that we haven't reached our ultimate goal, which is the NBA Finals," he said.

Is Embry to blame for that?

"I value intelligence and experience," Gund said. "I look at our franchise and it has been better than most NBA franchises during the last 10 years. I mean, only two teams play for a title every year—meaning 27 do not."

But what about Embry?

"I think he has hired two excellent coaches in Lenny Wilkens and Mike Fratello, and he has worked well with those coaches," Gund said. "Most of our moves have worked out relatively well. I thought Wayne was the right guy when we hired him [in 1986] and I still think he is the right guy for us. I believe in stability."

But some say the Cavs are complacent, that they refuse to drop back in the standings. . . .

"You mean to tank it?" asked Gund. "I won't allow that. I want the team to play as hard as it can. I want the players to give their best effort. We owe our fans that much."

But how do you build a championship team if you are stuck in the middle, winning 40-some games and losing in the first round of the playoffs?

"Some people may not agree, but I thought we were close to contending for a title with Price, Daugherty and [Larry] Nance," Gund said. "We will build the team again, and do it as we are now. We have added draft choices. We are well [about $6 million] under the salary cap, while most teams are now over the cap. I guess I'm saying we are in position to make moves to really improve the team."

Then Gund paused.

"I know it takes some patience," he said. "Look, I hate losing. But I also know the next few moves we make are critical to the future of this franchise. If we make the wrong moves, we are over the salary cap and we are stuck. We can't afford any mistakes."

So Gund plans to hold more meetings. He plans to listen to Player Personnel Director Gary Fitzsimmons, Embry and the Cavs' scouts to learn everything there is to know about this year's college players, possible NBA free agents and players who may be available in a trade.

"I like this part of it," Gund said. "I like sitting down, listening to these guys talk basketball. I like asking them questions, then watching us come to a conclusion on a course of action. I like trying to rebuild the team as we are right now. These are the reasons why I like owning the Cavs."

2/9/1997

Herb Score

IT WAS THE WEEK before Herb Score announced his retirement. As usual, Score and Tom Hamilton were in the broadcast booth, calling a Tribe game.

Between the sixth and seventh innings, the two broadcasters put their headsets down and relaxed during the 60-second commercial.

"Herb looked right at me and said he wasn't coming back next year," said Hamilton, his radio partner for eight years.

A stunned Hamilton stared at Score.

"I'm retiring," he told Hamilton.

"Herb, we gotta talk about this," said Hamilton.

"Ten seconds to air time," said the radio engineer.

Then Hamilton and Score put their headsets on and went back to work, the radio audience having no idea what Score had just decided.

Hearing the story, Joe Tait wasn't surprised.

"That's typical of Herb," said Tait, who was Score's partner on the radio from 1973–79. "He keeps his own counsel, and when he decides something—he tells you."

The Indians honored Score at Jacobs Field last night.

As usual, Hamilton was next to him in the booth.

Tait was there to represent all of Score's other partners. Score has worked with seven men in his 34 years' calling the Tribe games.

To understand Score, it's best to talk to the men who have sat next to him in the booth. Score is always friendly and pleasant, but you usually have a feeling that he's holding something back.

One of the few rules Score gave Hamilton was that they were not to talk about their personal lives on the air.

"Herb is a very private person," said Hamilton. "But I could never have had a better partner, and I doubt I ever will. For the seven months of the baseball season, you spend more time with your partner than you do with anyone, even your wife.

"That is why I'll always appreciate Herb. He was the same way every day. You never had to worry about mood swings with him. He's just a good person. Around baseball, no one ever says a bad word about Herb Score."

Tait was paired with Score from 1973–79.

"If you heard our broadcasts, you would have thought we were the best of friends on and off the air," said Tait. "We always got along, but away from baseball, Herb had his own friends and he went his own way. But when it came time for the broadcast, we had instant chemistry.

"I have never worked with a better person than Herb."

Score will never be considered a great broadcaster. He has no trademark calls. He might be best known for his blunders. Recently, he had Tony Bernazard at second base for the Tribe, even though he last played there in 1987.

"People just like Herb because he is so unassuming on the air," said Hamilton. "He doesn't think he's bigger than the game. There are no false pretenses, no phoniness about Herb. When you are on the air for 162 games a year, the listeners get to know you. You can't fool them, and Herb never tried."

Most fans know Score was a star pitcher with the Tribe in the middle 1950s before being hit in the eye with a line drive off the bat of Gil McDougald in 1957. He pitched several years after that, but was never the same.

Score was hired by the Tribe to do television broadcasts in 1964. He was 30 years old.

For the next 34 years, Score was always there for Tribe fans. He has a Cal Ripken–like sense of duty, even missing the wedding of one of his children because the Indians also had a game that day.

Score is old-school baseball.

You don't complain. You try to stay the same every day. You don't even read newspaper stories about yourself.

"A lot of guys say they don't," said Hamilton. "But Herb doesn't. I've seen people hand him stories, and he politely thanks them. When the person leaves, he throws them away without even glancing at the story."

Score has been a confidant of managers and general managers for most of his tenure.

"Herb understands more baseball than anyone I've ever met," said Tait. "Managers and GMs have always talked to him, even asked his advice. That's because they respect his opinion, and because they know he will never reveal their conversations to someone else."

It is like the old sign in the clubhouse: What you see here and say here stays here.

Another of his partners, the late Nev Chandler, said Score once gave him a slip of paper taped in an envelope. He told Chandler not to open it until the Indians hired a new manager.

About a week later, the Tribe fired Mike Ferraro and hired Pat Corrales.

Chandler opened the envelope and found Corrales name.

"Herb always knows what is going on," said Tait. "He's not psychic, he knows. And he knows all, because he never tells."

Score survived for 34 years, because broadcasting is the closest thing to playing, and Score loved being a ballplayer. He once said a player should stay in the game until they tear the uniform off your back, which is pretty much what happened to Score.

Now, he's 64. He has three children, eight grandchildren.

He also has no hobbies.

"But Herb has always told me that he likes to do nothing and he's very good at it," said Hamilton.

"Herb just sensed it was time to go," said Tait.

Score was originally offered a contract to call the games through 1999. He refused, signing a deal through 1998.

Now, he's decided he's had enough.

"And once he decides something, there is no changing Herb's mind," said Tait.

9/8/1997

Aeros help a special fan

ARIC MURRAY MAKES YOU BELIEVE IN BASEBALL.

Make that minor-league baseball.

"Nowhere else do people make us feel at home like here," said Tina Murray. "We go to the mall, and people sometimes look at us funny. We go to restaurants, and it's, well it's hard, because people look at us when I have to feed Aric."

But not at Canal Park.

Not Aeros fans.

Aric Murray is 16 years old and has a serious case of cerebral palsy. He can't use his arms. He's in a wheelchair. He is legally blind, although he can see figures on the diamond. Even speaking can be a struggle.

And as if that isn't enough, he has braces on his teeth.

But Aric Murray loves Akron Aeros games, because the management and fans treat him like everyone else—yet understand he needs a little help

They don't stare if he spills something. They don't make faces, wishing he'd hurry up. They assume he has every right to be there, because he's like them—just another baseball fan. Aric and his mother, Tina, went to 15 Aeros games last year. They still talk about seeing Jaret Wright at Canal Park months before the rest of America discovered him in the World Series.

"It's just more homey here," said Tina Murray. "This is our sixth game so far this season. We get tickets from friends or we buy them through the different promotions from the team. We usually can find discount tickets."

That's important.

That's because Aric already has had seven operations on everything from his ears to his toes. He is facing back fusion surgery coming up in the winter.

"So we watch our pennies," Tina Murray said. "We only made it to Jacobs Field once. This is a lot cheaper, and I really think it's more fun for us."

Tina Murray is a secretary at Children's Hospital Medical Center.

Her husband of 23 years, Paul Murray, works for Aircraft Braking Company in Akron. Tina works the day shift, Paul at night, so they always have someone home with Aric.

"During the week, I can take Aric to Aeros games when Paul is at work," she said. "On weekends, Paul takes him."

Baseball is more than a game to them.

"It's better than TV," Aric said, speaking slowly.

Canal Park isn't just a great place for the average fan to watch a game. It's a great place for Aric and his family. They can sit in the wheelchair section, yet still be behind home plate.

"Because of Aric's vision, it's important for us to be behind the screen so we don't have to worry about foul balls," she said.

He watches the games with an embroidered Aeros T-shirt, and a big purple hand with a No. 1 finger that reads "Akron Aeros."

"Getting the rubber hand was our treat for the night," said Tina.

Mom and son each have one.

They buy popcorn and soft drinks. They laugh at Orbit, the team mascot. They sing "Take Me Out to The Ballgame." Their favorite promotion is the Human Bowling Ball Contest.

"Baseball is a good game for Aric because it gets him outside," she said. "You don't know how great it is for us to get out of the house. Aric is very social, and here people aren't afraid to stop by and say hello to us."

You look at the Murray family, and you see smiles.

Aric tells you that Tina is a "super" mom.

Tina tells you that Aric "makes me feel good, because he's such a happy kid."

Paul is the kind of father who heads to Kenmore High every day at noon to help Aric get out of his wheelchair for a few moments, and just to be with his son.

And Rachel, Aric's 17-year-old sister, knows how to make her younger brother feel important.

But their life has been a series of hospital stays, operations and therapy sessions. It's a life that means you have to make sure you'll be welcome whenever you head out of the house.

Will there be enough room for the wheelchair? Are the restrooms equipped with handrails and ramps?

But even more important, how are the people?

"And nowhere do you find better people than at a minor-league baseball game," said Tina Murray.

5/21/1998

For Nev Chandler, smiles still linger

JEFF PHELPS REMEMBERS the first time that he talked to Nev Chandler.

It was in the mid-1970s. He was about 13 years old and Chandler was filling in for Pete Franklin on the Sportsline talk radio show.

"Nev took my call, and I said I wanted to be a sportscaster one day," Phelps said.

Chandler said that was great.

"Then I asked him something about [former Tribe infielder] Larvell Blanks," Phelps said. "Toward the end of the call, he told me to hang on. Then he talked to me for about 10 minutes off the air."

Phelps still can't believe it. He was just a yahoo calling a sports talk show. Chandler was a Cleveland TV star.

"He encouraged me to go into broadcasting and to stay in touch," Phelps said. "Then, when I was in college, I wrote him a letter and said I was still pursuing broadcasting. He invited me to spend a night with him in the radio booth, and I found myself sitting there with Nev and Herb Score as they called an Indians game."

An Akron resident, Phelps is sports director at WUAB-TV (Channel 43). As a young broadcaster, he sent tapes to Chandler, who replied with helpful hints.

"I'll never forget how kind he was to me," Phelps said. "When I finally got a job in Cleveland, he was really thrilled for me."

Doug Dieken spent 10 years sitting next to Chandler in the Browns radio booth.

"I have never been around a tougher guy," he said. "Not in football. Not anywhere. He'd come to the Browns games, just drained from the cancer and then chemotherapy. Then he'd drag himself up to the booth and he'd say, 'You have to cover for me.'"

Dieken stops as he tells the story, the emotion bubbling inside the former Browns offensive lineman.

"I don't care how sick he was, no one ever had to cover for Nev Chandler," Dieken said. "When the game began and he was behind the microphone, he was in Seventh Heaven. When I think of courage, I think of Nev Chandler. I think of how he'd complain bitterly about [Coach Bill] Belichick running Eric Metcalf up the middle, but he'd never complain about how sick he was."

"People in Cleveland loved Nev as a person and a broadcaster," said Kevin Byrne, public relations director of the former Browns. "But you should hear how the NFL people respected him."

Byrne said that video tape proved Chandler's calls were "right on the money."

How so?

"When Nev said a guy was on the 30-yard line, he was on the 30," Byrne said. "When Nev gave his trademark touchdown call of 5-4-3-2-1, it was as the guy was running over the 5-4-3-2-1-yard lines. NFL Films loved to use his voice because it was so enthusiastic, and he was so accurate."

Even in his final days when cancer was ravaging his body.

"Nev always was feisty," Byrne said. "He wanted no sympathy. Some days, he was so sick from the chemo, he looked green. But in the booth, he'd say, 'We're gonna get everything right today, and that includes you—Doug.'"

Chandler meant Doug Dieken, who sometimes cringed at Chandler's demands for excellence.

"I got a letter from a blind person who told me that he lost interest in football when he lost his sight," Dieken said. "Then, he said that he began listening to Nev and he could see the game again. That letter meant a lot to Nev."

Despite his enormous popularity, a part of Chandler was the kid in class who always wanted to hand in an extra-credit report or stay after school so the teacher would like him.

"He really worried about the Browns finding another announcer," Dieken said. "He'd worry that he wasn't good enough, or that some big name would come along and get the job."

Chandler just pushed harder, demanded more.

"Nev never talked behind your back," said Lana Durbin, a producer at Channel 5 who was hired as an intern by Chandler. "He told you what he wanted, and because you knew he really cared about the quality of the broadcast—and not his own ego—he made you want to work harder just to please him."

Dieken agreed.

"I just wished I had listened more to what Nev had to say about broadcasting," Dieken said.

Unlike many longtime members of the sports media, Chandler never lost his love for the games or became overly cynical about the people who played them.

"Nev was a true sports fan," Bill Wilder said. "When he was in the hospital, he couldn't get the Indians games on the radio. The AM band didn't come in, so we rigged up a wire from his radio out of the hospital window so he could hear the games."

Wilder is Chandler's doctor and longtime friend.

"Toward the end, when he obviously was in a lot of pain, he'd still be listening to the Indians," Wilder said. "And I asked him how it was going. He'd say, 'My poor Tribe, they're terrible.' I always wish Nev could have lived long enough to see the Indians in the World Series."

Chandler died a week before the 1994 baseball strike.

"He did get a chance to go to Jacobs Field," Wilder said. "That meant a lot to him. I have a picture of him in my office, and I think of Nev every day."

Lisa Bercu was hired by Chandler as an intern and became a producer and reporter for Channel 5. She now is director of broadcasting for the Baltimore Ravens, and still has a note from Chandler.

"It was telling me that he had to go see the doctor, that he just wasn't feeling well," Bercu said. "I guess I kept it because it was so rare to hear Nev say anything about his health. That visit was when he was diagnosed with [colon] cancer."

Bercu said that Chandler refused to indulge in melancholy—or to allow those around him to offer any sort of pity.

"I'd see him looking gaunt, tired and you knew he was hurting," she said. "But he'd just tell us how he planned to beat the cancer. He would try different treatments. He'd drink protein shakes and other vitamins. He'd get ornery and complain about things at the station, but never about what happened to him."

"It's hard to believe, but I never heard my father ask, 'Why me?'" Scott Chandler said. "Often I asked, 'Why my dad?' But not him. Until the last few weeks, he was convinced he was going to beat the cancer. He said things happened for a reason. I admired him so much for that."

"Nev wanted to stay on the air as long as possible, even when you could see the cancer was really taking a lot out of him," Bob Stevens said.

Now with ESPN, Stevens was Chandler's backup at Channel 5 when Nev was diagnosed with cancer in the spring of 1992.

"He never let us know how bad it was," Stevens said. "You'd see his shows, and there was no way you could tell. He was the conscience of the Cleveland sports fan. We had ratings surveys showing when a big sports story broke in Cleveland, more people watched us than ever—because they knew they could trust Nev to tell them the truth."

Stevens remains amazed at Chandler's ability to walk the thin line between being a broadcaster for a team and being an objective TV commentator.

"He had such respect from the local teams, he could criticize them, yet they'd still keep him on their payrolls to do the games," he said. "He was paid to do coaches shows with Bill Belichick, yet he criticized Belichick. His integrity was his greatest asset."

Most of his friends say that Chandler "made me laugh."

"I never heard him tell a joke," said Dieken, "but he could make me roar."

Chandler did it with his imitations.

"Nev did me better than I do me," former Tribe broadcaster Herb Score often said.

Tribe baseball writers remember an evening at a Japanese steakhouse in Minnesota where Chandler fell into Score's voice as he described a cook ("A fine young man") grilling a steak and chopping vegetables at the table.

"One time, he used Art Modell's voice and convinced Art's secretary to run out to the parking lot and move her car," Dieken said.

"Once, he started yelling at me about how no one in my office was working," said Byrne, the former PR director. "I could have sworn it was Art Modell, until finally Nev started laughing."

"I owe my career to Nev Chandler," said Matt Underwood.

Now the sports director at Channel 5 (Chandler's old job), Underwood echoes what you hear from so many young broadcasters: Chandler took time to meet and listen to them when they were nobodies. He offered advice. He helped them to find jobs.

In Underwood's case, he was a business student at Baldwin-Wallace who messed around at the campus radio station. A friend of Underwood's had a part-time job at Channel 5, and he played a tape for Chandler that included Underwood.

"For some reason, Nev liked what he heard of me," Underwood said. "One day, after a Browns practice at Berea, he stopped by Baldwin-Wallace to meet me."

Underwood is still astounded that Chandler would look up a college kid because of a voice on a scratchy tape. Chandler hired Underwood to an internship. Then to a part-time job. Then as a full-time reporter.

"He was a friend, a mentor," Underwood said. "I just think about him and I get emotional. It wasn't fair that he died so young. There was so much more he had to give people."

Underwood paused, regaining his composure.

"The night Nev died, I was watching the movie *Grumpy Old Men,*" he said. "I never saw the end of it. To this day, I still can't watch it."

Nev was married to Cindy Chandler for 24 years. Their daughter, Ashley, is a senior at Miami of Ohio. Son Scott is in sales in Jacksonville, Florida, although he'll be moving to Northeast Ohio, because his wife has found a job teaching special education in the Rocky River schools.

Cindy Chandler works part-time at the Animal Protective League, and has several dogs and cats at home.

"It was a love of horses that was the common bond between my mother and my sister," Scott Chandler said. "For Dad and I, it was sports. We never had a bad time at a sporting event, or when I was in the booth with him when he was doing a game."

Scott Chandler's favorite memories of his father are from Nev's final year.

"My mother and sister would go out of town for a horse show," he said. "Dad and I would grill steaks in the backyard, pop a few beers and watch the Indians game on TV. We were real friends."

It was only in the final few weeks, when the pain was so severe that Chandler had to be on medication, that it became clear that the end was near.

"My dad was always so optimistic," Scott Chandler said. "Here he was with cancer, and we'd see he had a bad day with chemo.

"But he always thought he'd beat it. He never let it drag him or the family down. I'm proud he was my dad."

Casey Coleman was the man who replaced Chandler as the Browns radio play-by-play voice.

"Talk about an impossible situation," he said. "He was so respected, so loved. It's just like the guy who comes after [Cavs broadcaster] Joe Tait. Heaven help him."

Coleman called the final Browns home game on December 17, 1995.

"I brought pictures of my father [Ken Coleman], Gib Shanley and Nev to that game," he said, referring to the three radio voices of the team. "There was a hole in the radio booth. When the game ended, I put those pictures in that hole along with the play-by-play sheet from that final game—sort of a Browns broadcasters' time capsule."

The old stadium has been torn down. The old Browns are in Baltimore. Some NFL owners now want a billion dollars from the next owner of the Browns.

"I miss my dad so much," said Scott Chandler.

"But in some ways, I'm glad he didn't have to see what happened to the Browns. It would have eaten him up."

8/9/1998

Embry a very good GM, better person

UNTIL HIS SENIOR YEAR in high school, Wayne Embry lived in a house without indoor plumbing.

He walked the streets of Springfield, Ohio, knowing there were some restaurants that wouldn't serve him, and that the only movie theater in town wouldn't sell him a ticket.

He wanted to play basketball at the University of Dayton, but discovered that the school never had a black player and was not ready to break the color line.

He attended Miami of Ohio, and learned that when you play in towns such as Louisville, the only place for a young black man to eat at the hotel was in the kitchen.

He came into the NBA, where the unwritten rule was "only three blacks on a team."

"But I refused to let race or other people define me," he said. "I never wanted to be a 'black general manager.' I just wanted to be a general manager, and a good one."

Embry is more than the outgoing general manager of the Cavs. He was recently voted to the Basketball Hall of Fame because of his overall contributions to the sport, ranging from his career as a five-time All-Star center to becoming the first black GM not just in the NBA, but all of the major professional sports.

"I don't believe being the first black GM is the only reason I was

picked to the Hall of Fame," he said. "At least, I hope not. It is a part of
me, of my history. But all I ever asked was to be judged like anyone
else, regardless of color."

He paused, reflecting on his front-office career of 27 years.

"The truth is every time I walked into a [corporate] board room, I
always felt I had to be the best prepared guy there," he said. "I knew people were looking at me, wanting to see if I really deserved the job I had."

He paused again.

"In a different way, I know what Jackie Robinson felt like," he said.
"I know what it feels like to know that if I didn't make it, then who
knows when the next opportunity would come?"

Embry didn't just mean for himself, but for the next black trying to
break through the glass ceiling that often has kept minorities out of
the top front-office jobs in all sports.

Usually, he was the only black in a world of well-educated white
men in suits and ties, men who were not accustomed to dealing with
minorities who were considered their professional equals.

"Rather than make that a dividing point, I wanted to use it to bring
people together," he said. "My goal has always been to bridge the gap
between people and races."

Embry is a quiet, shy man.

He grew up on a 70-acre farm in Central Ohio, milking cows and
plowing fields in the pre-integration days of the 1940s and early 1950s.

He is a huge man, 6-foot-8 and 300-some pounds with hands the
size of catchers' mitts. Yet his voice often lapses into a whisper, his
temperament is to think of others' feelings first.

"People stare at me without me saying a word," he said. "When
you're my size, all you have to do is walk in a room."

Yet this is a man who prefers to let his record speak for itself.

While his critics lash out that Embry's teams have never won an
NBA title, how many GMs can make that claim—especially in a sport
that has been dominated by Boston, Los Angeles and Chicago for most
of his tenure?

In Milwaukee, his Bucks won six division titles.

When he was hired as GM of the Cavs, he inherited the likes of
Edgar Jones, World B. Free, John Bagley, Phil Hubbard, Keith Lee and
Melvin Turpin.

Before Embry arrived, the Cavs made only four playoff appearances
in 16 years.

Nine of his 13 Cavs teams went to the playoffs, and 10 of the 13 years, the team had a winning record. Twice, he was picked as the NBA's Executive of the Year.

"I think my greatest contribution was to put together teams in Cleveland that the fans could be proud of," he said. "We had a lot of good people playing here."

The Cavs of the late 1980s and early 1990s were Embry's dream team.

Mark Price, Larry Nance, Brad Daugherty, Hot Rod Williams and Craig Ehlo were a mix of solid citizens, of black and white players coached by a black man in Lenny Wilkens.

But race was never an issue, which is exactly how Embry wanted it.

Embry isn't especially comfortable talking about race, because he is an idealist.

"I went through a lot [when it came to race]," he said. "But I always believed in the American Dream. I believed if you worked hard enough and paid your dues, you could succeed."

Embry is not naive.

"Sometimes, I know that race is a factor in how people look at you or the decisions they make," he said. "But I never let it be a factor in how I think or act. Yes, I had some people think that I would give blacks a break because I'm black, or that I wouldn't give whites a fair shake."

He pauses, shaking his head.

"Why can't we just judge people as people?" he asked. "That is what I've always been about. I was glad that as time passed, most people accepted me as a GM who just happened to be black."

Embry was so shy, that as a high school senior who was being recruited by colleges, he once hid in a barn rather than face one coach whose scholarship he planned to turn down.

For someone with that personality to be able to stand up in front of unrelenting TV lights and explain a major trade or coaching move shows how much a man can mature in a lifetime spent pursuing the right things.

"I grew up in modest circumstances," he said. "But I wouldn't trade the values I learned from that farm and my close-knit family for anything."

Embry is now 62, and he knows that a lot of people will dismiss what he says as outdated cliches, but he doesn't care.

"It's what I believe, what I am," he said. "Over the years, there have been racist letters, threats and slurs. But I refused to dwell on the negative, to let those things drag me down. My goal has always been to inspire people to rise above all that. If I can be remembered for anything, I hope it's that—helping us to move beyond race and just to be more accepting of each other as people."

6/27/1999

Dolan should hope the joke isn't on him

"ROBBIE ALOMAR WHO?"

That was not the wisest way for Tribe owner Larry Dolan to answer a question about trading the future Hall of Fame second baseman.

To Dolan's credit, he regrouped from a joke that drew nothing but grumbles from Friday's Akron Press Club luncheon to call Alomar perhaps the greatest second baseman ever.

But Dolan has found himself in a middle of the old debate that has always surrounded pro sports. In the movie *North Dallas Forty*, where a football player tells his coach: "Every time I say sports is a business, you say it's a game. And when I say it's a game, you say it's a business."

And Dolan called Alomar "an asset."

He added, "You don't fall in love with your assets."

But no one buys a ticket to watch "assets." The best players mean more than that to us. They aren't just bodies in uniforms.

Down deep, Dolan knows this.

When he overpaid to buy the Indians for $335 million before the 2000 season, he sounded a lot more like a fan than an owner. He told stories of keeping score at old League Park, of listening to Jimmy Dudley call games on the radio.

You didn't hear those tales from Dick Jacobs, the man who both revived the Indians and made a fortune off them by selling to Dolan. Rather, Jacobs liked to talk about being a teenaged car-hop at Swenson's and beating the other waiters to the cars that tipped the most.

Jacobs was always a bottom-line guy.

But he also left the Indians as perhaps the greatest owner in Tribe history. Twice, his teams went to the World Series (1995, 1997), and they dominated the AL Central Division. He gave former general manager John Hart enough financial ammunition to transform the Indians into a legitimate contender.

Dolan took over in 2000, and the Indians missed the playoffs for the first time since 1994. Last year, they were eliminated in the first round. Given the economic climate and the slippage in talent, it sure seems that Jacobs knew when to cash out and Hart was smart to bolt for Texas.

Meanwhile, Dolan finds himself sounding more like Dick Jacobs than Dick Jacobs. At one point Friday, he shrugged and said, "How do you get warm and fuzzy when someone makes $10 million?"

But that is what teams ask fans to do.

How else can you convince them to buy shirts with numbers and names of their favorite players? There has to be some emotional attachment, because there is nothing rational about dishing out $20-$40 a ticket to watch a bunch of millionaires play baseball.

Dolan also said the Indians didn't get "where we wanted to go" with Alomar, so that made it right to trade him. That's a poor argument, the kind former Tribe president Gabe Paul would make when he said, "We finished in sixth place with Buddy Bell and we can finish in sixth place without him."

It wasn't Alomar's fault that the Indians failed to reach the World Series.

Dolan said the problem is . . . pitching.

So true.

He said new general manager Mark Shapiro plans to build a team based on pitching, and he praised the promising young arms of Bartolo Colon, C.C. Sabathia and Danys Baez.

He correctly diagnosed the 2001 team as one where sometimes, "No one cared on the field, and I'd look in the dugout and see nothing."

The Indians do need better pitching, more intensity and a stronger farm system, because too many prospects were traded off for veterans to help the team stay in contention.

In Dolan's words, the Indians do "need a new direction, and we will go as far as the young pitching takes us."

Dolan knows the fans are upset. His Akron visit was the first of several appearances he's making, trying to preach the new Tribe gospel. He insisted that the Indians aren't returning to the dark ages of the 1960s, '70s, '80s, and he probably is right.

They already have sold 2.1 million season tickets. They remain among the top 25 percent in terms of player payroll. He's trying to say the Indians still will be a good team, just a different kind of team.

This season will determine if that's really the case.

1/13/2002

Memories

Thanks, Larry

WHEN LARRY NANCE WALKS on court at halftime tonight, he will be in the spotlight. The applause will embrace him—and Nance will wish he was anywhere but there.

Yes, he wants his No. 22 to hang from the rafters at Gund Arena, which will happen tonight when the Cavaliers play host to Phoenix. And yes, he knows he was the best Cavaliers forward—ever.

But Nance isn't the kind of man who talks about these things.

If you want to have an in-depth conversation with Nance, ask him about his wife, Jaynee, and their two children. Ask him about fishing. Ask him about his race car.

Just don't expect to talk about Larry Nance with Larry Nance.

"One time I was giving a speech in Norwalk," Cavs broadcaster Joe Tait said. "Afterward, a lady came up to me and said she'd heard that I knew Larry Nance. She asked if I could get this picture signed by him. It was a picture of Larry and her son. Larry had the little boy up on his shoulders."

Tait told the woman he'd see Nance in a few days at the Cavs game.

"She had no idea that Larry even played pro basketball," Tait said. "She just knew him as a car owner from Norwalk Speedway. To her, he was a nice man with a fast car who liked to hang around the track and play with the little kids."

That's a vintage Nance story.

Think about this: No NBA forward has blocked more shots than Larry Nance. None.

But Nance never talked trash.

No "In Your Face."

When he'd swat a shot, he'd give almost an embarrassed shrug as he'd run down to the other end of the court—sure not to look at the man he just humiliated.

"Larry played the game like you should," Cavaliers general manager Wayne Embry said. "He played it with class and dignity."

Nance wore his socks nearly up to his knees, as if he came from a more elegant era of basketball. He was a three-time All-Star, a career 17-point scorer and good for eight rebounds a night.

When he retired this fall, he was only 35, but seemed to have as much in common with this generation of screaming stars as canvas tennis shoes and the two-handed set shot.

That is part of the reason that Embry added Nance to Mike Fratello's coaching staff. Embry agrees with *Sports Illustrated*, which has a cover story this week about Petulant Prima Donnas and how many of today's young players are a bane to the NBA.

"Larry was always good with young players," Embry said. "He's a positive guy, an upbeat person and a man of tremendous integrity and work ethic. I worry about us losing those things in the NBA, and I want our young players to be around a guy like Larry and to listen to him."

Lawrence Donell Nance came from Anderson, South Carolina, a small town in the Appalachian foothills only a jump shot away from Clemson University.

His father drove trucks for a living. He also had a knack for fixing motors. If you had a problem with your car or pickup, a noise under the hood that baffled the boys at the filling station, you let Mack Nance listen and tinker with the engine.

At first, Nance didn't understand his father's fascination with cars, trucks and tune-ups. But soon, he found himself under the hood, poking around, tightening screws and checking alternators.

That passion remains. He owns his own race car, "Catch 22", and some of his happiest moments are when he's up to his elbows in grease with half of the car's engine dismantled on the floor of his garage.

Nance's mother, Minnie, was a cook. He had three brothers and a ton of cousins, and they often played basketball together on the hoop in Nance's backyard.

It was here that Nance grew up learning to say "Yes, sir" and "No, ma'am." His parents made him take three years of piano lessons, and he played for the church choir. He wasn't allowed to go outside and play until his homework was finished.

Nance was quiet and polite. He grew tall, all the way to 6-foot-5 at McDuffie High in Anderson.

But that put him near the top of no one's recruiting list. In fact, Nance was set to attend Anderson Junior College when Clemson decided to use its last scholarship on a local kid who would practice and not complain about sitting on the bench.

Between his freshman and sophomore years, he grew a half-foot and, suddenly, he was 6-foot-10 with the arms of an 8-footer. Just as remarkably, Nance grew into a starter in the Atlantic Coast Conference.

"We had the 20th pick in the 1981 draft," Phoenix Suns owner Jerry Colangelo said. "I scouted Larry myself and I loved his athleticism. I remember seeing him leap into the heavens to block a shot, but he had no outside shot, and was not much of an offensive player."

The Suns worried that the Los Angeles Lakers, who picked in front of Phoenix, might beat them to Nance.

"Jerry West loved Nance," Colangelo said. "But no one else in their front office did, and they took Mike McGee instead."

As the Suns debated Nance, several of their basketball people made the case for Michigan State's Jay Vincent, who was a far more polished player.

"The morning of the draft, I found myself going along with the people on my staff who said that Nance was a project, and if Vincent were there, we should take him," Colangelo said. "When it came time for us to pick, I grabbed the microphone with every intention of calling Vincent's name. But something just swelled up in me and I said, 'The Phoenix Suns take Larry Nance.' It was just a gut feeling."

It turned out to be a slam dunk of a decision, although not right away. Nance averaged only 6.6 points as a rookie.

"We told Larry what he had to do to become a better player," Colangelo said. "He had to do more than run and jump. We gave him a summer program, and he went to work."

Nance returned to the Suns as a starter, and became one of the league's premier players.

A true glimpse into the heart of Nance is the 1984 Slam Dunk Contest. It may have been the only time in his life that he actually showed off, as he took a basketball in each hand and dunked one after the other, like a windmill whirling.

He beat out Julius Erving—and never competed again.

"I was invited every year, but I didn't want to put that extra wear-and-tear on my legs. It also didn't make any sense to leave my family for that weekend just to dunk."

But those who know Nance insist he was embarrassed by the attention he received. In fact, he seldom dunked in games, preferring to gently drop the ball through the hoop.

The Cavs acquired Nance in February 1988 as part of the Kevin Johnson deal. It was a trade that made both Phoenix and Cleveland contenders.

With the Cavs, Nance added a new weapon—an accurate 15-foot jumper. He still ran up and down the court with that long, regal stride. He still blocked shots, including a team-record 11 in 1989 against the New York Knicks.

But what tells you more about Nance is how he had to give his wife and daughter a good luck kiss before each home game.

As the Cavs retire his No. 22, what comes to mind is that they are honoring more than a fine basketball player. They are paying tribute to a good person.

1/30/1995

Robinson was a ground breaker

IT'S HARD TO BELIEVE it was 20 years ago when Frank Robinson became the first black manager in Major League Baseball.

But as Robinson talks about it, you see that his hair is almost white. You also hear him mention the names of players such as Duane Kuiper, Rico Carty and Dennis Eckersley—players who are long gone from the Indians.

There has always been anger and fire inside Robinson, driving him to do what few men could. But at the age of 59, there also seems to be some peace about the man.

He remains a warrior at heart, but that heart has been tempered by wars from the past.

He praises the Indians for having the courage to break the color line, and he realizes that maybe only the Indians could have been so desperate to take that chance.

"I knew that some team was going to do it," Robinson said. "But I was surprised when it came as soon as it did. The old-boy network for hiring managers was so strong—it's still strong today. It took a special set of circumstances for it to happen."

Robinson is now the assistant general manager for the Baltimore Orioles, a position he has held for five years. He has done everything but run his own team—and that is what he views as the next step.

There are now three active black managers—but only one black general manager, Houston's Bob Watson. Robinson believes that this must change, and that he is qualified to change it.

As Robinson ponders his career today, he surprises himself when he admits that he is a part of the baseball establishment. He managed for 11 years with three teams.

Being hired, fired and hired again by another team is one of the signs that you have been welcomed to the club.

Now he has moved into the Orioles' front office. He has been a big-league coach, a minor-league manager and worked with the Baltimore farm department.

"I really don't want to manage any more," he said. "I've had three shots at it. Let the younger guys [manage]. But a chance to run my own team . . . yes, I think that I am ready for that. It is something that I have been preparing myself for ever since Cleveland."

Until recently, there was little in the last 35 years about which the Indians could be proud. But hiring Robinson in 1975 was one of the team's best moments, and it was the product of pure desperation.

"If the Indians had been winning—or even if they were drawing, they never would have hired me," Robinson said. "But let's face it, the situation back then wasn't very good. They felt they had to do something, and they thought that maybe by hiring someone different, they could turn things around."

Nick Mileti owned the team, along with 47 "partners." For as little as $50,000, you could be a partner in the Tribe.

The result was that the Indians were the worst-financed team in the majors during much of the 1970s. They traded and/or sold players who were on the verge of free agency because they knew that they'd never be able to afford them.

They also were banned from certain hotels and airlines because they failed to pay their travel bills.

Once, they were on a bus carrying them from the airport to a hotel in Detroit. About 10 of the seats were ripped out.

The players began to scream at the driver about wanting "a real bus." The driver yelled back, "When you guys pay your bills for the last three years, then you'll get a real bus."

The Indians were losing on the field and at the bank. Fans were beaten down by a franchise that had only two winning seasons since 1959.

Or how about this? From 1959–74, the Indians went through nine managers in 15 years.

When they went looking for No. 10, Ted Bonda had an idea.

Bonda was the team's president and Mileti's right-hand man. He also was a George McGovern liberal who had a passion for civil rights. He was appalled where the world was in the middle 1970s, but baseball's Jim Crow mentality still dictated that when a team needed a manager, only white men should apply.

"Phil Seghi was the general manager, and Ted Bonda always let Phil take credit for hiring me," Robinson said. "But it was Bonda's call. If Seghi had his way, he'd have hired one of his buddies. Bonda was not a part of the baseball establishment. He wanted to do something dramatic, something he hoped might help the attendance—so he tried a black manager."

As usual, the Indians were hunting for a bargain.

Robinson was acquired by the Tribe late in the 1974 season to help the team with a pennant drive that never materialized. He earned $180,000 as a designated hitter. He finished that season with 22 homers.

When the Indians asked him to manage, they also wanted him to still play. The offer was $200,000—his old salary plus $20,000 to manage.

At first, Robinson wanted to hold out for more. He was inclined to pass up the job, period, because he knew the Indians were in sad shape. If he flopped with them, then he or another black man might never manage again.

But then he considered something else. If he turned down a chance to be the first black manager, then the baseball establishment could say, "We tried to hire a black, but Frank Robinson wouldn't do it." They could use that as an excuse not to hire any other blacks.

"I had to take the job almost under any circumstances," he said.

Robinson was neither a good manager for the Tribe—nor a bad one.

"In retrospect, I think it was important that they didn't feel that they had to fire me at midseason, or even at the end of the first year," he said.

If Robinson had embarrassed himself or the team and was canned by the All-Star break, then that would have become reason in the minds of many baseball people not to hire a black manager.

"I didn't like it, but in the beginning, everything was about race," he said. "Some of the people in baseball didn't think a black could or should manage. Some of my players with the Indians didn't want to play for a black manager."

On opening day, April 8, 1975, Robinson put himself in the lineup as the DH. There were 56,715 fans at Cleveland on a brisk afternoon. In his first at-bat, Robinson faced Doc Medich of the Yankees. Medich slipped two quick strikes past Robinson, then Robinson barely fouled off a third pitch to avoid striking out.

He called time out and collected himself. Suddenly, he was angry. Maybe it was from all the pressure that came with his first managerial job. Maybe it was from the racist letters that showed up at his mail box, or even the death threats.

But suddenly, he was really mad at Medich, who didn't even bother to waste a no-ball, two-strike pitch. "He's trying to embarrass me in my home park on my day," Robinson thought to himself. He also was aware that more than 100 reporters from across the country were in Cleveland to see what a black manager would do in his first game.

He fouled off a few more pitches, ran the count to two balls and two strikes, then homered over the left-field fence.

"I floated around the bases," he said. "You know, I don't think about it that much now. But as I get older, I'm sure that I'll make it even bigger. I'll say there [was] standing room only at the old 80,000-seat stadium. I'll say I hit the ball into the third deck (even though there was no third deck). I'll have fun with it."

For now, Robinson is simply proud of that day.

As a manager, Robinson made some mistakes. He dueled with players such as Gaylord Perry, Larvell Blanks and Rico Carty. While he had managed for eight years in the Puerto Rican winter league, he was still a rookie big-league manager.

"It was hard for me to relax in those first few years," he said. "It's like being the only black in the room. You know you are as good as anyone else in that room and better than a lot of people—but you don't feel comfortable. Rather than respect you, they sort of tolerate you."

Along with being black, Robinson also was fighting the label that superstars don't make good managers because they can't tolerate the weaknesses of average players.

"It was hard for me to let things go, with either a player or the umpires," he said. "With the Indians, I took too many things personally. If I thought someone crossed me, I held it against them for a long time. Criticism would just stick to me."

One of the incidents he regrets is punching out a minor-league pitcher named Bob Reynolds, when the Tribe played their Class AAA Toledo team. He threw a pitch behind Robinson's head, and the manager charged the mound and clocked him.

But Robinson did improve the Indians. He inherited a 77-85 team, and raised the record to 79-80 in 1975 and 81-78 in 1976. He was fired midway through the 1977 season after a 26-31 start.

"I was a decent manager with the Indians, a better one with the Giants and a good one with Baltimore," he said. "I'm proud that I was good enough to be hired by other teams."

Robinson's record is 738-814, and he was the 1989 American League Manager of the Year with the Orioles. Robinson calls himself "a survivor" and wants other blacks in baseball management to be able to say the same.

"I'm glad that we have had minority managers, and I'm glad some teams are willing to hire a minority because they believe he's the best man for the job," he said. "But there still are some teams where skin color is an issue, and that bothers me.

"As long as that is the case, we can say that things are better, but we have to keep pushing for more minorities to get a chance."

5/18/1995

Graham still one of "Paul's Guys"

OTTO GRAHAM meets you at the door wearing a golf shirt that says "Paul's Guys" over the pocket.

That's Paul—as in legendary Browns coach Paul Brown.

It has been 40 years since Graham threw his last pass for the Browns. He retired after leading the Browns to the title in 1955.

Paul Brown was fired as Cleveland's coach by Art Modell in 1962.

Graham is now 73, retired and living in an upscale ranch home with a screened-in swimming pool on a quiet street in Sarasota. He can walk out his door and step on to a local golf course.

Eighteen years ago, Graham fought and beat rectal cancer. He recently suffered some heart problems, but they are under control.

He comes across as a nice man, a thoughtful neighbor—the kind of guy who has a black Labrador retriever at his side. In Graham's house, the Lab is named Cleo—and she has trained her owner to rub her stomach on cue.

Graham reminds you that he is far removed from pro football, here on the West Florida coast. But he still considers himself one of "Paul's Guys," even though the two men banged heads over plays.

"Paul Brown ruled with an iron hand, and I really think that is the way you have to coach," he said.

Even today?

"Especially today," the Hall of Fame quarterback said. "That is why I was happy to see Art Modell give [Bill] Belichick a chance to run the football operation himself.

"If I were to coach today, I would have it in my contract that I'm in charge of coaching 110 percent. The owner should be in charge of the finances, but the coaching and disciplining [of] the team—that is my department entirely."

Graham likes Modell as a person, but he believes the owner made a mistake when he dumped Paul Brown.

"I heard that Art liked to sit in on the football meetings," Graham said. "You can't have an owner putting his two cents in there, and I know Paul Brown told him that. If Art has backed off and given Belichick more freedom, that's good."

Graham is an expert on this subject. He was the coach of the Washington Redskins from 1966–68.

"I was too nice of a guy to be an NFL coach," he said. "You have to be part SOB to be a good one, I'm convinced of that. Look at the guys who have been the most successful—Lombardi, Noll, Shula, Landry, Parcells and Paul Brown—in their own way, they all could be an SOB. They all made their players fear them a little.

"Heck, when I coached, if a guy was five minutes late for a meeting and we hadn't started yet, I just let it go. I knew that I should come down hard on the guy, but I just didn't."

Graham is a stand-up guy, the kind who treats everyone as he'd like to be treated. Coaches can't always do that, and Graham tells a Paul Brown story to prove the point.

"My rookie year with the Browns was 1946, and our team captain was Jim Daniell, a lineman from Ohio State," Graham recalled. "We had won our division and were waiting to play the winner of the Colts-Buffalo game for the old AAFC title.

"Daniell and some other players were out on the town. Daniell had a few drinks, and he pulled his car up behind a police car. I don't know about you, but when I'm behind a police car, I don't honk the horn and tell him to get out of the way—but Jim did.

"The policemen got out of the car, came up to Jim and a confrontation ensued. They took Jim down to the station. He said he wasn't drunk and demanded a sobriety test. Well, it turned out that he had drank enough to be legally drunk."

Graham read about the team captain being arrested in the morning newspaper and wondered what Brown would do at practice the next day.

"Paul called the team together and said, 'Jim, is what I read in the paper true?'

"Jim said it was.

"Paul said, 'Fine, then turn in your suit. You are through.'

"Jim said, 'Do you want to hear my side of the story?'

"Paul said, 'No, you are through.'

"Jim got up and left. Then it hit us. Paul Brown had just thrown the team captain off the team right before the championship game. We were a young team and he had us in the palm of his hand.

"What I didn't know until later, was that Jim's backup was just as good as Jim. So Paul was able to make a point with us and not hurt the team, either."

Graham recently was named one of the four greatest quarterbacks in the 75-year history of the National Football League—the others are Johnny Unitas, Sammy Baugh and Joe Montana.

The Browns won seven titles with him and went to 10 consecutive championship games with him as quarterback.

"For the first five years, I called my own plays and we won championships," Graham remembered. "Then one year, Paul Brown told me that he was going to call the plays."

And what did he think of that?

"I didn't like it," Graham said, laughing. "We had some real battles. But Paul said that between him, his coaches in the press box and talking to players coming out of the game, he could see things and process information better than I could."

And?

"And he had a point—sort of. You know those movies where you see a quarterback look over the huddle at the defense and he calls the perfect play for a touchdown? Hell, that never happens. You can't be sure what kind of defense they'll play, because they disguise it. But the coach doesn't know, either.

"With Paul, he didn't want us to change the plays at the line of scrimmage. It was a guessing game. Me, if I saw eight guys to the right, I didn't think it was a good idea to run a play to the right."

But did you?

"He was Paul Brown," Graham said, looking at you as if you should know better than to ask the question. But once in a while, I'd change a play," he confided. "I'd tell the guys in the huddle, 'We better make this work, or I'll never hear the end of it.' If it worked, I didn't hear a word. If I changed it and it didn't work ... boy, I never heard the end of it."

Graham speaks reverently of Brown's innovations and organizational abilities.

"If we had a guy who was a drunkard or a troublemaker, Paul Brown would get rid of him," Graham said. "I admired him for that."

The ultimate tribute to Brown is that 40 years later, Graham remains in awe of the man—even if they didn't always agree.

When Graham coached the Redskins, who called the plays? The answer to this question tells you the difference between Brown and his old quarterback.

"Sonny Jurgensen was my quarterback," Graham said. "I let him call about all the plays. He was a terrific quarterback, so why not?"

As a pro coach, Otto Graham discovered he couldn't be another Paul Brown.

"There was a game in Washington where we had a rookie who fumbled a punt and we lost the ball deep in our own territory," he said, beginning another story.

If Paul Brown had coached the team, he either would have melted the kid with a steel glare, or simply turned his back on the young man as if he weren't there.

"Me, I put my arm around him," Graham recalled. "And 50,000 fans booed me. Can you believe that?"

Graham was fired after three years and a 17-22-3 record, and was replaced by Vince Lombardi.

He returned to college coaching at the Coast Guard Academy in New London, Conn.

"It was small-college football, but I loved it," he said. "Those kids aren't great athletes, but they are top-notch people with tremendous intelligence and desire. They would go through a wall for you.

"I hated getting beat, but I can't make every game life and death. Maybe that is why I wasn't suited for coaching in the NFL."

But Graham had a tremendous impact on the cadets he worked with for 23 years. They respected him for his honesty and decency. His old Browns teammates talk about him the same way.

As a player, Graham never earned more than $25,000—his salary in his last season of 1955.

"What is that worth, maybe $400,000 in today's dollars?" he asked.

"But I never made money into a big issue like some of the older guys."

Why not?

"I don't resent all the money that these kids are paid today in the NFL. The more they make, the more they pay in taxes," he said.

"Well, between the time I spent in the service during World War II and then the time I worked at the Coast Guard Academy, I now have a $50,000 annual pension—tax free.

"And the way I see it, the players today are helping to pay my salary."

9/10/1995

The Toe

LOU GROZA wears a friendly smile and a nice blue tie. His steps are small, slow but certain—souvenirs of two hip replacement operations and 21 years of pro football.

Groza lives in a comfortable house in Berea, the same house for the last 34 years. That tells you a lot about the man.

So does this: "I hate controversy."

And this: "My parents always told me to treat people how I was treated, and I took that to heart."

And this: "When the Browns moved, I felt like I lost a close relative. I mean, I was so upset that I couldn't even talk to anyone the day it happened. I now know why it happened, but I still don't understand why. I just know it still hurts."

No one played for the Browns longer than Groza. Most fans remember him as "The Toe," who kicked for the team for 21 years and was the only player to have been on all eight of their championship teams. He also was an offensive tackle from 1946–59.

"I'd block some guy, he'd step on my foot—then I'd have to get out of the mud and go kick a field goal on the next play," he says. "I wore my square-toed kicking shoe even when I was playing tackle."

Groza was 6-foot-3 and weighed more or less 250 pounds (well, probably more than 250) when he played for the Browns. Most of us remember him approaching the ball—then taking exactly 2 1/2 steps each time, every time—and booming the ball through the goal posts.

We also remember a healthy gut hanging over his football pants.

"I tried to watch my weight when I played," Groza says, laughing. "And I just kept watching it. Believe it or not, I was the smallest of the four boys in our family. My father weighed over 300 pounds."

Groza is now 72 years old. He is from the Bob Dole generation, the people who grew up during the Depression, fought the last great war to keep America safe—then set out to make life better for their children.

Groza tells you about Martins Ferry, an Ohio River town near Wheeling. He tells you how smoke in the air and soot on the windows were good signs.

"That meant money and that meant jobs," he says.

He was born above Groza's Tavern on Main Street. His father had immigrated from Hungary at age 12. He worked in coal mines, then the steel mills. He wanted more. So he opened a pool hall, then the tavern.

Groza tells you that his father kept order because he was all of 300 pounds—and he had a pistol behind the bar, even though he never needed to use it.

"It was a situation where you never really left that tavern," he says. "Each of us had chores and we did them. My father never tolerated much nonsense."

Groza learned his kicking from older brother Frank, and he practiced booting footballs between telephone poles and over power lines. They played pickup games at a place called Mill Field, near the steel mills. There was ash in the air, but no one much cared. Afterward, they swam in the Ohio River.

"No one talked about pollution," he says. "We knew the river was dirty, but no one worried much about it."

All he knew was that his parents demanded that he study hard, that he attend college and that he become somebody. So Lou Groza . . . All State football player, All-State basketball player . . . member of the National Honor Society, and the kid his friends call "Big Chief" . . . earned a scholarship to play football for Paul Brown at Ohio State.

As you listen to Groza, you realize that he loves football. But it wasn't the game that shaped him. It was life on the Ohio River, and his time in the Pacific.

That's because after a year at Ohio State, he was drafted into the U.S. Army. The year was 1943.

At first, Groza tells you that his time in the Pacific was no big deal. He tells you that millions have stories like his. That you went out and did your duty—that he was nothing special.

All of that might be true, but those of us from the generations that followed still need to hear what these men did in the war. Their stories are important, because they tell us a lot about that generation and about the country.

Groza was a "surgical technician," which means he helped the first level of doctors, guys in tents only a few miles behind the front lines. His first stop was Leyte, in the Philippines, then Okinawa.

"I remember getting out of a [landing craft] on the beach at Leyte," he says. "It was the first time I saw combat. A guy about 10 feet from me was shot. I mean, it about took his face off. Then another soldier went over and took money out of his wallet."

Groza stared at the man robbing the dead. "The guy said, 'Well, he won't need it any more,'" Groza says, shaking his head. "That shows you how brutal it can be.

"My job was to get guys ready for surgery. You have to remember, it was always dirty and muddy over there. Guys would be wounded and brought to us caked with mud. I'd wash them down, especially around the wound, so that the doctor could operate. Then I'd do anything else the doctor wanted."

Groza spent nearly two years in the Pacific. He was to have been part of the invasion of the Japanese mainland. Those who criticize Harry Truman's decision to drop the atomic bomb never talked to men such as Groza.

"If you were there, you know he did the right thing. That saved a lot of lives, both Japanese and American. You have no idea how fierce the fighting was over there."

Was he ever wounded?

"Nah," he says. "Just a terrible case of round worm. I got it while taking a shower. Made me sick as a dog."

Paul Brown began sending Groza letters and a contract to sign with the Cleveland franchise in the new All-American Football Conference.

Groza signed for $7,500—"very good money for 1946," he says. "I went to my first pro training camp in army fatigues and carrying all my clothes in a duffle bag."

He played tackle and kicked for the Browns in the late summer and fall—then went to Ohio State in the winter.

Groza was an All-Pro football player and an honors student at Ohio State, earning a degree in business in 1949.

"None of us thought football would be anything but a job for a few years," he says. "We all figured we'd have to get real jobs. That is why I sold insurance."

Groza then takes you into his study. He shows you a gold shoe, the one he used to kick the winning field goal in the 1950 championship game.

Groza says he never felt special pressure on that or any kick. He says the key was his four-step approach to kicking: stance, approach, contact, follow through. He shows you a football and how he aimed for a spot near the middle of the ball, "on the seams, just under the center part."

He is now in the Hall of Fame. The days of tackles who kicked are over, and straight-on kickers such as Groza are extinct.

"I don't know why all the kids kick soccer-style," he says. "They kick the ball with the side of their foot, which is supposed to give them better control. I don't know, I never tried it."

He is a man who has been married since 1950, and who, along with his wife, Jackie, raised four children. *Sport Magazine* once wrote: "Lou Groza doesn't break training, punch referees or insult reporters. As a result, he only gets his name in the paper when he kicks."

As Groza shakes your hand and thanks you for dropping by, you think about that.

How often this man has been called just a kicker. He really is so much more.

4/7/1996

Retiring Lemon's number

HE LIMPED UP to the podium near home plate, his gnarled fingers clawed around a cane.

This is the man who could drink all night and pitch nine innings the next day. This is the man who won 20 games in 1948, and 10 of them were shutouts.

Today, his voice is slurred by a stroke, his eyes sensitive to the sun.

This man who was strong enough to manage and win two pennants for George Steinbrenner . . . this man who could (and did) knock out a teammate with one punch . . . this man could barely find the words on this special day.

The Indians retired Bob Lemon's number 21 yesterday, and not a moment too soon.

It doesn't matter that many of the 43,259 fans at high-tech Jacobs Field had little idea who the old man was, or why he was on the field.

Most of them applauded politely, perhaps remembering hearing something from their grandparents or parents about Lemon.

But there was little passion. You could tell a few moments later, when Kenny Lofton was introduced as the Tribe's leadoff hitter—and he received five times the ovation of Lemon.

But that's OK.

That's life. That's the passage of time. That's what happens when we live in an era when baseball is no longer king, when the lore of the game is not passed down from one generation to the next.

Bob Lemon was never on ESPN or David Letterman, so who cares?

Well, we should.

It doesn't matter that 1948 was 50 years ago, or that most of the players from that World Series–winning Tribe team are deceased.

Robert Granville Lemon is still with us. He is 77 years old. His body is riddled by years of drink and a stroke, his legs betraying him due to poor circulation.

But somewhere inside is the Bob Lemon who completed 20 games in 1948, the Bob Lemon who won two games in the World Series and the Bob Lemon who batted .284 as a pinch hitter in his Tribe career.

He's the Bob Lemon who threw a no-hitter in 1948, a no-hitter unlike any other.

That's because he was at a bar for a few drinks the night before.

Well, more than a few. And more than a few hours. Then again, he really wasn't supposed to pitch for two more days.

Or so he thought.

So Lemon figured he'd drink away the night—and some of the morning. He'd catch a nap at the ballpark, then sit in the sun that afternoon in the bullpen, sweating out the evils of Old Panther Juice.

He stayed in that bar until 6 A.M. A few hours later, he staggered into the dressing room, sat down by his locker and found a surprise.

Manager Lou Boudreau had placed a baseball under his cap.

That was Boudreau's way of telling a pitcher that he was to start that game. Lemon held the ball in his hand, and got sick.

After returning from the bathroom, he looked at the ball again. He told Boudreau he wasn't feeling well. Boudreau told him to warm up.

He warmed up.

He threw up.

And for nine innings, no one touched him, even though he retched again during the game. True story. A Bob Lemon story. The same Bob Lemon who was at Jacobs Field yesterday.

Lemon is in the Baseball Hall of Fame. He won 20 games in seven different seasons. He finished with 207 victories, not bad for a guy who was a third baseman until his 24th birthday.

Lemon roomed with catcher Jim Hegan.

"Never saw two guys who slept so much," remembered veteran sportswriter Hal Lebovitz. "And Lemon liked to drink, while Hegan never touched the stuff."

But Hegan would lead the team to the bar, where he led them in song.

As Lemon said, "In 1948, we had the kind of team where 10-to-12 guys would go out together."

They sang. They drank. They played cards.

After beating the Boston Red Sox in a one-game playoff to win the American League pennant, Tribe third baseman Ken Keltner and backup catcher Joe Tipton began yelling at each other about a game of cards.

Lemon stepped between them to break up what he thought would become a fight. Lemon claims Tipton swung at him—and like most who tried to hit Lemon, Tipton missed.

Lemon didn't.

One punch, Tipton went down.

One bloody lip. One mouth shut.

Just imagine what would have happened if Lemon had broken his precious right hand on Tipton's jaw—on the eve of the 1948 World Series!

But Lemon was in his prime. He was a Hall of Fame pitcher. And even if we weren't alive back in 1948, that is how we should remember him.

6/21/1998

Cleveland asked, Hal answered

WARNING: This story contains absolutely no objectivity. For that, I offer no apologies. It's about a man I've known for 20 years, a man I deeply admire, a man whose career inspired my own. His name is Hal Lebovitz, and he will be enshrined Sunday in the writers' wing of the Baseball Hall of Fame.

He stood over my desk, shaking his head.

"I read your story today," he said. "There's no such thing as 'road trip.' The Indians are either on the road or they are on a trip. The phrase 'road trip' is redundant."

With that, Hal Lebovitz walked away.

This was 20 years ago. Lebovitz was the sports columnist at the *Plain Dealer*; I was the 24-year-old baseball writer.

Lebovitz was my favorite sports writer. He was my father's favorite sports writer. He was Cleveland's favorite sports writer.

I desperately wanted Lebovitz's approval. He wanted to make me a better writer. Lebovitz continually gave me tips: Write simply. Interview a player's wife, parents, friends. Report, report and report some more.

At the time, I acted as if I really didn't want to hear it. But I remember it all, and I never used the phrase "road trip" in a story again.

When I was in high school, I sent Lebovitz copies of my stories from the *Twinsburg Bulletin*. He sent back notes, telling me to keep writing.

After the third batch of stories, he mailed back a note, saying, "Please don't mail me any more stories until you grow up."

That's not really what he wrote. He was much kinder. But I was bombarding the poor man with my stories. He just was begging for mercy.

"What people don't know is that Hal felt compelled to answer every piece of miserable mail that he received, and he got thousands," said Dan Coughlin of WJW-TV (Channel 8), who worked with Lebovitz at the *Plain Dealer*.

But receiving those letters on Plain Dealer stationery is part of the reason that I became a sports writer. The writer I respected most took the time to notice me, only 18 years old.

Lebovitz is 83 years old. He still writes sports, his main paper being the Lake County *News-Herald* in the Cleveland suburb of Willoughby. His work also is published by papers in Mansfield, New Philadelphia, Lorain and Massillon.

And he's being inducted into the Baseball Hall of Fame, only the second area writer so honored. The other was Gordon Cobbledick, one of Lebovitz's mentors.

"Even though Hal doesn't write for the dominant paper in the area, he is still considered the authority on area sports," said veteran *Beacon Journal* baseball writer Sheldon Ocker. "People want to know what Hal has to say about anything that happens, so they read his Sunday notes."

Ah, yes, the Sunday notes. I shamelessly stole his idea for "View From Pluto," which runs Sundays in the *Beacon Journal*.

Lebovitz's notes are an epic production, offering tidbits from every Cleveland sports team and filling nearly a page. The remarkable thing is that Lebovitz still breaks stories, that he still has such incredible contacts.

Former Browns public relations director Kevin Byrne told this story: "It was my 15th wedding anniversary, and my wife and I were going to spend the weekend at a local hotel. No one was supposed to know where we were. Ten minutes after checking into our room, the phone rang."

It was Lebovitz.

"He was looking for Sunday notes," Byrne said. "He called all my relatives until he found my one brother who was watching our kids, then he convinced him to give up the phone number of our hotel."

Person after person can tell story after story about Lebovitz tracking them down in unusual places, about Lebovitz relentlessly chasing information, about him checking and double-checking facts.

That's why his Sunday notes remain mandatory reading for members of the area media.

This man had his first article published in 1938. It's now 2000, and he has virtually no interest in retirement.

"Hal still runs two miles a day," Coughlin said. "He out-works most of the young reporters. He doesn't drink. He doesn't smoke. He doesn't play golf. He eats kosher. He goes to temple. At 83, he's physically and mentally able to do the job as well as anyone."

Lebovitz has one secret: Write for the people who read the paper— the people in the factories, the offices, the barber shops.

"Writing is not a flash dance," he said. "You don't write to show off. You should write like you talk to people. John Steinbeck and Ernest Hemingway did it that way. Keep your sentences short and to the point. You want the guy in the bar to read your story and talk about it. This is sports, not brain surgery."

Or as Coughlin said: "Everything with Hal is the reader. All that counts is the reader, the average guy. He never wrote for the head of the English Department at Case Western Reserve."

Lebovitz outlines every story before he writes, so he has a clear idea of what will be the beginning, middle and end.

"Writing for me is hard," he said. "I'm careful what words I use, and it kills me when I don't do a good job."

His regular column runs under the headline "Hal Asks?" in which he presents his ideas in the form of a question. He occasionally employs a format of talking to himself, question-and-answer style, which I also swiped from him.

Lebovitz never has considered himself an artist. His goal always has been to be informative and entertaining for the fans, not to impress other writers or win awards, although his work was published in magazines such as *Collier's*, the *Saturday Evening Post* and *Newsweek*. *Newsweek* even offered him a job, but the native of Cleveland's East Side could not imagine living in New York, and quickly turned it down.

He has been married for 62 years to Margie, who still checks his stories for grammar and spelling before he sends them in. This is the woman he still calls "my bride"—and means it. All you have to do is hear him talk to her on the phone. He never fails to end a conversation without saying, "I love you."

Lebovitz didn't set out to become a sports writer. In the 1930s, he was a science teacher and coach at old Central High School in Euclid.

"I taught six classes a day, coached the three major sports and was paid $1,300 a year," he said. "I was glad to get it, because that was good money. This was still the Depression."

In 1938, he talked to the old *Cleveland News* about upgrading its high school sports coverage. He began assembling statistics, using his slide rule to figure out batting averages and ERAs. The paper loved printing all the names, because it helped circulation.

Soon, they asked Lebovitz to write stories about high school athletics, offering him $15 a story—three stories a week, no byline. Because Lebovitz was a high school coach, he had tremendous access to all the goings-on, and suddenly, he made the *News* the paper to read for prep sports.

By 1943, the *News* started to give him bylines. He was up to $20 a story, still teaching, still coaching.

Here's another twist. In 1946, he was hired full-time by the *News*—not as sports writer—but as a science writer! He was supposed to help out in sports for a while, and he never left.

"I want from making $40 a week as a teacher to $75 in the newspaper business," he said. "And I got to do something I love."

For the next 14 years, Lebovitz worked for the *News*. From 1950–60, he was their baseball writer, riding trains with the likes of Bob Feller, Bob Lemon and Al Lopez.

"It was an era when you really got to know the players," he said. "You spent so much time with them on those long train rides. You ate with them. You played cards with them. A lot of the writers went to bars with them. You really knew the people you covered, and became friends with some of them."

But it still was very competitive. On the road, Lebovitz hung out in the hotel lobby until he was sure every player had gone to bed. He wrote an 18-part series on Satchel Paige in 1948 that later was published as a book, *Pitchin' Man*.

"Back then, there was no TV, no talk radio," he said. "Today, it's much more adversarial [between the players and the media]. Everyone is looking for every little thing. The writers can't write just about the game, because everyone knows what happened from TV. That creates some tension."

One of Lebovitz's columns each week is called "Ask Hal, the Referee."

That's because Lebovitz spent much of his life officiating basketball, football and baseball. High school games. College games. Top amateur games. Even major-league spring training games and games in the National Basketball League, forerunner of the NBA.

Several times, he was offered a chance to umpire in the minors, but turned it down to stay in the newspaper business.

"Hal is considered the ultimate authority on rules," Coughlin said. "He started that column where fans mailed in their questions about game situations and trivia. He'd use some of them in the paper for his column, but he answered them all, and he was constantly looking up obscure facts."

The volume of mail became so overwhelming that Lebovitz had to hire a secretary to help with the 7,000 letters he received annually. This was in the 1960s and 1970s, when he was sports editor of the *Plain Dealer*.

His "Ask Hal" column still runs in several papers, and Lebovitz still is trying to untangle such bizarre baseball situation as: "A man hit a fly ball to left field. The ball hits a pigeon. The left fielder catches the ball, but not the pigeon—which died. Is the batter out?"

Somehow, Lebovitz patiently answers every question.

Lebovitz's real legacy is the team that plays today at Jacobs Field.

"They ought to build a monument to Hal for all the times he saved the Indians for Cleveland," Coughlin said. "The team was about to be moved to Seattle, and another time New Orleans. Both times, he exposed the plans, putting pressure on the local people to keep it here."

Lebovitz is unashamed to admit that he's a fan of all the local teams, especially the Tribe.

"When the Indians are losing, food doesn't taste as good and I don't sleep well," he said.

"Hal always knew how important the Indians were to Cleveland," said Chuck Murr, who worked with Lebovitz at the *Plain Dealer*. "He may have been a little easy on them during the 30-some years where they were awful, but he also knew that having a bad team here was better than no team."

Coughlin said that Lebovitz pushed the Indians to have promotions such as Bat Day and Ball Day to help the gate. He had contests in the *Plain Dealer* in which fans could express their opinion on sports issues of the day and receive free Tribe tickets. It was an effort to fill some of the usually empty 80,00 seats at the Stadium.

Lebovitz never has been an overly critical writer, but he took on the Cavs during the Ted Stepien era, and he was morally outraged when Major League Baseball picked Cleveland to hold its 1981 All-Star Game, played immediately after the 81-day players' strike.

"Hal was ripping that game for weeks, because he knew the players weren't in shape and it wouldn't be a true All-Star Game," Coughlin recalled. "The executives from baseball met with him, trying to get him to change his mind. Hal wouldn't be moved. One executive told me, 'Hal has too much integrity for a sports writer, he's too highly principled.'"

That also extended to former Browns owner Art Modell.

"They used to be so close," said Byrne, who now works for Modell in Baltimore. "Hal and Art talked at least twice a week. But when Art moved the team, Hal vowed he'd never talk to Art again—and he hasn't."

To Lebovitz, it was a betrayal of a city and fans, both of whom he loves. The wound still bleeds a bit.

Lebovitz will tell you that there are sports writers today of the caliber of Ring Lardner. He insists that Robbie Alomar and Omar Vizquel are the best second baseman/shortstop combination he has seen—and he's watched them all for 75 years, dating to when he sold hot dogs at old League Park.

"Hal prides himself on keeping current," Byrne said. "He never wanted to be one of those guys always talking about 'the good old days.'"

Lebovitz was born during World War I, lived through the Depression and World War II and knows the meaning of hard times—and lousy baseball teams. Perhaps that's why Lebovitz generally is optimistic about the local sports teams and athletes.

"To me, the most impressive thing about Hal is how he can look through all the garbage around professional sports and still see the good things, and that's awesome," said Joe Tait, longtime Cavs broadcaster.

That's because bitterness and cynicism has sapped the joy of more than a few writers and broadcasters. Lebovitz never fell into that trap. Perhaps that's the best compliment of all.

7/19/2000

Thornton and Tribe: Tough love

WHEN HE WAS WITH THE INDIANS, they never finished higher than fifth place. They never were closer than 11 games out of first place, and the only move they ever seemed ready to make was out of town.

Ten years of bad baseball, in front of small crowds, in a lousy ballpark, with owners counting rubber bands and dodging bill collectors.

Few Tribe fans remember those bad old days. Now, they whine when the team loses in the first round of the playoffs, or wins "only" 90 games.

When Andre Thornton played first base for the Indians (1977–87), there was no pennant race. The season was over by the All-Star break, although most of the players knew it was over in spring training.

As Thonrton said yesterday: "We either had teams with good hitters, or good pitchers. Never enough of both."

And they were continually trading the hitters for pitchers, or pitchers back for hitters.

All to little avail.

During Thornton's era, they finished in sixth place six times.

And in seventh place . . . three times.

And they had five managers in 10 years.

These were the dark ages of Cleveland baseball.

"About 2,000 fans in that big, old ballpark," Said Thornton. "Those fans who stuck with us were great, but a situation like that—it doesn't exactly help your career."

Thornton played with guys such as Jack Perconte, Jerry Dybzinski, Ron Pruitt, Paul Dade, Toby Harrah, Bert Blyleven, Rick Manning, Larry Littleton, Joe Charboneau, Mike Hargrove, Len Barker and Gary Alexander.

As Thornton said, "Some were better players than others."

And all of them came and went during Thornton's era, an 11-year span (minus 1980, when he was on the DL) during which he hit 214 homers. He was a constant, not only staying on the roster for those 11 years, but also living in Chagrin Falls in the off-season.

"I was the one who always heard the snickers about the Indians or the one whom they always asked, "What's wrong with the Indians?" he said.

The answer . . . well . . . about everything except Thornton.

That's why it's fitting that the Indians are featuring Thornton on a poster with Jim Thome. They announced the promotion yesterday as part of the franchise's 100th-year celebration.

Other present Indians will be on posters with Tribe players from the past, such as third basemen Travis Fryman and Al Rosen, and pitchers Bartolo Colon and Bob Feller.

Yesterday, at a press conference at glorious Jacobs Field to announce 2001 promotions and ticket-sales information, Thornton and Thome represented Indians, present and past.

"To me, it's an honor to be on the same poster as Andre Thornton," said Thome. "I've only seen films of him at-bat a few times, but I know him and he's such a classy person."

Thome doesn't know the half of it.

Yes, he played for two years at the old Stadium in the early 1990s, but even then, there was hope. A new ballpark was coming. A young team with Sandy Alomar, Kenny Lofton, Albert Belle, Carlos Baerga, Charles Nagy and Thome was being assembled.

Thornton's old boss, Gabe Paul, used to call Cleveland "a sleeping giant." Well, after nearly 40 years of slumber, it was about to awaken, and Tribe baseball never would be quite the same, as baseball's longest sellout streak was about to be born.

When Thornton was with the Indians, the franchise was in a coma.

Players had to buy their own weights to lift. The team was banned from some hotels because it hadn't paid its bills during the previous visit.

So it was no surprise that when the team moved into Jacobs Field, it tried to distance itself from the grim past.

"One of their advertisements was 'These are not your father's Indians.' It was like we were the plague," said Thornton.

And it hurt.

So the Indians were wise to choose Thornton as a bridge to the past—the muscular first baseman, a man of steel faith who never gave up on the home team.

"I really think the tragedy cemented me to the team and the fans in this area," he said.

He was referring to an auto accident on October 17, 1977, in which Thornton's wife and daughter were killed when his van slipped off an icy road. Thornton and his son were unhurt. He had been with the Indians for only a single season, but saw the town open its heart to him. He never forgot that.

While so many of his teammates demanded to be traded, Thornton was content to stay.

"After how well people treated me, if I had run, it would have been like I ran away from my own house," he said.

Thornton is 13 years away from his career. He's 51 years old, and runs a consulting and management firm that specializes in diversity training. His clients include some of the area's major companies.

He also bought into Applebee's restaurants, and his group expanded to 20 before he sold them back to the parent company in 1997. He has been as successful in business as he was in baseball.

"This franchise had a lot of peaks," he said. "I sort of fell into the valley between them."

So it's about time that Thornton is raised up by the team and the fans who really remember what Indians baseball was all about.

1/11/2001

Prospects

On the bus to nowhere, hoping to get somewhere

GENE ROBINSON IS BEHIND THE WHEEL. He doesn't have arms, just tattoos—machine guns, daggers, flowers, snakes . . . and only his needle man knows what else. On each hand is a black glove with the fingers cut out. A Camel dangles from his lips and his black, skull-and-crossbones T-shirt is sweat-soaked.

It is midnight and he is wearing shades.

Meet the man the Canton-Akron Indians call "The Bussie From Hell."

While Robinson drives the Class AA baseball team to Williamsport, Pennsylvania, team trainer Dan Redmond walks up and down the aisle, handing each player an envelope. They quickly tear them open and find $10 bills, 12 of them. Over and over, some of the players finger the bills, continually counting. But the amount never changes. No miracles on the order of the loaves and fishes, just a dozen $10 bills.

That makes $120 meal money for a 10-day trip.

"I think there's a Silvers in Williamsport," says infielder Rob Swain. "At least I hope so."

Silvers is Long John Silvers to the uninitiated, home of the massive $2.95 fried seafood platter and salad bar. Lots of food for little money, which is what you want when your salary is $5,000.

On any summer evening there are busloads of minor-league teams on the highway. In early June, the Canton-Akron Indians were on a safari to Williamsport; Albany, New York; and London, Ontario. That's 12 games, 10 days, 1,259 miles.

These Indians will play 140 Eastern League games in 147 days. Their average trip covers nine days and 996 miles. When the season's over, they will have ridden 8,964 miles covering 194 hours. In other words, that's a little more than eight full days on the bus—morning, noon, night and morning again.

"After a while, you don't know what day, it is and you really don't care," says Mike Snyder. "Really, all that matters is what time the bus leaves. There's always another game, another bus trip."

Mike Snyder is 36 years old. He has been married for six years and is the father of a 4-year-old daughter. He is a local journeyman broadcaster, having called games for the University of Akron, Kent State, Cleveland State and the Cleveland Force soccer team before becoming the voice of the Canton-Akron Indians.

"The other day I called home and I was talking to my daughter," Snyder says. "Suddenly, she says, 'Daddy, where are you going to work after baseball season?' I was stunned that a 4-year-old would ask that, and making it even worse is that I have nothing concrete lined up. I'm playing this out and hoping something breaks for me. All I know is that this life is totally different from anything I've ever been through."

Snyder and the Indians will visit Williamsport; Albany; London; Reading and Harrisburg, Pennsylvania; Hagerstown, Maryland and New Britain, Connecticut—places where no one goes unless they must.

Actually, they don't truly see these towns. Their motels usually are right off the interstates on a main, four-lane road of neon signs, doughnut shops, hamburger joints and car washes. It looks like the Montrose section of West Market Street. So when the guys tell you that all the towns pretty much look the same, it's because they do.

The bus dominates a minor-leaguer's life because it is where he spends so much of it. Players board with pillows, with Walkmen, with bottles, cans and bags. They establish a territory in their favorite seat, and getting a good seat by yourself is crucial because the bus isn't big enough for one-man, one-seat, and nobody wants to double up.

Putting 25 guys on a bus for endless hours is not something you want to think about . . . or smell.

Beer isn't allowed, but chewing tobacco is. Gatorade is popular, but you can't be sure if it's because they like to drink the stuff or because the bottles make great spittoons. In baseball, you always must be careful when you see someone holding a bottle or a cup because you never know if someone is drinking out of it or spitting into it.

Card games are important. Coolers are placed in the aisle, a pillow on top and guys play something called "pluck," with two-man teams. These games can easily last six hours.

And unless it's about 4 in the morning and the card games have folded, five minutes won't pass without hearing the ultimate four-letter word—the "F-bomb," as it's called by one player.

Most of those not playing cards are wired for sound, courtesy of their Walkmen. A few, not many, read.

Twenty-eight-year-old Dan Boever sits near the front. He had very serious knee surgery in 1983 and is a lifetime .300 hitter in the Eastern League who failed to stick in two shots at Class AAA. He reads a book called *How To Talk To God*.

Which brings up another minor-league terror—that no one is watching, no one is listening, no one cares what they do in the Eastern League.

Players try not to think about that. They'd rather attack each other or the bus driver:

"Hey, bussie, a guy in a wheelchair just passed us."

"Hey, bussie, the guy in the wheelchair is in the lobby of our motel right now, getting our rooms."

Or to pitcher Paul Kuzniar, who had served up a 400-foot homer: "Hey, Kuz, how did you like your trip to Cape Canaveral?"

Or to the players in the front of the bus looking at a map: "Hey, you four guys, put your heads together and make a rock pile."

Or to Jeff Shaw, who has a plug in his jaw: "Your wife know you're chewing?" (Shaw only chews on the road precisely so his wife won't know.)

Then there's pitcher Carl Keliipuleole explaining why he missed a team meeting in the afternoon: "Man, I don't know what happened. I had a brain fart or something."

One of the prevailing themes on the bus is the temperature:

"Hey, bussie, turn up the A.C. [air conditioning]."

"Hey, bussie, throw a log on the fire [turn off the A.C.]."

All night long, at about 15-minute intervals, it's turn up the air conditioning, turn off the air conditioning.

Why?

Because when you take the bus, it's always too hot or too cold.

Putting 25 guys on a bus that sometimes gets too hot, 25 guys whose eating habits match the typical teenager's, 25 guys together so long in such a small space also leads to all sorts of emissions from all sorts of places.

When nature calls, no one wants to answer. There is a toilet in the back of the bus, but it's hard to get there with all the card games, legs, feet and even prone bodies in the aisle. To move from one end of the bus to the other is a monumental task that means climbing on the seat handles while hanging on to the upper luggage compartment (assuming no one is sleeping up there).

Besides, even if you do reach the toilet, common sense would tell you not to go in there.

Near the end of the trip, bottles and cans on the floor roll in one direction when the bus starts, the other direction when it stops. The bus becomes a long, stinking cigar and when you get on it the next day, the stench is there to greet you.

This isn't unique to the Canton-Akron Indians, who are more orderly than most minor-league teams. It's just how it is and always has been in places such as the Eastern League.

It should be no surprise to learn that no one really wants to be here for long. Not the players, the manager, the coaches, the trainer, the announcer.

"And we all do know what we want," says Canton-Akron manager Bob Molinaro. "We all want the big leagues. I tell the players that my job is to get them the hell out of this league, to get them to Class AAA and then maybe to Cleveland."

The Eastern League is about cliches that are true. These Boys Of Summer, these Boys On The Bus, are Good Enough To Dream. Unlike so many people today, these guys know what it means to want something so badly that they'll give up the good life, the normal life. They're willing to pay dues, to climb on the bus and go along for the ride. Unfortunately for most, this bus won't take them there.

Instead, it goes to the Holiday Inn "on Williamsport's Golden Strip," according to the local chamber of commerce.

The Golden Strip?

Across from the team's hotel is a K Mart, a Rax, and (yes, thank God) a Silvers.

The players carry their luggage off the bus, to the lobby and then to their rooms, and that's two players to a room.

"Remember the boiler room?" asks one of the players. Suddenly, you get the feeling that this motel is not exactly the jewel of the Holiday Inn chain. The guys indeed remember the boiler-room incident from their first trip here.

There was smoke, there was a rumor of fire. There was the Loyal Sock (Pa.) Volunteer Fire Department on hand, "and every fireman had a jacket that said 'Assistant Chief' on the back," Snyder says.

While there was smoke, there was no serious fire and the hotel remained standing.

Good or bad break? No one is sure, and it doesn't matter because the bus leaves for Williamsport's Bowman Field at "4:15 on Gene's watch," Molinaro says.

The Bussie From Hell smiles at the mention of his name. His old job was to keep America safe for democracy as a member of the Army special forces. He trained for jungle warfare in Panama and for Arctic fighting in Alaska and can tell some mind-boggling stories about a Korean woman in a basket.

He says he has been around the world three times, and you have a feeling that none of the trips was easy. You also have a feeling that he revels in this $4.50-an-hour job, a demanding job that means he'll be up at 7 in the morning to drive the trainer to do the laundry, at 11 to drive a player and the trainer to a doctor's office and to make a couple of trips to and from the stadium in the afternoon to deliver the players.

During the game, Gene Robinson sits atop his throne, the roof of the bus, still wearing his black driving gloves and swatting mosquitoes while he watches his team play. He also is Mike Snyder's roommate, an odd-couple combination that delights the players.

As the team arrives at Bowman Field and starts batting practice, a scratchy oldie, "Eve of Destruction," comes over the public-address system. The temperature is 52 at game time and it will be 40 before the night is over. You won't find any Bull Durham glamour or anyone like Susan Sarandon in the stands at Williamsport.

Actually, you won't find hardly anyone at all, even though the home-team management insists on announcing attendance of 744, which must include the folks driving by.

Snyder has to broadcast the game from a bench-like seat and a wooden table in the stands. The players carry their own equipment on and off the bus, something that never happens in the majors.

There is no "clubby" to help trainer Dan Redmond, who has to find a Laundromat so he can wash the players' uniforms. The players dress and undress at the hotel because of the primitive dressing-room and shower facilities at the stadium.

A humbling moment comes after each game when Redmond stands up on the bus and says, "Guys, you got a half-hour to bring your uniforms to my room to get cleaned. If you didn't play, you don't get it washed."

Don't blame Redmond. He already puts in an 18-hour day, and it begins at 8 A.M. at the local Laundromat. Nothing can be taken for granted in the minors, not even a clean uniform. In the minors, everyone works hard, but Redmond works harder.

Every hour of every day, something happens to remind you that this isn't the big leagues, be it the bus rides, the dirty uniforms, the skimpy paychecks or the $2 fines for missing a sign.

Two bucks?

Two bucks is a lot on $10 meal money. It means no post-game beer. Actually, most guys will drink the beer and skip breakfast at the ever-popular Dunkin' Donuts.

Which goes to show you that on every level, minor-league baseball is a numbers game.

So Bob Molinaro knows the odds are that only five of his players will make the majors and that no more than two will have a significant career. He knows that 75 percent of the players under him aren't considered prospects, they are just bodies so the five guys favored by the Cleveland front office will have someone to play with.

The players know it, too. They know the front office is watching Joey Belle, Jeff Shaw, Beau Allred, Greg McMichael and Kevin Bearsc.

But what about the others?

Molinaro knows that feeling and he knows his players. He knows that they're worried, worried about what Cleveland thinks of them, worried about not hitting, worried about hanging curveballs and sore arms, worried about getting too old too fast.

Now you know why these guys adopt a macho pose and curse in the face of fear as the bus goes slicing through the night.

"It took me 10 years to get out of the minors," says Molinaro, who is 39. "I was supposed to be a Class AAA hitter, a lifetime bush-leaguer. Everybody wrote me off but me. Every year, I'd go out and I'd hit my .300 and I'd steal bases and I'd never strike out when it mattered. I made them take me to the big leagues and I got my six full years in and I got my pension."

Molinaro prides himself on his ability to motivate, to communicate, to "help these guys fight their way to the majors."

In the dugout, he has grabbed a bat and smashed the valuables box, he has whacked the walls, he has kicked helmets. Intriguing combinations of F-bombs have fallen everywhere.

Molinaro will pace the dugout during a game and say:

"Don't you guys want to get out of this league? Don't you want to make money, to make a better life for your family. One day, you'll be out in the world with a real job and you'll wonder how you screwed up your life when you were playing in Canton. You'll wonder why you didn't put out when you had to. "The only way you can look at yourself

in the mirror, the only way you can enjoy the winter is to give 100 percent in the summer. Somebody do something that will make me pick
up the phone, call Cleveland and tell them to take you up, to get you a
ticket to Colorado Springs [the Indians' Class AAA club]. Make me
pick up that phone."

Molinaro is relentless. He knows that minor-league players desperately crave attention and he gives it to them. He talks to players at
breakfast, at lunch, on the bus, even in the dungeon-like weight room
of the Williamsport YMCA.

Yes, these guys go to a health club or YMCA every day, on the road
to lift weights, ride exercise bikes and stay fit. Pumping iron with the
troops are Molinaro and his coaches, Eric Rassmussen and Billy
Williams.

"If they see old guys like us on the weights, then they have no excuse
for not lifting, too," says Molinaro.

He has opinions on everything:

"I tell the guys that if they want to find a girl, don't hang around in
the bar at 3 in the morning, go to the mall at 3 in the afternoon. That's
where you find a lot of nice women just looking for someone to talk to.
Me, I met my wife at the bank."

Molinaro is a man of passion and compassion, of endless energy, a
short fuse yet with the marvelous capacity not to hold a grudge. It is
the personality of a young Earl Weaver.

"I tell the guys that if I made it, they can make it," he says. "And because of what I went through, I'm very reluctant to give up on a player.
I'll scream at these guys and probably be more critical of them than
any manager ever has, but I do it because I want to get them out of this
league and I get excited when I see a player I can send to Class AAA."

Molinaro will tell you that he has a gut feeling about such supposedly marginal prospects as Rob Swain, a barrel-chested, 26-year-old
infielder "who can become a good utility man in the bigs, I don't care
what anyone says. In a year or two, Robby can help a big-league team."

He'll tell you that 26-year-old shortstop Julius McDougal has "as
good an arm as you'll find in the big leagues. If we can work on his hitting, we can get him there."

On and on it goes.

You can do it. You do have a chance. You must believe in you because I believe in you.

Molinaro is always sending messages.

This is Molinaro's second season as a manager. Two years ago, he
was 91-48 for Hagerstown of the Class A Carolina League. Last season,

he was Cleveland's roving minor-league hitting coach.

Where people have been and what they have accomplished in base-ball is important on the bus as the guys sometimes play trivia: Who was the last right-handed hitter to win the American League batting title? Who was the last American League pitcher to hit a home run?

Molinaro has his own trivia question: "Who was the only guy to take Goose Gossage deep in 1980?"

Silence as players fear the worst.

Molinaro: "Hey guys, it was good old Bobby M. He threw me one inside and I turned that [bleep] around."

Groans.

Then outfielder Dwight Taylor asks, "Who was the only guy ever to pinch run for Willie Wilson?"

Molinaro stares at Taylor: "You?"

Taylor: "Yeah, Willie got thrown out of the game and they put me in."

Taylor was in training camp with the Cleveland Indians in 1984 and actually made it to The Show with Kansas City for three weeks and two official at-bats in September of 1986. Taylor is the only player on the bus to ever cash a big-league check.

Now Taylor is 29, the father of seven and he has just been sent down from Colorado Springs. Now you know why he spends some of his bus time reading the Bible though his black, horn-rimmed glasses.

Which is why Molinaro may be the ideal manager for these guys. After 10 years in the minors, he did make it, batting .264 with 14 homers and 90 RBIs in 803 at-bats during parts of eight big-league seasons. The Canton-Akron Indians will hear more than they care to about the career of Robert Joseph Molinaro, a former theater pop-corn-maker from Trenton, New Jersey.

But the point is that Molinaro did beat the odds, he did room with Pete Rose, become a close friend of Mike Schmidt—and it happened simply because he wouldn't listen to what the scouts said.

It happened because Molinaro willed it, and his players are trying to do just that.

There's Casey Webster, 25 years old, bald spot on the back of his head and in his second Eastern League season—his second Eastern League season trying to hit .250.

Poor Casey Webster, he of the wonderful baseball name. He is the guy they always ask for directions: "Case, do we make a right or a left to get to the YMCA? . . . Do we go get off here to go to the hotel?" The Indians' travel strategy seems to be, aim the bus in the general direc-tion of the destination and Casey will handle the specifics.

On the field, Webster is a fearless third baseman, sticking his chest, even his jaw, in front of anything smashed his way. The game is a tough proposition for Webster, who refused to flinch even when the eye doctor said those spots he was seeing were no real problem, "just floaters." That night, Webster played through the floaters, got a broken-bat single and started two double plays with neat grabs at third base.

Minor-league buses are loaded with guys like Webster, guys who deserve at least one day where their uniforms will be cleaned even if they don't play; one day of $50 meal money; one day on a baseball charter plane where they have the choice of steak or lobster, red or white wine.

"This is my first real extended experience with baseball," says Snyder, "and you grow close to these people quickly when you ride the bus with them. You think about the sacrifices they make, how they got on a bus after a night game in Albany and then rode all night to get to London the next morning at 9, caught a few hours of sleep and then played a double-header that night.

"Frankly, I respect these guys a lot more than I did before for what they endure, and I know that I'll never be able to see a bus, or even hear the hum of its motor, and feel the same way about it again."

7/16/1989

Kid pitches the biggest game of his life

YOU'LL TELL YOUR KIDS ABOUT THIS GAME.

You'll tell them about the night Jaret Wright took the ball in Yankee Stadium in a game the Indians had to win.

And how he helped the Tribe beat the Yankees, 7-5.

You'll tell them how Wright was only 21 years old, only three months removed from kicking the Canal Park dirt out of his spikes— right there on Main Street in Akron.

You'll talk about the kid with the baby face and the brush cut... the kid whose old man was a big-leaguer named Clyde Wright... and how the old man, the kid (and mom, too) went to see *Phantom of the Opera* on Broadway.

Just a family taking in a show before the kid would pitch the biggest game of his life. Can you believe that?

It will be an amazing story that you'll tell, the kind that still is hard to believe if you are a hard-core Indians fan.

Things like Jaret Wright just didn't happen to your Indians.

Only you can believe it.

You try to temper yourself. You know he is only 21, and a lot can happen between now and Cooperstown.

But you can only believe what you see, and you saw a star in the sky over the South Bronx.

You saw a kid who had every reason to be rattled, a kid who was put into an impossible situation . . . Only he made it possible.

You'll remember watching Jaret Wright that night in New York— and how he made it possible for you to dream again.

To understand what Wright did last night in Yankee Stadium, you had to have spent the week in New York.

You had to see the tabloids full of huge pictures and glowing stories about young Mr. Wright.

All of them said he wouldn't choke, even though this was his first start in Yankee Stadium. Even the usually harsh Gotham media treated Wright kindly, as if they were fattening his ego for the kill that night in the Bronx.

For goodness' sake, his own manager compared him with a young Roger Clemens.

Now, imagine being Wright.

On Tuesday night, you watched Orel Hershiser blow a 6-1 lead after three innings. Hershiser is one of your heroes, one of the greatest clutch pitchers of any generation.

But he took the apple in New York.

Now, it's your turn.

Now, your team is down 0-1 in this best-of-five series. If you lose, it's all over but the second-guessing.

You walk out to the mound, and feel 100,000 eyes bearing down on you.

These are not your friends.

This is New York.

In fact, these people hate you—just ask them.

So what do you do?

You walk the bases loaded.

Three times, people have come to the mound, telling you to cool it.

Easy for them to say.

They're not pitching with the season on the line, you are.

They're not 21, you are.

Their knees aren't shaking . . . palms aren't sweating . . . hearts aren't pounding . . . the 57,000 fans on their feet, screaming and stomping, demanding you throw another stupid pitch.

The lousy ball just won't go where it should—where it usually does when you pitch.

Then Tino Martinez swings late . . . the guy seemed fooled . . . and swats an ugly double to the opposite field.

When the first inning is finally over, the Yankees have three runs.

Suddenly, you realize you're not at your dad's pitching school in Southern California anymore—nor even at Jacobs Field.

The heat is on, the stakes have been raised and you suddenly realize you have never been on the spot—or in the spotlight—quite like this before.

You sit in the dugout and try to take a deep breath.

How can you be so tired after one inning?

You tell yourself there are eight more innings to go, that just because your team is behind 3-0, it doesn't mean the game is over.

Three runs don't mean you let your team down.

The top of the second is almost over before it starts—three up, three down for the Tribe.

You're on the mound—again.

Only this time, it feels right.

The dirt under your spikes. The ball in your hand. Your windup, your release—the pop of the ball as it smacks into Sandy Alomar's catcher's mitt.

You suddenly realize this can be your game, your night.

So you make it happen.

Five scoreless innings.

No runner past first base.

You blow away Martinez with a 3-ball, 2-strike fastball. You fool Charlie Hayes on a 3-ball, 2-strike slider.

Your last inning is the sixth, and you blow away the side.

Three up, three down.

Not a loud foul to be heard.

Then Manager Mike Hargrove pats you on the back. Your teammates shake your hands.

At age 21 and on this October night in New York, Wright was more than the winning pitcher.

He became a warm memory.

10/3/1997

Starting on the lowest rung

FOR THE CLEVELAND INDIANS, Burlington, North Carolina, is where it all begins.

It's staying at Kirk's Motor Lodge, where as many as four ballplayers share a room—a room with just three beds and where the laundry is done in the bathroom sink.

It's the Kentucky Fried Chicken where the Latin players eat chicken at least twice a day.

It's where many of these same players turn their paychecks over to the trainer, who doles out $5 and $10 bills—helping the kids to save so that they have money to send home at month's end.

It's where the best gift is a long-distance, prepaid telephone card, because these kids are away from home for the first time.

Burlington is where Manny Ramirez began his pro career, shattering nearly every franchise hitting record. But it also is where Tribe phenom Richie Sexson batted only .186 with one homer in 40 games.

Burlington is where the Indians send the rawest of their raw recruits. It's where 33 kids are in uniform, but odds are that only three will have significant careers in the big leagues.

Burlington is where you find Jack Mull, batting coach and 30 years in pro baseball. It's where Mull laughs and says, "Some of these kids have never used a hanger before. They just throw their clothes into the lockers."

Burlington is where you meet a shortstop named Maicer Isturiz. He is 17 years old. He is from Venezuela, just like the Tribe's Omar Vizquel. He wears No. 13, just like Vizquel. And on some ground balls, you'd swear it was the Tribe's All-Star shortstop. Burlington also is where you meet Jason Farmer, who will soon turn 25. He is a pitcher with an 8.08 ERA. The oldest guy on the team. It is his first year in pro ball, and it could be his last. He'll have memories of a couple of early-season saves before a gathering of 300 or so folks in places such as Bristol, Tennesee, and Princeton, West Virginia, before it all wilts in the heat of August.

And it's where you meet C.C. Sabathia, the Tribe's No. 1 draft pick who signed for a $1.3-million bonus, but also stays at Kirk's Motor Lodge. "We're all the same down here. We're all trying to make it," he says—and honestly means it.

Burlington is where every player's salary is $850 a month—about

$666 after taxes—and only for the three summer months when they play. It's where they eat at Burger King, at Taco Bell and at the revered KFC.

"Sometimes, I save up and go to a good restaurant," says Paul Day, Burlington's star third baseman.

And what's a good restaurant?

"A place like Cracker Barrel," he says.

Burlington is a land of dreams and bad food located in the center of North Carolina, between Greensboro and Durham. It's all-night bus rides through the Blue Ridge Mountains. It's playing a game at 7 P.M., staying up until 2 and then sleeping until noon.

"I'll tell you what this is," says pitcher Donnie Suttles. "It's the greatest. It's what I've always dreamed."

It is one of those endless bus rides through the heart of America.

Burlington's radio voice/public relations director is Larry Blucher. He is sitting with Dennis Malave, an 18-year-old outfielder from Venezuela.

Malave is determined to learn English. Blucher would like to pick up some Spanish. So they teach each other phrases such as, "How is the weather?"

A few seats behind is a pitcher named Martin Bautista from the Dominican Republic. He also is taking English lessons, but from some of his teammates.

Suddenly, Blucher hears Bautista slowing say, "You can kiss my. . ." with a few profanities dropped in as punctuation.

Blucher tells Malave, "You really don't want to say those words."

The manager is Joe Mikulik, a 34-year-old former minor-league outfielder. He made it as far as Class AAA. Fifteen years as a player, coach and manager—but not one day in the big leagues. Not unless you count that exhibition game in 1995 at Jacobs Field. He was a replacement player.

Mikulik makes about $25,000. He and Mull, the pitching coach, live with a local fireman to save money. He also finds himself teaching his players how to dress.

"For real," he says. "We don't allow earrings on the field. We make them tuck in their shirts. We make them wear their caps straight. I've had kids tell me Ken Griffey wears an earring and his cap backward in batting practice."

How does the first-year manager answer that?

"I tell them: 'When you're Ken Griffey, you can do what you want. But right now, you're in Burlington.'"

And Burlington is in the Appalachian League, as low as you can go and still be affiliated with a big-league organization. It's a league in which only 12 players on any team can be 21 years or older. It's the sixth farm team in the Tribe minor-league system, and it's at the bottom.

It's the kind of place where players such as Matt White say, "Next year, if everything goes right, I'll be in Columbus."

Not the one in Ohio.

The young pitcher from Clemson is talking about the Columbus in Georgia—the Tribe's Class A team.

Paul Day sits in front of a blue cinderblock dugout that looks more like a World War I trench than a place to watch a game. He holds his bats and stares off into space.

Day is 22, the leading hitter on the team. He was a star at Long Beach State, received $50,000 to sign. He also is an excellent student in computer science, a couple of semesters away from a degree.

"I remember the day I wanted to become a ballplayer," he says. "I saw *The Natural* with Robert Redford. I wanted to be like that."

The game does not come naturally for Day. He is a gutsy, but shaky, third baseman. He can hit, but some scouts say that he should rack up big numbers because he is one of the most experienced players in this league after coming out of the College World Series.

But on this night, he strikes out three times. He had whiffed five times in a row, counting the previous game. He looks as if he's never seen a curveball before, as if his head is somewhere else.

Which is the case.

"We talked to Paul about playing in our fall instructional league program," said Tribe scouting director Josh Byrnes. "But he wants to go back and finish his degree. He's pretty torn up on what to do."

For many of the Latin players, there are worries other than continuing a college education.

Some of them still are getting used to the fact that there's hot water in their rooms. Just turn the knob and out it comes—doesn't happen at home.

A few had to learn not to throw used toilet paper in the wastebasket, that you really can flush it down—that doesn't happen at home, either.

Former Tribe pitcher Julian Tavarez had stomach trouble when he pitched in Burlington. He loved to drink milk before going to the park. He'd buy some, keep it out overnight. He didn't know how to use the refrigerator.

Never had a refrigerator in the Dominican Republic.

Bautista, the pitcher learning the blue vocabulary, wanders into the trainer's room. He tells Dave Lassiter: "You are like a father to me. A lot of kisses to you."

Lassiter has had the trainer's job at Burlington since 1991. But it's more like being a big brother, banker, dietitian and psychologist. He's helping Bautista to save enough money to buy shoes and clothes for his family in the Dominican.

"Chicken," says Bautista. "We must have chicken in the morning, chicken in the night."

He sings it over and over, "Chicken in the morning, chicken at night."

Lassiter has peanut butter and jelly sandwiches available for the players before the game.

"The peanut-butter-and-jelly buffet," pitcher Matt White calls it.

The trainer also arranges for well-balanced meals such as chicken and vegetables after the game. And yes, it's heavy on chicken at the request of the 13 Latin players.

"I don't like no McDonald's," sings Bautista. "No pickle. No lettuce. I like chicken. Chicken in the morning, chicken at night."

Radio voice Larry Blucher is walking past the clubhouse.

Maicer Isturiz stops him and asks, "Larry how are you?"

Real slowly.

Real carefully.

But it's English.

"I'm fine," said Blucher. "Your English is getting better."

The young shortstop smiles, and walks off proudly.

All of the Latin players have been taking English lessons at least once a week from a Burlington fan who also is a college professor. The Indians also have English courses for their Latin players in the off-season.

"Know the best place to learn English?" says Angel Bastardo. "It's the TV, man. You get lots of English off the TV."

Bastardo is 19 years old. He's from Venezuela. He loves American television.

Do you remember your first time away from home? It could have been in college. The military. Or maybe just out on your own in a strange town. So it is for the kids in Burlington.

They come from California, Venezuela, the Dominican Republic, the East Coast and the Midwest. They don't know anyone. They have a suitcase packed with dreams and a head full of fears.

They are the chosen few, the ones who leave their hometowns to go off and play pro baseball. Their families, their friends—everyone seems to expect them to play in the majors.

Million-dollar contracts. National television appearances. Maybe a commercial. When they sign their contracts and leave home, it all seems possible.

But after 10 weeks at Burlington, reality sets in. For many of these kids, it's the first time that they haven't been the best players on their teams. Some suddenly realize that they are just hanging on, that they could be cut.

Then what?

What do you tell your friends? Your mother? The coach who believed in you, the girlfriend you write to every day.

About 20 players sit in the grandstand an hour before the game. A local preacher is speaking to them about the importance of God in their lives. With wide eyes and open hearts, they listen. They pray. They ask God to heal sore shoulders, to make bats well.

When it's over, they form little groups.

Venezuelans hang together.

Dominicans hang together.

The high school kids.

The college kids.

They look for something in common. Maybe they played against someone who once played against someone else they knew. Or maybe they come from the same part of Latin America.

These frightened kids reach out, trying to make a connection—trying to hang on.

8/23/1998

Kid gloves, wooden bats

MATT WHITE COULDN'T BELIEVE IT.

He is in his first year as a pitcher in the Cleveland Indians farm system.

There was one out in the seventh inning.

He had allowed only one hit.

That's it, one hit.

His team was leading. He never felt better in his life. But over his shoulder, he caught a glimpse of someone warming up in the bullpen.

Why would someone be in the bullpen?

And here came pitching coach Carl Willis to the mound. White was confused. He had just struck out the last hitter he faced.

"Matt, that's it," said Willis, putting out his hand for the ball.

"That's what?" asked White.

"Nice job," said Willis. "You're done."

"I'm done?" asked White. "Why am I done?"

"Ninety pitches," said Willis.

That was it. White was done. Done with a one-hitter. Done in a game where he had struck out 10. Done because this is how baseball is played in Burlington, North Carolina, the lowest rung on the minor-league ladder.

Here, every starter is on a pitch-count. Here, everything is development. Here, no pitcher is allowed to throw more than 30 pitches in an inning, or 90 for a game.

No questions asked. No chances taken with young arms just out of high school or college. This year's first-round draft pick, C.C. Sabathia, was yanked from a game in the second inning of his second pro start—30 pitches did it.

"One time, we had a kid get to up 27 pitches before he finally got out of the first inning," Willis said. "I told him that he was close to getting the hook."

The kid stared strangely at Willis for a moment.

"Well," said the pitcher. "Next time I get close to 30 pitches, just give me a signal from the bench and I'll throw a couple a pitches they'll hit for ground balls."

"Just like that?" asked Willis.

"Just like that," said the cocky pitcher, whose 5.55 ERA hardly merited such confidence.

Burlington is the first time many of these kids have used wooden bats.

"A huge, huge adjustment," said hitting coach Jack Mull. "These kids are used to getting a fastball on the fists and lining it to left field with those aluminum bats."

But now?

"The fastball shatters the bat right in their hands," said Mull. "I've seen a half-dozen kids break a bat on a pitch, and just stand there at home plate, holding the broken handle in their hands. They were so surprised, they didn't even run."

Meanwhile, pitching coach Willis has another problem.

"All these kids used to pitching to metal bats hate to throw the ball inside," he said. "I tell them please, bust them on the fists. You'll break the bat right off."

But they don't always listen. Having spent years facing hitters with those indestructible aluminum bats, they have learned to just nibble at the outside corner. In pro baseball, that's a disaster. It means the pitcher has surrendered about half of home plate to the hitter—and they are throwing pitches where they can be hit by the thickest part of the wooden bat.

"These kids will run through a wall for you," said Mull. "But they don't always understand what you're teaching them."

Sometimes, they can barely play catch.

Before the game, you better keep your head up. Balls seem to be flying everywhere. Yes, we're talking about guys just warming up before batting practice.

The games themselves are wild affairs with walks, strikeouts, ridiculous throws and outrageously fine defensive plays—all sometimes within the same inning.

Burlington plays in the Appalachian League, where no team can have more than 12 players who are 21 years or older. The season is only 68 games, June through August, and it's the lowest of all the minor leagues still directly affiliated with Major League Baseball. It's where there are 33 players on the roster, 15 of them pitchers.

And only three are likely to have a major-league career of any significance.

Here, kids learn how to act like professional players. They learn to practice. They learn to travel. They learn to be away from home for the first time.

Shortstop Maicer Isturiz, he had to learn to play under the lights— the 17-year-old had done it maybe only five times in his life before signing with the Indians.

And Carlos Batista received a standing ovation from his teammates for drawing a walk.

That happened last week. It happened after Batista had come to the plate 172 times as a professional, swinging every time. It happened after three months of his coaches begging him to be patient, to take a few pitches.

Finally, after 10 weeks and those 172 at-bats, he walked.

Later he said, "They gave me absolutely nothing to hit."

Three days later, he walked again.

Even though Batista has been hitting only .230, that second walk was considered real progress.

"Down here, a lot is measured in baby steps," Manager Joe Mikulik said.

The best hitter Burlington has ever seen is Manny Ramirez, the Tribe's star right fielder. In 59 games, he hammered 19 homers and drove in 63 runs while batting .326.

But Tribe phenom Richie Sexson batted .186 with one homer in 40 games. This from a kid who four years later would hit 31 homers at Class AAA Buffalo.

"We called Sexson 'Pine Tree,'" trainer Dave Lassiter said. "That's because he was only 18 years old, and so tall and skinny. He'd work out like crazy in this heat and he'd just wilt."

Sexson was from Washington state, where humidity was rare. In the summer, Burlington can feel like a marathon runner's sweat socks. Every day, it's 90-something. Every day, the humidity pulls the water right out of your pores. Every day, you feel a little more tired than the last.

"Especially since this is the first time these kids have played base-ball every day," said Mikulik, in his third year at Burlington.

Watching baseball in Burlington shows what you don't know.

You don't know who will make the majors. You don't know who will gain 30 pounds of muscle, or who will blow out their arms. You don't know who will grow up, or who will lose their careers to something as simple but heartfelt as homesickness.

Yes, sometimes there is a sure thing such as Ramirez. And you can usually guess that about half the players have no chance whatsoever to make it, and you wonder why they were signed in the first place.

"But anyone who can look at a bunch of kids in this league and pick out the big leaguers will have a job for life," said Willis, the pitching coach who spent six years in the majors, mostly with the Minnesota Twins.

Burlington is about dreams.

Matt White has won eight games. He was a 15th-round pick out of Clemson. Not exactly a phenom. Not a hard thrower. But he's left-handed. He throws strikes. He has some guts.

Matt White has a chance.

Then there are broken dreams.

There is a kid named Ryan McDermott. He was the Tribe's second-round pick in 1996. He is 6-foot-9 and 230 pounds. He just looks like he'd throw a ball hard enough to knock the gun turret off a tank.

And he did, when the Indians signed him.

Only, it's three years later. Only, McDermott had major shoulder surgery in 1996. Only, last year, he stopped to help someone change a tire and was struck by a drunken driver, causing back and other problems.

Only now, it's 1998, and this hulking young man can't get his arms and legs to work together. In his third year at Burlington, he is reduced to the last pitcher on the staff. His ERA is over 10.00. His fastball can't even break 84 mph. He's thinking about going to college, maybe playing basketball.

At age 20, his career is probably over.

Burlington is in another universe from Jacobs Field.

It's an aging ballpark dating to the 1930s. Actually, the park itself was built in 1959, but pieces of the park were imported from Danville, Virginia, sold for $5,000 and transported to Burlington by trucks.

Those parts—including much of the grandstand and light stands—go back to the 1930s. They were reconstructed in Burlington, and have been painted countless times.

But this park still has the feeling of baseball in an era before corporate boxes and even minor-league palaces such as Canal Park. It reeks of stale beer, grilled hot dogs, old cigars and stories of players from before the war—as in World War II.

With a fine young general manager named Mike Edwards doing some earnest promotion, this team averages about 1,200 fans—fourth best in the 10-team league. Teams such as Johnson City (629 fans), Elizabethon (356) and Pulaski (279) barely draw anyone to watch these games.

At Burlington, you see old men in overalls with crew cuts and pipes. You hear a woman stand up and belt out the theme from "Green Acres" every night. You hear them talk about Jim Thome, Brian Giles, Bartolo Colon and others who have passed through Burlington and made it to Cleveland.

And like everyone else, they wonder which of these kids they'll see one day on national TV.

8/24/1998

Remember, he's only 19

THE MOTHER OPENED the refrigerator and found a bottle of water, a can of V-8 juice. She checked the freezer and found nothing but ice.

"Son, you're gonna starve," said Margie Sabathia.

Not likely. Not at 6-foot-8 and 268 pounds, and not with the eyes of the entire Cleveland Indians front office on him.

But you should know that C.C. Sabathia is more than the hottest prospect in the Tribe's farm system, more than a man blessed with a magical left arm that sends his fastball to home plate with a vapor trail, a fastball that lights up these soft North Carolina spring nights with readings of 97 mph on the radar gun.

Sabathia is still only 19 years old.

He is still a kid who had his parents and his godmother in Kinston last week to watch him pitch for the Tribe's Class A team. He still needs his mother to shop for him, to buy chicken and break it down into little bags that can be quickly opened and nuked in the microwave.

He still runs up phone bills of at least $200 a month, talking to his mother.

He signed for $1.3 million in 1998 and has such a pleasing, mature personality that you'd never guess he was anything besides another young man in Class A baseball. He dreams those big-league dreams on those endless bus rides as he tries to stretch that $20-a-day meal money at those Bojangles chicken restaurants that dominate the Eastern Carolina landscape.

Sabathia shares an apartment with two other teammates—Byron Ewing and Albert Garza. He walks the mall, he watches ESPN, he laughs at the same stupid baseball jokes. He's excited about the George Foreman grill he bought so that he and his roommates can cook out at their apartment. He brags to his mother about his ability to make eggs and grits.

Just remember, he's only 19.

Remember that as you read about his 43 strikeouts in 34 Carolina League innings this year, compared with only 16 walks and one wild pitch. Remember that as you check his record and see he's struck out 111 hitters in his first 86 pro innings heading into this season.

Remember that as you hear Tribe general manager John Hart say that no player in the Tribe farm system is asked for by more teams than Sabathia—and Hart adds that he'd rather slice off his own left arm than part with this left-hander from Vallejo, Calif.

Finally, remember that as you hear the comparisons with Randy Johnson, the ultimate left-handed power pitcher.

"I just worry that C.C. is growing up too soon," Margie Sabathia said. "He is such a good person, kind of shy and trusting. He never really got in any trouble, but. . . ."

But Margie Sabathia knows that her son can be a target, that word of his talent, his $1.3-million bonus, and his easy-going, kind personality won't be much of a secret for long.

"That's why I'm glad that they started him in Kinston, away from everything," she said, watching her son at Grainger Stadium last week. "Down here, it's just baseball, and that's good."

Believe or not, Hart and the Indians agree with Mom.

"We thought about having him open the season at [Class AA] Akron, but that's really a mini-Cleveland with everything from the great stadium to the media attention," said Hart. "In Akron, Cleveland isn't just 35 miles away. It's so close, you can taste Jacobs Field and that can screw up a player's thinking. C.C. will get to Akron soon enough, but we want him to get his feet on the ground."

Kinston is the smallest city with a full-season, minor-league team. It's 25,000 people in a town where the best place to stay is the Hampton Inn, where there are few distractions and lots of fast-food and barbecue joints.

It's a town that sprang up from the sandy soil, a town that is the hub for the local tobacco, cotton and tomato growers. It's not near an interstate. It is not served by a commercial airline. It's a place that celebrated the arrival of the Wal-Mart.

"I like it for C.C.," Margie Sabathia said. "This is exactly what he needs right now."

At Kinston, he can throw a seven-inning shutout (nine strikeouts, two walks) as he did 10 days ago, and no one clamors for his immediate promotion to the Indians to replace Charles Nagy in the rotation.

Or he can be distracted as he was in his last start. He learned right before the game that his favorite uncle had died. He gave up one run in each of the first four innings.

Four times, runners stole bases against him. He was hurt by his inability to field a bunt. He allowed batters to lean over the plate and take soft swings, hitting singles to the opposite field.

He had to feel like Goliath, being pelted with pebbles until he was driven into utter frustration. There is no reason to panic. That game was just a reminder that Sabathia is still 19, that he's thrown only 120 pro innings, that despite his fine control on and off the field, he's still a babe in terms of baseball.

If this had happened in Akron, the temptation would be to say that Sabathia is carrying too much weight on that wide frame, that maybe 250 is a better number than the 268 he sees when he steps on the scale.

"We really don't know C.C.'s best weight, because we don't know how big he'll be," Hart said. "He's still growing. Maybe it's 265. Maybe it's 245. We have given him a nutritional program, but in the minors they ride the buses, they eat the junk food. We don't want him to get any bigger, but we won't make a big issue of his weight, either."

What has impressed the people in Kinston as much as Sabathia's arm is his attitude.

"He's just a nice guy," said teammate Matt White.

"He doesn't act like he thinks he's a big deal," teammate Mike Bacsik said. "You look at him and you know that he's going to be a No. 1 starter in the big leagues. You know that he got the big bonus. You know he's a Top Dog, that he's going to be pushed along. But with him, it doesn't bother you."

That's not always the case. No. 1 draft picks can quickly alienate their teammates in the minors, who believe they don't receive the same attention, the same breaks, as The Chosen Few.

But Carsten Charles Sabathia, Jr. acts like the son of a man who worked in a warehouse, like the son of a woman who still works the graveyard shift at the phone company. He seems grounded in the values that came from all those Sunday services and youth-club meetings at the Baptist Church.

Though his parents divorced when he was 13, his father remained close to their only child. In high school, he had a 3.2 grade-point average as a senior. He played three sports, and was a good enough tight end to be offered scholarships to several mid-level Division I schools, such as Hawaii and Fresno State.

His father coached him in youth baseball. His mother played catch with him in the back yard, and he'd insist that she wear a mask and chest protector as they played imaginary games.

"We did that until he was 12," Margie Sabathia said. "Then he threw a fastball that about broke my hand, it stung so bad."

"He's a good kid who is very competitive and is willing to listen and learn," Kinston Manager Brad Komminsk said. "He works his butt off, and the other guys see that."

With his bonus, Sabathia bought his mother and himself each a Ford Expedition, a nice sport utility vehicle. But that's it.

"I want to get my mother a new house, but she refused," he said. "Just like she has kept her job. We don't want to make a big deal of the money."

The Indians appreciate Sabathia's parents, who are a part of their son's life, but don't overwhelm him. Tribe officials tell stories of other top picks whose parents quit their jobs, followed their sons to the minor-league cities where they became a general nuisance, because they have nothing better do to. They live through their sons and make life miserable for coaches and managers while turning their boys into baseball brats.

That's why Sabathia's humility is so refreshing.

"I know that I'm like the other guys here," he said. "I have to work my way up. It didn't bother me to start in Kinston. I just want to stay healthy, start 25 to 28 games and see where I end up."

Sabathia talked about coming to Kinston at the end of last year, where he had a 3-3 record and a 5.34 ERA.

"Now I can see it was good for me," he said. "It showed me that I'd have to earn my way to the big leagues, that I don't have all the answers. My goal is to be able to go out there and dominate the other team, to get a guy with two strikes and then finish him off, just bury him."

5/8/2000

A big change for Baez

LISTEN IN as two members of the Class A Salem Avalanche farm club talk about Cuban pitcher Danys Baez:

"Who's pitching for Kinston tonight?" asked the first.

"That Elian Gonzalez guy," said the second.

"Who's that?"

"The Cuban guy who got the $14 million."

"Right, him. Maybe he'll boycott the game."

"Man, nobody boycotts a Carolina League game."

Before he even threw his first pitch for Kinston, Danys Baez was known all over the Class A Carolina League—even if most of the players couldn't remember his name.

He was the guy who bolted the Cuban National Team during last year's Pan Am Games in Canada, the guy who had teams bidding wildly for him—even though they barely had scouted him.

The finalists were Tampa Bay, Cleveland and Atlanta.

They had so little hard information. Scouts saw Baez at the 1999 Pan Am Games. There was a video of another game in international competition. There were whispers from those who had seen him pitch in Cuba, saying he would be the next gem to come from this country that is the last bastion of hidden baseball jewels.

But that's it. No statistics. No long interviews. No extensive background checks.

The Indians committed $14 million to someone they barely knew. Then again, the Braves offered nearly as much, and Tampa Bay's bid was even higher!

After a rocky spring training in which it was obvious Baez was rushed into big-league camp too soon, the Indians assigned him to their Class A team in Kinston, a town of 25,000 in eastern North Carolina.

Here, he is away from the pressure and media scrutiny that would find him even at Class AA Akron.

At Kinston, most players are paid $1,200 a month, $6,000 for the season. Most signed for a bonus less than $50,000. Most try to squeeze every dime out of their $20-a-day meal money, and most live 3 to 4 people to an apartment, the odd man out having to sleep on the sofa.

Baez's teammates like him personally. They see a sincere, open-faced man who works hard at everything from running sprints to learning English to going by the American version of his first name—simply being called "Danny."

But like most scouts, they don't see a $14-million pitcher.

They might not know exactly what a $14-million pitcher should look like, but they expect more than the 90-mph fastball that Baez usually throws.

They expect more than the 1-1 record and whopping 6.10 ERA in his first six starts.

If Baez were just another 22-year-old prospect, say a 15th-round pick out of Kent State, scouts would be pleased because he has 35 strikeouts in 31 innings.

He has displayed a sharp breaking ball. At times, his fastball has been as high as 93 mph. He looks like he eventually could develop into a useful major leaguer, especially since he has been pitching for only three years.

But put the $14 million next to his name in a league where a great night out on the town is a bucket of Bojangles chicken, and there is bound to be a certain amount of jealousy, especially when they see him driving that Mercedes.

"Danys knows that," said Jackie Minges, a Cuban-born attorney who has been Baez's interpreter in Kinston. "Some of the Latin players ask why he gets his own interpreter. Others think he shouldn't have his own place."

It's not like Baez lives in luxury. His place is a modest one-bedroom apartment. He just wanted a little privacy, somewhere to cook his fa-

THE VIEW FROM PLUTO

vorite Cuban rice and bean dishes. He wanted something he didn't have in Cuba—his own home.

"When I was 12 years old, they took me away from home and sent me to a government camp where I picked oranges. We used to play catch with the oranges, like they were baseballs. Then, I spent two years in the military. Then, I went to college to study physics. Since I was 12, I've spent far more time away from home than with my parents." — Danys Baez

Baez won baseball's version of the Powerball lottery.

One day, he was pitching for $10 a month in Cuba; the next day, he had that outrageous four-year contract.

One day, he finally had a pair of spiked shoes that he didn't make himself, tennis shoes in which he had pounded some screws through the soles to give him better traction.

The next day, he has all the gloves and shoes and clothes he'd ever want, enough to outfit his old Cuban team.

One day, he's riding a bike in Cuba, his only mode of transportation.

The next day, he's driving the Streets Of Gold—or at least, the interstates of Miami—in a Mercedes.

One day, he was a poor kid with a physics degree scheming of a way to sneak into the United States, to crawl out from under Castro's oppressive thumb and make a decent living like his relatives in Fort Lauderdale.

The next day, he seemed to be rich enough to buy Fort Lauderdale.

"I never imagined this kind of money," Baez said. "I remember when [agent] Joe Cubas told me that the bidding would start at $10 million. I thought he was crazy."

Cubas knew how desperate teams were for pitching. He knew how intrigued scouts were with Cuban pitchers such as Orlando and Livan Hernandez, who both have starred in the World Series. He knew Baez looked like a pitcher at 6-foot-3, 225 pounds of muscle. He knew the radar guns tracked Baez's fastball consistently in the 93 mph range during the Pan Am Games, where he also displayed a sharp curveball and a deft change-up.

He knew he could turn Baez into a pile of cash, $10 million more than any Cuban pitcher had ever received.

"At first, you think that you'd do about anything for $14 million. But then you realize Danys will probably never see his family

again, that he put himself in real danger to come here. It makes
you think twice." — Kinston pitcher Mike Bacsik

Here is Kinston, home of the Indians' Class A team.

Here is where Baez arrived "like a turtle with his head in a shell," according to team general manager North Johnson.

Here is where Baez goes to his apartment, where he sits alone in front of the TV, trying to learn English. Or where he calls his parents back in Cuba, and wonders if the authorities are listening.

"I know the line is tapped," he said. "I'll be talking to them, and suddenly, they cut us off. Then I can't get through again."

Here is where the Kinston team set up Baez with Minges, the Cuban-born lawyer who is helping him learn English and other nuances of his new home.

"In Cuba, Castro controls everything," Minges said. "My parents left Cuba 30 years ago when I was 6. I have not seen that side of the family. It's so hard to get news back and forth. When you leave Cuba, there is always a sense of guilt, of knowing you've cut the cord. Danys is dealing with that now."

Baez is trying to cope with everything: a new culture, new wealth, a new way of playing baseball, "Where when they say be there at 11 o'-clock, they mean 11 o'clock," he said. "Back home, that can mean 1 o'-clock or even later."

And it's not been easy.

In one start, he'll allow one run in seven innings. In another, he's shelled for five runs in four innings. The next start, three runs in six innings. Then comes six runs in three innings. He seems to struggle when there are men on base, unsure of what pitch to throw to slip out of a jam.

"The kid is a real work in progress, and Cleveland just better accept that. He's not like C.C. Sabathia or some phenom who can come quick." — A baseball scout

Sabathia is the pitching jewel of the Tribe farm system, the No. 1 draft pick in 1998 who signed for $1.3 million and looks like a blue chip investment. He's a 6-foot-8, 268-pound left-hander with a consistent 95 mph fastball and remarkable control for someone only 19 years old.

This summer, he'll appear at Akron's Canal Park. Some time in 2001, you'll probably be able to catch him at Jacobs Field. He's on the fast track to Cleveland, and no one holds it against the friendly and unassuming young man from Northern California.

But Baez pitches in the Kinston rotation the day after Sabathia, and he suffers from the comparison.

One of Baez's Kinston teammates said, "C.C. looks like the next Randy Johnson. He can be overpowering. Danys may become the next Rick Helling; he's really going to have to use his head and pitch to be effective up there."

"Danys is just a great dude. When he comes into the clubhouse each day, he shakes hands with everyone. We like him. We're pulling for him. But you can see that he's put too much pressure on himself, that he has all these outside influences working on him. He just needs to relax and pitch." — C.C. Sabathia

How can any of us know what it's like to be Baez?

How would we feel if our parents were college professors, yet they were paid only $10 a month? How would we feel if our older brother became a math professor like his mother, and he earned $10 a month?

How would it feel to know that the only reason we had a television set was because our relatives in the U.S. managed to slip us some money?

How would we feel if we knew that no matter how hard we worked, no matter how many college degrees we earned, no matter what we did—we were doomed to live a life of poverty?

"Before I even got serious about baseball, I was determined to leave Cuba and get to the U.S.," Baez said. "What good is it where everyone makes $10 a month? Where U.S. dollars are the only thing that count? My family couldn't afford a car, but if they had one, they never could buy gas. That's like $4 a gallon."

Baez talked about July 9, 1999, the last day he saw he parents. He talked about going with the Cuban National Team to Winnipeg, Manitoba, for the Pan Am Games. He talked about how he had to somehow, some way, get to America.

But he won't say much about how it happened, how he came into contact with Cubas, the man who has helped other Cuban players defect to the U.S.

"We were staying at a military base in Canada," he said. "We wanted to go to McDonald's and the Pizza Hut, but they wouldn't let us leave the base."

Baez shook his head.

"Security was everywhere," he said. "You didn't know if the player sitting next to you was really a player or a government agent. They didn't want anyone to defect, and you didn't tell anyone that you were thinking about it."

At this point in his story, Baez stood up and shook his legs, as if he was having a sudden attack of nerves.

"That's how I felt, real scared," he said. "I told the security people that I was going to get some tape for a VCR. Then I went to one part of the building, way in the back, and opened this door."

Cubas and the road to the U.S. was on the other side.

"Danys wants to be a good pitcher. He is so generous, such a nice guy. He works hard. He likes to be coached. On the mound, he tends to nibble too much, to give the hitters too much credit. But in time, I think he'll be fine."
— Kinston manager Brad Komminsk

Baez didn't pitch after the Pan Am Games in August until spring training in February. In that time, he lost his natural pitching motion—and some of the power off his fastball.

One scout who saw Baez early in the spring said it looked as if he were "spearfishing" when he threw to the plate. The Indians have simplified that once funky and awkward motion.

"We're relieved that his throwing mechanics are straightened out," Tribe general manager John Hart said. "His curve is his best pitch right now. We like his change-up. His fastball is 89-91 range, and we just don't see the velocity that he showed last year. We know he'll get to the big leagues; it's just a matter of when."

Last week, Baez's fastball consistently hit the big-league average of 90, with a high of 93. He has no explanation of what happened to his natural pitching motion, other than he "got into some bad habits" during his time away from the game.

One theory is that he's still building up his arm strength after that long layoff, that his fastball will show more life the more he throws.

Another theory is that Indians really won't know what they have in Baez until next year, that he's coping with so much all at once right now that he doesn't seem very relaxed or confident on the mound.

"I do feel the pressure," he said. "I remember one game, there were 15 scouts watching me. I know that I'm supposed to do well. I know I'm supposed to get to the big leagues. I know I can be a much better pitcher than this."

As Baez said that, he sat in an empty Grainger Stadium in Kinston. He stared at the mound.

"So much has happened so fast," he said. "So much. . . ."

5/9/2000

Great expectations for LeBron James

HOW GOOD IS LEBRON JAMES?

Howard Garfinkel paused for a long time before answering.

For 35 summers, Garfinkel has run the famed Five-Star camp for the nation's top high school players. Name a great player, and he probably has passed through Garfinkel's camp.

Today's name is LeBron James, the 6-foot-6 sophomore from St. Vincent-St. Mary.

Dick Vitale says James is among the top five sophomores in the country. He doesn't rate them in order. In *ESPN Magazine,* he writes, "James is a tall, athletic point guard with serious skills and a brilliant first step."

The *Sporting News* says James is the second-best sophomore in the nation.

A magazine called *Athlon* has James at No. 1.

Garfinkel doesn't care about the rating services. He isn't concerned that St. V-M was 27-0, that it won the Ohio Division III title last spring, or that James had 25 points, nine rebounds and shot 8-for-11 in the championship game.

Garfinkel has even higher standards, a historical perspective. He talked about the 100-plus NBA players who have attended his Five-Star camp, names such as Grant Hill, Stephon Marbury, Rasheed Wallace, Christian Laettner, Elton Brand, Dell Curry and Bobby Hurley.

"I'm afraid to tell you the truth about James," Garfinkel said.

Why?

"Because I don't want to ruin a kid," he said. "I've seen a lot of kids get big heads, stop working "

His voice trailed off.

"I'll say this," he said. "You heard all those NBA guys I mentioned? LeBron played as well or better than any one of them when they were sophomores at my camp. It was ridiculous; he totally dominated. I've never seen anything quite like it."

How so?

"In the middle of the week, we had some guys hurt in our NBA [high school junior and senior division], and we moved him up," Garfinkel said. "He was playing four games a day, with both the sophomores and our NBA divisions."

Garfinkel's gravelly voice rose.

"He made both all-star teams," he rasped, "both of them, in his own division and the NBA division. In the 35 years that I've had this camp, that's never happened before. He can shoot it. He can pass off the dribble. He knows the game. He seems like a great kid. Like I said, I don't want to say too much, but I like this kid a lot. I don't want something to happen to him."

That's because LeBron James is a kid. Just 15 years old.

Remember that as you hear the things said about him. Remember that even if, right now, he would be good enough to make most Division I college teams.

Remember that he's 15, that his friends tease him about his big ears and he talks about their teeth or their feet.

Remember at 15, you're supposed to be silly.

But at 15, he has already played summer basketball in Utah, in Memphis, in Las Vegas, in Pittsburgh, and, believe it or not, in Milan, Italy.

He talks about a stretch last summer when he attended camps in Pittsburgh, Orlando and Tennessee. "I was gone almost all July," he said.

Then he sounds like a weary businessman, saying next summer he plans to cut down on his travel schedule. That's because all the camps and tournaments want a piece of LeBron James. They want a seat, even in the caboose, just in case his train carries him all the way to the NBA.

James has people telling him that he'll be the next Kobe Bryant or Tracy McGrady, the next kid to go right from high school to the pros. And he has pictures of them in his room.

But his favorite player is Michael Jordan. He even tells everyone he's 6-foot-6½, because that is Jordan's exact height. Jordan is the perfect role model for James, and not just because he is arguably the greatest basketball player ever. Jordan had strong values from his family. He played three years of college and considers North Carolina's Dean Smith to be a father figure, a man he still calls "Coach Smith." Jordan went back to North Carolina and earned his degree, even though he had enough money to buy the library and name it after himself.

Those pictures on the wall of James' room demonstrate the war for this young man's soul.

Jordan—who waited for the game and fame to come to him.

Or Bryant and McGrady—who went directly from the senior prom to the NBA.

"I try not to think about that stuff," James said. "I have Dick Vitale's magazine on the wall of my room. To see my name there, I want to live up to that. It's like Dick Vitale invented college basketball, you know what I mean?"

To a 15-year-old reared on Vitale screaming about "Diaper Dandies" on ESPN, maybe the bald former coach of the University of Detroit did start college basketball. Or at least, Vitale helped make it what it is today: An industry where 15-year-olds like James are rated and then dated by the top colleges and even the pros.

More than 100 colleges have written James. The coaches can't talk to him until his junior year, but they all know his name. Coaches from Michigan State, Duke, North Carolina, California, Ohio State—virtually every major basketball school in the country—are in contact with St. V-M coach Keith Dambrot, telling him of their interest in James.

LeBron James, 15 years old.

Gloria James loves her son, wants him to be 15, to enjoy high school.

"He keeps telling me that soon I won't have to worry about a thing," she said. "I'll have a house, a car, everything paid for. I tell him to take his time. I tell him that I don't need those things. My dream is to have my own chef, because I love to eat."

Then Gloria James laughs. She is 32, meaning LeBron was born when she was very young. She's only 5-foot-5 and played volleyball at Central-Hower. She is astonished at how her only child has grown, how he is blessed with such God-given athleticism.

"When he was 4 years old, he was dunking on our Nerf basketball hoop," she said. "I kept raising it, and he still kept dunking."

In the eighth grade, James was 5-foot-8.

When he enrolled in high school, he was 6-foot-2.

Now, he's 6-foot-6, oops, make it the Jordan-like 6-foot-6 1/2.

His arms seem to hang down to his knees. His hands are huge, his fingers long and delicate. His body flows like a river, and his rangy legs seem to cover the court in but a few incredible strides. Despite the growth spurts, he's never endured one of those uncoordinated stages where arms and legs refuse to function in harmony.

Gloria James talks about her son, the student. His grade-point average is a 2.8, which is a B-minus. His freshman English teacher, Jake Robinson, says James "has excellent penmanship and wrote some nice essays. He still has to work on his writing, but he cares about it."

Dambrot and his assistant coach, Steve Culp, the former head coach at Firestone High, run a study table each afternoon for the St. V-M players. James willingly finishes his work, even if he does it in between jokes.

"I never had to spank LeBron, not even once," Gloria James said. "When I tell him something, he listens."

That's because James truly loves and appreciates his mother. He talks about the hard times, especially when he was in the fourth grade and they "moved from place to place to place" because of money problems.

He says things are better now, adding, "My mother is my mother. But she also is my sister, my brother, my best friend, my uncle, my everything."

He has a tattoo on his arm, a woman with the name "Gloria," his way of honoring his mother.

James is at St. V-M because of Dru Joyce.

That's Dru Joyce, Sr. and Dru Joyce, Jr.

Dru, Sr. is "a special person to LeBron," according to Gloria James. He is a summer league coach.

James said, "Coach Dru teaches me a lot, like how to be polite to grown-ups."

On that count, the pleasant James certainly has listened.

Meanwhile, Dru, Jr. is St. V-M's point guard, the wisp of a lad who is only 5-foot-2, 102 pounds. Yet, he swished seven outrageously long and high-arcing 3-pointers in the state title game last spring.

James got to know the Joyce family when he was 11 years old. Dad coached the AAU team; the son played. As did Sian Cotton and Willie McGee.

"We called ourselves the Fab Four," James said. "We decided we'd all go to the same school together. We promised that nothing would break us up—girls, coaches, basketball. We'd hang together, no matter what."

They're doing it at St. V-M, partly because the Joyce family was very impressed with the summer basketball camp run by Dambrot and the academics offered by the private Catholic school in central Akron.

"Dru [Jr.] was the first to say we should go to St. V's," said James. "The rest of us followed."

When the Irish were 27-0 last season, they were led by senior Maverick Carter, now playing at Western Michigan. He also is James' cousin. But four of the top eight players were freshmen, the Fab Four as they called themselves.

Dru Joyce, Sr. and Lee Cotton (father of Sian) help out as assistant coaches at the school. Dambrot likes having them around, not only because he considers them solid basketball men, but strong, positive influences on all his players, not just James. When Dru Joyce, Sr. or Lee Cotton talk about James, they both immediately start with, "He's a good kid." They mention his loyalty to the other players on the AAU team and his unselfishness with his high school teammates.

Last year, James led the Irish by averaging 17 points and shooting 50 percent from the field.

"If he wanted, LeBron could have scored 25 points a game, easy," Dambrot said. "But he'd rather pass than shoot. That's why I think he can handle things and still fit in with the rest of the team."

At 15, LeBron James made a decision that surprised a lot of people.

He played football, catching 42 passes, 14 for touchdowns. He was picked as St. V-M's Most Valuable Player on offense this fall.

Not bad for a sophomore.

"Some people said I should just stick to basketball," he said. "But I like football. I like being with the guys on the team. It's fun."

Nothing wrong with a 15-year-old saying that, at least when the subject is football. He likes being a part of a team. In the 1999 regional semifinals, James caught six passes when his school lost 15-14 to Wickliffe. After the game, he was in tears, unhappy that the season had ended—especially for the seniors.

"He's a heckuva football player," Dambrot said, "probably one of the best receivers in the state. I wouldn't be surprised if he played again next year."

That's rare in an era where great athletes are pressured to play one sport.

"I just want to make sure LeBron does well academically," Dambrot said. "All the big schools already want him. We are already preparing him for the standardized tests. We want to give him every chance to get the scores he needs, because it would break my heart if he ends up at a junior college."

Dambrot is a former college coach at Ashland and Central Michigan. He is 43-9 in two years at St. V-M.

"LeBron is one of those players who comes around every 25 years," he said. "He knows he's good, but he doesn't seem to be very caught up in all the hype around him. He's really just a nice kid."

And those who know James are praying that he doesn't change.

11/26/2000

Tribe prospect turns scouts' heads

THEY TOSS AROUND THE NAMES RECKLESSLY.

He can be another Barry Larkin. No, he's Paul Molitor. He's more advanced than Alfonso Soriano at this stage.

In every minor-league park, he hears the same thing: There's the guy in the Colon deal.

Brandon Phillips, the future of the Indians.

"I try not to pay attention to that stuff," he said.

Then, he smiled.

That's one of the reasons scouts love Phillips.

The smile.

The enthusiasm.

The sense that baseball still is a game, and it's fun—especially when baseball comes as easily as it does to Phillips.

"The more I think about the trade, the more I like it," he said. "It feels good that the Indians care about me, that they wanted me and they like my game."

That's wrong.

They love his game. They are infatuated in a heart-pounding, starry-eyed way with their young shortstop.

"He's dynamic," General Manager Mark Shapiro insisted. "He has a presence. He brings energy. You just sense that he'll be someone special by being around him."

Naturally, Shapiro has a huge stake in this young man. He traded his emerging ace in Bartolo Colon for three kids in the Montreal farm system—pitcher Cliff Lee, outfielder Grady Sizemore and Phillips.

Baseball America oozed over the deal. The magazine is considered the bible of minor-league baseball, and it puts enormous effort into rating (and re-rating) prospects. It says Phillips is the most talented young player traded this summer, "a potential 20-20 man," meaning 20 homers and 20 steals per season.

It also ranked Lee as the fourth-best prospect and Sizemore the 10th-best prospect to switch teams.

Ask Phillips for a scouting report on himself, and he pauses for a moment, giving it serious thought.

"The man can hit," he said.

His smile lights up the Buffalo dressing room.

"Yeah, the man can hit, and he uses the whole field," he said.
Then he laughed.
It was the right touch—confidence with a touch of cockiness.

Phillips was just named the Class AAA International League Player
of the Week, as he batted .484 between July 29 and August 4. He carried an eight-game hitting streak and a .287 average into last night's
action.

Keep in mind that he turned 21 only a few weeks ago. He opened
the season in Class AA, where he savaged the Eastern League (.327,
9 HR, 35 RBI in 60 games) before being promoted.

While he's more of a line-drive hitter than a power man, he does
have 15 HR and 55 RBI in 102 games.

As Shapiro said, "Most kids at his age are still playing in college, but
Brandon is already at Class AAA."

The Indians are trying to be careful with Phillips. They believe his
immediate future is at second base, but they are keeping him at shortstop for now.

"We just want him to be comfortable," Shapiro said. "We can work
Brandon at second base in the Arizona Fall League."

That's what he played in that same league a year ago when he batted .344.

"Brandon can play second, short or third," said Jason Phillips (no
relation), the Tribe pitcher who was a teammate in Arizona last fall
and with Buffalo this summer.

"He's really a good athlete," Jason Phillips said. "He's a good guy, too."

Like most young shortstops not named Omar Vizquel, Brandon
Phillips makes errors—often on easy chances—while turning in star-
tling, spectacular plays on seemingly impossible balls to reach.

Buffalo manager Eric Wedge is impressed with Phillips' quick adjustment from Class AA to Class AAA and how he's done it under the
glare of the trade and the pressure that brings.

Phillips is at the park early most days, taking extra infield practice
before all the regular pregame drills begin.

He seems to glide on the field, his arm is strong, although he sometimes doesn't set his feet before he throws.

That leads to some needless errors.

At the plate, it's a right-handed, line-drive swing. His bat is a whip,
a white blur, and it's hard to imagine many fastballs getting past him.

Phillips wears No. 7, partly because Kenny Lofton was one of his favorite players.

He also likes the Reds' Barry Larkin.

While he grew up in Stone Mountain, Georgia, he says he really enjoyed watching the Indians of the mid-1990s. He ticks off the names: Belle, Baerga, Lofton, Ramirez, Thome.

He says he'd like to be a Robbie Alomar–type player.

It's nice to be around a young man with a sense of baseball history, albeit recent. But he's smart enough to know the game didn't just begin when he first laced up a pair of spikes.

He says he was good enough to be offered a scholarship to play basketball and baseball at the University of Georgia. He averaged 16 points as a 6-foot high school guard. His sister, Porsha, is 15 years old and rated one of the top high school girls players in Georgia.

Watching him on the diamond, there's little reason to doubt Phillips' word. He's one of these gifted athletes who probably can play anything and play it remarkably well.

"I feel confident about helping the Indians," he said. "I'll be second, third, whatever they want.

"It would be fun to play next to Omar.

"He's really great."

Phillips probably won't be too bad, himself.

8/7/2002

More than a Game

Baseball still holds sway over its fans

IT WAS THREE O'CLOCK and Jacobs Field was locked, but that didn't stop some fans from staring through the bars at a stadium where there was supposed to be baseball last night.

I'm talking about maybe 20 people pressing their faces against the gates when there was really nothing to see.

"I just like looking at the field, even if it's empty," said one middle-aged fan. He said he didn't have tickets for last night's Indians-Milwaukee game. He just was in the neighborhood and stopped by to stare.

For John Chlebo and Ken Peters, it was different. They should have been at last night's game. "Right there, that's where our seats are," said Chlebo pointing to a spot in the upper deck behind home plate.

Peters and Chlebo were behind the right-field gate, maybe 600 feet from their seats.

"I grew up in Cleveland, but I live outside of Chicago," said Peters. "I came to town this weekend to see my friends and go to the game—my first game at Jacobs Field. It's sad because finally, the Indians are good and this happens."

So why were they there?

"I've got a package of tickets for 20 games," said Chlebo, who lives in Parma. "So I've been here before, but I wanted Ken to at least see the park."

Whenever the strike ends, will they be back?

"I'd like to say no," said Chlebo. "But I know better. I love baseball and the Indians are really entertaining this year, so I'll watch 'em again."

What strike?

As you walked around Jacobs Field, you saw fans posing for pictures in front of the stadium, by the Bob Feller statue and even by the closed ticket windows. You would never have known that baseball was on strike.

One of the ticket windows had a sign that said, "Today's game sold out." The others had information about strike refunds. But at the refund window, no one was in line.

Where you found a lot of people was at the window set up for vendors who were supposed to work last night. As I watched them with glum expressions on their faces, I thought of a truly insulting strike story that was carried on a local news station last week. The theme was, "What impact will the strike have on panhandlers?"

Here was this TV "reporter" interviewing street folks about their possible lost income if baseball stops and there will be fewer people to put money in their cups.

"It will probably cost me $40–$50 on a game night," said one guy.

As I talked to Nichola Woodward, I thought about this. She was walking away from the vendors window with a check—perhaps her last check of the summer.

Nichola is a high school student, but when the Indians are home, she works at a concession stand.

"I make $6.25 an hour," she said.

I did some quick math and realized that she'll lose $40–$50 on most game days. She isn't begging, she wants more work, more hours—and baseball has taken that away from this inner-city Cleveland area student whose values are in the right place.

Nichola showed me a sheet she received, telling employees that they either have to turn in their uniforms next week—or pay $50 to keep them.

"Don't worry, I'll give it back," she said. "I just hope I don't have to because that means I can work some more."

As you talk to fans on Day 1 of the strike, you can't help but get mad. The players and owners have no appreciation of those who pay the freight.

Take a woman who only wanted to be identified as Cathy. She is blind and has two teenage sons. They came out of the Indians' gift shop, and I asked her about going to the game.

"No, we weren't doing that," she said, while petting her guide dog. "But we went to the store because I promised to get my son an Indians jacket."

Even though there's a strike, that didn't stop her from spending money at Jacobs Field.

"My son wanted the jacket," she said with a shrug.

The gift shop was crowded yesterday afternoon, maybe 30 people.

"It has been like that all day," a clerk told me. "We are always busy. People always want souvenir."

You hear these stories and you realize the power that the game has on the people who follow it. No sport has treated its customers as shabbily as baseball—this is the eighth labor problem in 22 years. If this were any other business, the doors would be closed—forever.

But there was a man who didn't want to be identified. He was with his 10-year-old son.

"Me, I wasn't going to the game to see those schmucks, no way," he growled.

Now that sounded like a common-sense response to the strike. But then the man pulled out a camera and took a picture of the vacant diamond and empty seats. That's when it really hits you, the power baseball has on the fans. It tells you that no matter how stupid the players and owners are—and reminds you that no matter when the games begin—the fans may grumble and moan, but they will be back.

8/13/1994

Many need baseball as companion

THERE ARE THOSE OF YOU who think that if the major-leaguers stay on strike, then there shouldn't be any baseball.

You say that people should find something else to fill the hours.

Read a book, maybe a classic like Milton or Proust.

Go to the ballet.

Start a diary.

All of that sounds fine, but before you decide that we don't need baseball, let me tell you about my father.

He is 75 years old. He is the reason I grew up loving sports and why I am a sportswriter.

He also is a stroke victim, one of more than 1.3 million per year.

He likes to read but he can't. Amazingly, the stroke short-circuited his brain so that all he can read are nouns—and not all nouns.

He was never much of a letter writer, but now he can't write at all. The stroke zapped the right side of his body, and his favorite arm just hangs there—forgotten and useless.

Yes, he can print with his left hand—but only his name and my name. He really doesn't know what the letters mean—the stroke ambushing him again—but he has learned to make a few of them so he can sign papers that he really can't read.

My father used to love to talk on the phone, only he can no longer do that, either.

His speech is pretty much limited to one word—man. He must say, "Man . . . MAN . . . MAN!" a million times a day.

How he says it and where he points tell you what he wants, but it doesn't do much for telephone conversation or meetings with strangers.

He used to love to go out, but the stroke caused chaos with his bladder and kidneys. He now feels as if he needs to go to the bathroom—constantly.

This is a guy who can't use his right arm or right leg, so going to the bathroom often is like climbing a mountain of loose gravel.

Where do I put my arm?

My leg?

Will I slip?

This makes it easier and safer to just stay home.

Ah, yes, the leg. I almost forget to tell you that the stroke also attacked him there, stealing the leg's power from this big man who was once a minor-league first baseman. He finally learned to walk about 25 steps with a cane after 18 months of grueling therapy—then he fell down last week and broke his hip.

Now he has just finished surgery to install a metal plate and six screws in his right hip. He will be mostly bed-ridden for one month.

I tell you this for one reason—because my father misses baseball.

The place where he finds most of his pleasure is from sports on television.

Basketball and baseball are his favorites. The first numbers he pushes on his remote control dial up ESPN, and it is his constant companion.

He is almost as mad at baseball as he is at the fate that has sentenced him to this kind of life. He knows that life isn't fair—which was one of his pet phrases when I'd whine about something.

But he just can't understand why baseball is gone. He is sick of the strike . . . of seeing sniveling Bud Selig and sneering Donald Fehr on "SportsCenter."

He can't understand why there have been no games, no World Series, nothing much on ESPN but a tractor-pull and beach volleyball.

I wish I could push his wheelchair into the middle of these strike talks, and let Tom Pluto wave his fist and scream, "Man . . . MAN . . . MAN!" at the men who stole his game.

I'd like these guys to tell him how they can't figure out how to divide up a couple of billion dollars—and maybe seeing him would remind these guys what is important.

But probably not.

They'd probably just blame each other for my father's stroke and then argue about that for three months.

Of course, that misses the point. My father is like most fans today— he has no power, no voice. What baseball needs to know is that there are millions out there like my father.

They are stroke victims, heart patients, people who have lost limbs and nearly their lives. Baseball isn't everything to them, but it's something and it's soothing.

They will take replacement players or any games they can dial up. It's better than nothing.

But baseball also has a moral obligation to ask itself why it is selling out people like my father—the people who need the game the most.

3/5/1995

E pluribus champion

THE PITCHER WAS from Nicaragua, the catcher from the Dominican Republic.

The greyhound center fielder is from the projects of East Chicago, Indiana, and the strong, sometimes sullen left fielder is from Shreveport, Louisiana.

Their boss is from the dusty Texas panhandle.

We are talking about the manager and players who helped deliver the first World Series to Cleveland baseball fans in 41 years.

We are talking about guys from Latin America and the American South. Some of them are black, others white, a lot are Hispanic.

We are talking about men who probably wouldn't spend five minutes with each other if they all didn't happen to play baseball with the Cleveland Indians.

But they have lived together for six months, almost like a Martin Luther King Dream Team—a group of folks of different races and backgrounds working together for a common goal.

This is how life is supposed to be.

But we live in an age of rage. It is an age of Rodney King, O. J. Simpson and Mark Fuhrman—an age of hating those whom you don't know.

That is why it was so satisfying to see all these players covering every color of the human rainbow jumping, hugging, pouring champagne and celebrating what they have in common—rather than dwelling on what easily could have driven them apart.

It's good for our children to see this. It's important for them to know that a city kid from East Chicago such as Kenny Lofton can work between a fellow black from Shreveport in Albert Belle and a Dominican by way of New York City in Manny Ramirez.

And Lofton's job in the outfield is to cover up for both of them.

It does say something when a white pitcher who attended Bowling Green can throw to a catcher from Puerto Rico—and he trusts the catcher to make the biggest decisions on his job.

The pitcher is Orel Hershiser. He became the Most Valuable Player of the American League Championship Series, and he'll tell you that he loves how Sandy Alomar, Jr. calls a game. He appreciates Alomar's physical talent—and his brains.

The playoff clincher was pitched by Dennis Martinez, the recovering alcoholic from Nicaragua. His catcher was Tony Pena, who came from a farm in the Dominican Republic. The man who saved the game, Jose Mesa, grew up picking tomatoes and sweet potatoes on the family farm in the Dominican.

And all these guys won a pennant for Cleveland, Ohio.

This is not meant to romanticize the 1995 Cleveland Indians.

They can be a hostile, surly group. There are days when Belle doesn't just refuse to talk to the press or fans—he barely says a word to his teammates. It is known as Albert having One Of Those Days, and those who work with him have learned to give him wide berth.

Eddie Murray can give you a stare that would crumble Pikes Peak, and there are days when the players know it's not wise to mess with Eddie.

Lofton can be so suspicious of strangers—or even his bosses—that it borders on paranoia. Jimmy Thome is well meaning, but his hayseed kid from Peoria act can occasionally wear thin because he can seem so dazed about things. Remember, Thome is the one who thought it's only a two-hour drive from Cleveland to Toronto.

Then there are the Latin players chattering in Spanish, and sometimes making the Americans feel a bit left out.

They are managed by Dudley Michael Hargrove—and you can bet there were very few folks like these around when he was growing up in little Perryton, Texas.

All of this could lead to a clubhouse war, but Hargrove has a wonderful mix of patience and grit—and most of all, his honesty means that his players can trust him.

But as Hargrove said, "Every day there are a few brush fires to put out."

The Latin players want Salsa music on the clubhouse stereo. Most of the blacks want rap. Some of the whites try for country, although they are a definite minority in this matter.

These guys aren't thrilled when one group hogs the music. But at least they don't end up in a wrestling match as former Tribesmen Rick Sutcliffe and Broderick Perkins did in 1982. Sutcliffe wanted country music, Perkins pushed for soul—then pushed Sutcliffe. It took four players to separate them as suddenly this fight was about far more than music.

Think about your office, your classroom or anywhere you come across people who are foreign to you. Think about how easy it is for a simple, honest misunderstanding to ignite into something very ugly— something that strikes at the dark side of the human heart.

Those who have been there will tell you that sports and the military are great equalizers. People from everywhere are tossed together.

In the military, the issue can be as grave as life and death. It can be leading your squad through boot camp and out of maneuvers with everyone's health and sanity intact. You pull together, or you sink alone.

That also happens in a ballgame, where the passion to win takes precedence over racial prejudices. You have to rely on each other, and then you learn that the person next to you looks different, talks differently and maybe thinks differently—but you can still count on him.

It is like that with the Indians or any other successful athletic team.

These guys don't all love one another, but they have come to accept and respect each other.

Too bad the rest of America can't do the same.

10/19/1995

Unlocking the bars on men's souls

HIS NAME IS ROGER and he is in jail all because of a bar of soap.

"Can you believe it?" he asks. "A bar of soap, and they said it's an illegal substance."

You don't believe it.

But that doesn't matter.

You are with the Bill Glass Prison Ministries group at the Cook County Jail in Chicago, where there are more than 10,000 men and women behind bars, all wearing tan or blue pajamalike clothes with the letters D.O.C. on the back.

That's Department of Corrections.

Roger is jailed because of drugs. You didn't have to ask him. As one of 500 counselors who went into the jail with Glass, you are told never to ask why an inmate is there.

Besides, most of them tell you—or at least give you their version of events.

Roger is one of six convicts you meet—all of them say they didn't do it. They also say that everyone in jail claims they didn't do the crime—but they are the exception.

"I mean, I really didn't do it," Roger says. "It was a bar of soap, man."

You might remember Bill Glass, a former defensive end with the Browns in the 1960s. Glass has spent the last 25 years speaking to prisoners. It is his job—and his calling.

"I visit 200 jails a year," Glass said. "I have spent so much time in jail, if I robbed a bank, I'd never have to do the time."

Glass didn't want the prison ministry.

"I wanted to be like Billy Graham, speak to people in stadiums," he said. "But I was asked to talked to a prison when I was still with the Browns."

That was at Marion in 1972. He wondered what he could tell these men. Glass always had been a Christian. He had followed the rules. He is white and grew up in Texas, very middle class. Many convicts are poor, black and from the inner city.

Glass talked to friends who had dealt with prisoners. They told him how 90 percent of those behind bars eventually will be released.

And most of them will be back in jail within two years.

THE VIEW FROM PLUTO

"They used to think that just giving them a job was enough," Glass said. "But if you don't change a man's heart, he won't keep the job. He'll be back doing the same things he was before."

Roscoe first went to jail when he was 14.

"Juvenile home," he says. "Spent four years there. My mother could have taken me out earlier, but she said she couldn't handle me."

Roscoe is in his early 30s. He hates his father, and still is mad at his mother. He has two children—one is 9 years old; the other is 15 months.

He is incarcerated on some sort of drug charge.

"It was stupid, I know," he says. "I really didn't do what they said."

He pauses.

"I'll be clean for a while, have a job and everything. . . ." His voice trails off.

Then the drugs.

Then back to jail.

"My wife, she wanted to be with this other guy while I'm here," Roscoe says. "I said it was OK. Now, that didn't work out. I mean, I guess she's back with me. But I worry about the kids."

Why?

"She has the problem, too," he says.

Drugs?

"Drugs," he says.

He pauses again.

"I want to be a good father," he says. "I really do. When you are in a place like this, it makes you think."

A place such as the Cook County Jail is a small city, taking up nearly 10 blocks and housing 10,000 prisoners.

A place such as this has guards everywhere, men with hard faces.

A place such as this is always having to watch your back . . . your front . . . even the top of your head.

A place such as this leads to hollow eyes and cold hearts. It's convicts preying on other convicts, the strong taking everything from the weak.

It is scary days and long, sleepless nights.

Bill Glass will tell you that most men end up in a place like this because of their fathers.

"I was recently on death row in Mississippi, the same jail that John Grisham wrote about in *The Chamber*," he said. "There were 22 men waiting to die. All of them said they had a mother or grandmother who loved them and was praying for them."

The fathers?

"To a man, every one of them hated their fathers or the male figure in their life," Glass said.

There's more.

"I was recently at a juvenile facility in California. Three hundred kids there," Glass said. "In the last year, only one of those 300 kids had a father who visited him. One out of 300.

"Fathers are not teaching their children how to be good fathers."

One of Glass' messages is that even though you are in jail, you can be a father. You can bless your children, tell them that you love them. You can talk to them. You can write to them.

"I don't care who you are or how old you are, you need a blessing from your father," Glass said. "Unconditional love. A hug. All of us need to know we will be loved, no matter what—and no strings attached."

Glass is tired of watching sports events where players say, "Hi, Mom," into the camera.

"Just once, I'd like to have them say, 'Hi, Dad,'" Glass said. "You start to change that by fathers giving a blessing to their sons. If you say that your family doesn't act that way, I say change it.

"If not, you can visit your son in the penitentiary."

Thomas is 38 years old and knows he blew it.

This is his first stint in jail. He has four kids. He had a job in the sanitation department.

"I made up to $18 an hour," he says. "I tell that to the guys in here, and they ask me what I'm doing here."

Good question.

Thomas tells a long story, the point being he's jailed on a bum rap. But at the root of it are drugs.

"I stole, but I never hurt anyone," he says. "In the beginning, I could afford the drugs. Then, it got to be more. But I'm telling you, I never laid a hand on anyone. And the money I took, I didn't use all of it for drugs. Some went to feed my family."

Thomas wants you to believe that he is a decent guy. He wants his kids to think so, too. He thinks about that $18-an-hour job as he sits in a place outside a unit called "Lockdown."

Here, prisoners are pulled out of the general population and shoved into little holding cells—either for their own safety or because they broke rules.

It is a jail within a jail.

"I won't blow it again, I promise," he says.

Glass arranges what he calls a "Weekend of Champions" when he enters a prison. He brings in guys on motorcycles, yo-yo champions, basketball dribbling artists and former athletes, such as Bears star Mike Singletary, to talk to the prisoners.

The idea is to attract the attention of the inmates, then the counselors go to work, religious material in hand. They spend three solid days with prisoners who are interested.

They talk to inmates in the yard, in the cafeteria and even through the bars of the cells of those deemed too dangerous to ever leave those confines.

"We don't meet in the chapel," Glass said. "The guys we want to reach, they won't go to the chapel. They may know they need God, but they are too tough, too macho, to step into the chapel."

A surprising number of inmates are willing to listen.

Some are just bored.

Some are con men who think this will help them with the parole board.

Some are just lonely, frightened and know they need something in their lives.

So the counselors talk about God and fatherhood.

The counselors are, for the most part, average people—all colors, all faiths and all incomes. But a number seem to be recent retirees. Most never imagined that they'd end up talking with prisoners. They all are volunteers, paying their own way. More than 16,000 people have helped Glass over the last 25 years.

But Glass makes a compelling case for them to do so.

Most of these inmates will be back on the streets. Unless they find faith and some reason for living, they will end up back in jail.

That will cost you more money.

It also could cost your car—even your life. Most will commit another crime, and you might be the victim this time.

"Most people would like to see the men in prison put on a boat and sent out to sea forever," said Tully Blanchard, a former professional wrestler and one of Glass' speakers. "But these men aren't going away."

They won't change unless someone helps them.

Instead, they will create more criminals—unless someone teaches them how to be fathers.

His name is Al.

He says he is 24. He has a soft, pudgy body. He has trusting, but frightened, brown eyes.

He wants to talk, but the words just won't come.

He starts every sentence with, "You know what I'm sayin'. . . ."

Then his voice turns into a whisper.

It's hard to know what he's saying, but he wants a friend.

You extend your hand. You ask him to pray with you. He holds on as if the hand is a lifeline.

"I pray," he says. "I know what I'm sayin', I really do."

GLASS' MINISTRY does not take federal money. He doesn't do this to get on TV or to build a political power base. No collection plates are passed in prison, and certainly no one can accuse him of preaching to the choir. He has a small, full-time paid staff.

He does this because few others do.

Glass persuades men such as Singletary to help. A 10-time All-Pro selection as a middle linebacker with the Chicago Bears, Singletary also talks to the prisoners about fathers and sons.

He is the youngest of 10 children. His father was a minister "who lived one way on Sunday, another way the rest of the week."

When Singletary was 12 years old, his father walked out on the family. Six months later, his 14-year-old brother was killed by a drunken driver.

"My mother called me aside," Singletary said. "She asked me to be the man of the house, to help her. I never felt so important, so needed."

Singletary talks about trying out for the high school football team.

"The coach told me to tackle this guy named Cookie," he said. "Cookie was one of those huge dudes with a deep voice and hair growing out all over his face. Cookie ran right over me."

But Singletary hung on, Cookie dragged him 50 yards across the field.

That's his message—hang on, no matter what.

Then came a great pro career.

"But something was missing," he said. "God was telling me to reconcile with my father."

Singletary said he'd call just once. He'd let the phone ring just once. If his father didn't answer, that was it—he tried.

His father picked up the phone in the middle of the first ring.

"I hated that man so much," Singletary said. "I'd hated that man every day of my life. I'd waited for the day I could pay him back for all the pain he caused me and my family."

Instead, he discovered he had to forgive his father.

"It wasn't easy," Singletary said. "That first day, we talked for 3½ hours, and we yelled for most of it. I remember when God first told me that I had to talk to my father. I told Him, 'God, tell me something else.' But that is what you must do. You must talk to your father."

You look at the faces of these men and you aren't sure what to say. You are in the Lockdown unit. Concrete walls and floors. Dark yellow. The smell of stale sweat and urine.

No one would ever want to come back to this place, yet so many do. You meet a guy named Charles.

Says he is an ordained minister. Says he had good parents. Says his parents put him through college, and he has paid them back by what he has accomplished.

As he tells you this, he is wearing tan prison pajamas. He is wearing the shower shoes that everyone wears in Lockdown. He is quoting Scripture to you, and says he has it all figured out.

All you can do is shake your head and move on.

Then another inmate pulls you aside.

He tells you that this is all part of the military-industrial complex. The prison system. The drugs. The rehabilitation centers.

"We are good for the economy," he says. "They want us here."

You think of the story that Glass tells about the inmate who had a huge tattoo on his chest. It extended from his navel to under his chin. It was a huge extended middle finger.

"If you go through life giving the world the middle finger," Glass says, "the world gives it right back to you."

Prison guards will tell you that few inmates have dramatic conversions. Usually, things are better for a week or so after Glass' ministry.

"Then the bad guys take over again," a guard said.

Prison is a battle between good and evil. The men behind bars have a little of each inside their hearts.

"If nothing else, we've never had a riot when Bill Glass is here," a guard said. "The inmates are on their good behavior."

Wardens will take that. Wardens are thrilled that Glass and his army of volunteers have the courage to go behind the bars, the patience to listen to the inmates.

After a while, the faces of the convicts run together in your mind. Nearly all have had drug problems. Nearly all know that something is wrong with their lives, but have no idea how to fix it.

Glass' message about the power of God gets their attention, at least for a while. Just as most successful alcohol and drug rehabilitation programs have a religious element to them, Glass believes that the same must happen with criminal rehabilitation.

His name is Jackson and he's scared.

He is only 18. In a few days, he will be getting out. He won't talk about why he is in prison, but says it's not drugs. He says it's his first time.

"I was on house arrest," he says. "They say I broke it when I went outside to talk to the mailman."

Who knows?

But Jackson is listening. He says he is thinking about himself, about God. He says he has no children, but wants to be a good father one day.

He promises to go to church when he gets out.

You think about the 500 volunteers. According to Glass, about 10 percent of them were in prison once themselves. Some say that they changed their lives after encountering Glass' ministry while they were in jail.

Now, they have jobs, families and faith.

You wonder whether Jackson can become one of these. He is young enough. He wants something. He says he'll listen as long as you want to talk.

You take his hand. He closes his eyes. Together, you pray.

9/21/1997

A missing father matters

MY FATHER COULD BE SILENT, brooding and sarcastic.

I still cringe when I remember his calling me, "Half-a-job Terry."

My father was not the warmest man in the world. His hugs were stiff and forced, at least until his stroke.

But my father was there.

That's what I thought about as I read the *Sports Illustrated* story about pro athletes who father out-of-wedlock children.

Good mood, rotten mood—my father was there.

He was there to drive me to church. He was there to take me to Indians games.

But sometimes, it was utterly impossible to talk to him. Still, he was there—even if his mind was somewhere else and he didn't say a word during supper. The *Sports Illustrated* story dealt with numbers. How many fathers have had how many children by how many women—and how much they pay in child support.

But a father is something that can't be defined by numbers or dollar signs. A kid cares about one thing: Is the father there, or not?

Sports Illustrated reported that the Cavs' Shawn Kemp has seven children by six different women. Supposedly, he supports them well, at least, when it comes to mailing out checks each month. Kemp and the Cavs have declined to comment on the story.

But how can anyone—even an all-pro power forward—be a father to seven kids who are in six different households? No matter where he happens to be, at least five of the children won't have a father in the home.

No amount of money can change that fact.

New York Knicks forward Larry Johnson has five children by four different women. The old coach choker, Latrell Sprewell, had three children by three women by the time he was 21.

Seattle's Gary Payton has one son named Gary Payton, Jr. and another named Gary Payton II—with two different women.

Kemp did not have a strong father presence in his life. You wonder how many of these men who have had several children with several women grew up in homes without fathers. And if they did, you'd like to think that they wouldn't want to subject their children to the same fate.

But that apparently doesn't matter.

While a recent survey by the National Center for Health Statistics found that birth rates among teenagers dropped 21 percent from 1991–96, out-of-wedlock births remain high.

The agency found that one of every three children born in 1995 was out-of-wedlock. Compare that with 18 percent in 1980.

In some inner cities, the numbers are staggering—as high as three of every four.

The mothers, grandmothers, grandfathers and uncles do the best they can. In some situations, the women in these single-family homes often are the real heroes.

But a family is best when the father is there. And too many fathers choose to make children, then go elsewhere—often to make more children without fathers.

What is gong on?

What happened to the fathers?

Why is it that as the country has become more affluent, the illegitimacy rate has risen among all races and economic classes?

Sports Illustrated doesn't address that issue.

The magazine doesn't talk about the changing moral values in society and the decline of strong churches as the center of family life.

But that's really what this is about.

In the late 1960s, more absolutes crumbled. Church ceased to be important to a large segment of society. As former president Jimmy Carter once said, "We moved from the era of the Ten Commandments to the Ten Suggestions."

Suddenly, we have too many kids with no fathers in the home—and some of them will grow up to make more children without fathers.

And all of us are worse for it.

5/3/1998

It's time for Chief Wahoo to go

I GREW UP WITH CHIEF WAHOO.

I love Chief Wahoo.

But I also know it's time for Chief Wahoo to go.

Some of you will stop reading right here. Some of you will mumble about bleeding hearts, about Native Americans having better things to do than to worry about what logo is used by a baseball team.

They should worry about the lack of jobs on reservations, the lousy educational system and the poverty.

Chief Wahoo has no bearing on their lives, right?

Others will say you're Irish and you don't care that Notre Dame uses a silly leprechaun for a logo, so why should Native Americans care about Chief Wahoo?

None of that changes the fact that many Native Americans do care, and most of them consider it insulting. They think Chief Wahoo looks like a drunken Indian with the wild eyes and the big red nose.

How do I know this?

I've not taken a Gallup Poll, but I've traveled across several reservations in the West. I've talked to people who live there.

It comes down to this: Most don't like it. I didn't say all. I've even seen a few wearing Chief Wahoo caps. But the overwhelming majority object.

And it comes down to this: I'd be embarrassed to wear a Chief Wahoo cap in front of them, the same Chief Wahoo who was on so many of my clothes as a kid.

A few years ago, I stood at the site of the Wounded Knee Massacre in the Badlands of South Dakota. I stared at the church. The cemetery. The eerie rock formations and the empty land that somehow digs deep into your soul.

A lot of women and children were gunned down at that spot by jittery young soldiers. They were thrown into ditches and buried in cold, mass graves. It is one of the bleakest chapters in American history, and hardly the only one. You don't have to be historian Stephen Ambrose or filmmaker Ken Burns to know the native people in this country get a raw deal.

And I'm not naïve enough to think the Indians dumping Chief Wahoo will change the past or the future for the members of the Pine Ridge Reservation.

But I do know that it bothers a lot of people, and it's something the Cleveland Indians can fix.

Bob DiBiasio is the Tribe's Vice President of Public Relations. He has been dealing with this issue for years.

He's not a dummy.

He knows that this "is a very sensitive issue."

He explains how the Indians "don't make a mockery of Chief Wahoo. We don't play tom-tom music. We don't have the tomahawk chop. We don't have any mascots wearing head dresses, and we don't have anyone sitting in a tepee."

He says the Indians will keep Chief Wahoo as a caricature, a cartoon character.

He adds that some Native American groups want the Indians to change Chief Wahoo. Others want to change the team nickname and Chief Wahoo. Some don't care.

But the man whose opinion matters the most is team owner Dick Jacobs.

"Mr. Jacobs has gone on record as saying as long as he owns the team, the nickname and the logo will remain," said DiBiasio.

Let's give Jacobs a benefit of the doubt and say he probably likes Chief Wahoo. He grew up in Akron. He probably had caps and shirts featuring Chief Wahoo.

But Jacobs also is a bottom-line businessman.

The Indians have just become a publicly traded company, whose stock has been in a deeper slump than Sandy Alomar and David Justice.

Major-league records reveal that the Indians sell more souvenirs than any other team except the Yankees, and most of those things feature Chief Wahoo.

It is not in the interest of Jacobs' wallet to mess with the Chief.

Would you?

But what about the issue of right and wrong?

Would Dick Jacobs or anyone else in power with the Tribe want to wear a Chief Wahoo cap on the Pine Ridge Reservation? Would you want to do it?

If not, then it's time to change the logo.

If there is a certain queasiness, a lingering doubt about wearing the Chief in front of Native Americans—then there's a problem with the Chief.

The Chief Wahoo we see today is not the same Chief Wahoo that was around 80 years ago . . . or 50 years ago . . . or 25 years ago. The drawings and image have changed. The Chief Wahoo we see today is not set in stone like the Ten Commandments.

What the Indians should do is put together a list of six top Native American artists whose work is recognized nationally. That can be done with little homework.

Give them the major-league guidelines for the size of the logo, then ask them to submit drawings. The team should pick the top three, then put it to a vote of the fans through area newspapers.

Four things would happen:

1. There would be tremendous interests and debate about which logo was best. Fans (especially casual fans and kids) love to talk about this stuff.

2. It would create a consumer run on items with the old Chief Wahoo, making more money for Jacobs.

3. Items with the new logo would also be an economic boom to Jacobs. If the fans voted for the logo, they should buy it.

4. The Indians will have done the right thing, and this is what matters the most.

8/18/1998

Akron's Dave Young starts over

DAVE YOUNG WALKS the streets of downtown Akron alone.

Sometimes, he thinks of the 1980 Bluebonnet Bowl, when he caught the winning touchdown pass from Purdue quarterback Mark Herrmann.

And sometimes, he thinks about the nights spent sleeping in an abandoned van that was parked behind the mayor's office.

He thinks about rooming with Lawrence Taylor with the New York Giants in 1981, and he thinks about the $100,000 bonus he got as a second-round NFL draft pick in 1981.

And he thinks about the days when he'd want to disappear when he met an old high school friend on the street, a friend who was now a policeman and wanted to buy him a meal or drive him to a homeless shelter.

He thinks about being 40 years old and going for his driver's license test this week, and he thinks about the Mercedes he owned in 1982 when he was a tight end in the NFL and making $107,000.

Dave Young thinks a lot these days.

He thinks about being off booze and drugs for 17 months, the longest he has been sober in 20 years. He thinks about being one of the finest high school football players Akron has ever seen, when he was a star at East High in the 1970s.

He thinks about all that he had, and all that he lost. And often on those lonely walks, Dave Young prays that finally, just finally, he has been found.

Dave Young is an intern at Haven of Rest, Akron's private Christian mission on East Market Street. This is where the former 1980 first-team All-American from Purdue has lived for the last 17 months.

He sits behind the desk of the "Day Room," the area where men come off the street. It's a place to sit and watch a little TV. It's a place to take a shower, to have a few cookies, to sleep in a straight-back chair, to wait for the next meal at the mission.

"It's a safe place," says Young. "I know, I used to come in here—a lot."

The Day Room is where men see Young and say, "Big Dave, you doin' all right?"

And Dave Young can smile an honest smile of a man whose life he says is no longer ruled by drugs, but by Jesus.

"But I know what some of them are thinking," says Young. "They remember me from the street. They think I won't make it. Or they say that now I think I'm better than they are because I'm on the other side of this desk."

Young shakes his head.

"I look at so many of them and I see me," he says. "The bloodshot, sunken eyes. The dark rings under those eyes. The shaky hands. That attitude where you think everybody owes you something—and you really ain't done a thing to earn it."

Dave Young sits behind that desk to make sure there is order in the room, to check that none of the men who had been expelled for violent behavior or verbal attacks have tried to sneak in.

"At the end, I got banned from here," he says. "I never was physical with anyone. But I got angry, and I'd yell at people for no reason. But the guy who worked the night shift, he'd let me sneak in and sleep on the floor."

Melvin Fields overhears Young and laughs.

Fields is a social worker at Haven of Rest. A former addict for nearly 30 years, he has been sober since 1991. He also was one of the men on the other side of the desk at the Day Room, one of them whose first thought of the day and last thought was always the same—where can I get my next drink, my next fix?

"I knew Dave was sneaking in, we all did," says Fields. "That was back in 1997. Hey, when you're as big as Dave [he played football at 6-foot-5 and 240 pounds], you can't hide. We let it go because we always believed that down deep, Dave is a good guy."

Dave Young lives in what amounts to a tiny dorm room. There is a humble single bed that can't quite hold his hulking frame. There is a small dresser. There is a little TV, something he had to wait a year before he was allowed to own.

What makes him happiest is his closet.

"I came here with one pair of shoes, one pair of pants, a couple of old shirts and a worn-out coat," he says. "Now, I got nice shirts, pants, socks, a couple of coats. Clean underwear."

Haven of Rest supplies clothes to anyone who comes in and asks. They are limited to five items per month, two coats per year—although exceptions are made.

Tons of clothing are donated each month to the mission, and the items are cleaned, pressed and hung neatly on racks that would make any store proud.

During the day, Young feels contented. It's been a long time since he had this much to call his own—a room, a bed, some clothes, good meals.

Then come the nights.

"I have the most unbelievable dreams," he says. "The other night, I dreamed I was being chased by a straight-shooter [a cocaine pipe]. Some nights, I wake up in a cold sweat, I swear I'm back in a crack-house."

When that happens, Young paces and prays. He tells God that he can't do it alone. He tells himself that addicts who have been clean for five years say they still dream of drugs.

People want to know why addicts just can't quit.

The truth is the hideous secret of drugs. They make you feel good. They make you not worry about anything else but the high. They make you forget how you feel the next day, or what it cost you to get the drugs. They entice you to live totally in the hazy, soft-as-a-pillow, drug-induced present.

"The other day, I was sweeping up the Day Room and I found a straight shooter," he said. "Before, I'd have kept it, or gone out and got high. I admit, I can almost taste it, feel it when I see a pipe. Or even when I smell a guy who has been drinking, that makes me want a beer."

But Young was able to throw the pipe away. He has been able to close his eyes and ask the Lord to keep him from heading to a bar whenever he sniffs a whiff of alcohol.

"I'd go a couple of months totally sober," he says. "Then I'd tell myself that I'll just have a beer or two. I'd go into a bar, and five hours later, I was still there."

But that wasn't all.

"After a while, I needed more than alcohol," he said. "So I'd head off to the streets."

And he was smoking crack cocaine again.

Young is part of the Men's Residential Program at Haven of Rest. Twenty-four men spend anywhere from five months to more than a year living at the mission. They awake at 6 a.m. They must attend two Bible studies a day. There are church services.

Sometimes, Young preaches the gospel to men who have just come off the street, many of whom sleep in folding chairs waiting for the 20-minute service to end so they can have a free meal.

The rules are strict for residents such as Young: No drugs. No booze. No swearing. No visitors, other than immediate family and approved friends. Random drug testing. Very little time away from the building. Lots of manual labor.

Young's first job was washing dishes in the soup kitchen. Then, he set up tables in the dining room. Then, he cleaned up the dorms, the 100-bed area where men off the street spend a free night in a bunk bed.

"Most men don't make it through the first few months," said Rev. Marshall Brandon, who is in charge of the program for Rev. Curtis Thomas, who runs the Haven of Rest.

It has been in Thomas' family for 56 years. In that time, the mission has taken no government money, no United Way dollars. The $3.5 million annual budget is paid by contributions from corporations and individuals, and Thomas says the mission has no debt.

Brandon said helping people who have struggled for years such as Young is what the mission is all about. "That is why we are so encouraged about Dave," he said. "Seventeen months is a long time, a lot of self-discipline."

His longevity has enabled Young to earn his current status as an intern with responsibilities in the Day Room.

"I first went into the program in 1991," he says. "I lasted about four months. Then, I decided I had it [drugs] beat. I was feeling good about myself. I had saved some money. I broke one of the rules about having a relationship with one of the females who were staying at Harvest House [Haven of Rest's women's mission], and they put me out."

Out on the street.

"I was a phony," he says. "I acted like I cared about God, but I just went through the motions. With God, you can't fake it, they teach you that here."

Young first used cocaine when he was still at Purdue in 1980. He never thought it was a problem, "because I didn't do it during the season."

It was injuries, not drugs, that ended his NFL career in 1984.

Since then, Young usually worked, albeit seldom steadily. He was a day-laborer, doing everything from moving furniture to working on an assembly line to clean up. Temporary agencies liked Young because he was a strong guy with a kind nature who wasn't afraid to sweat.

"But I smoked up everything I made," he says.

Young says he had no major brushes with the law.

"I'm not a violent person," he says. "I stayed away from dealing, because when you're a user and you're dealing, you use up your own product—and the supplier doesn't like that. You can end up dead."

There was something else.

"I never wanted to be hauled away in handcuffs," he says. "I have a son in Akron. I have friends. I never wanted them to see me like that."

So Young worked for his drug money. Seasonal jobs with the post office. A six-month stint at a paper mill. He made decent money on some of the jobs, but he'd lose them because of his drug problems—and sometimes end up sleeping under a bridge.

"My mother had to use tough love and put me out of the house," he says. "That's how I started coming to Haven of Rest, or sleeping in that van behind the mayor's office. One day, they towed the van away and I had nowhere else to go."

A friend said he could stay in his old car.

"So I slept there," he said. "But they towed that, too."

He stared in the mirror at Haven of Rest. It was September of 1997. He had been at the mission on and off since 1990. He had tried The Program and failed. He had tried the streets and failed.

"Everything I tried, I failed," he says. "I was finally humbled."

And he went back into the program, where he'll remain at least until the end of August.

Young is only 11 academic credits short of his communications degree. He has been able to get his coursework from Purdue transferred to Akron, where he'll start college in the fall.

In the meantime, he has been working on his computer skills in the mission's learning center, where other men are able to do everything from earning their high school diploma and mastering Windows 95 to being tutored on the nuances of filling out job applications and interviewing with prospective employers.

"I'd like to teach and coach," says Young.

And he has a chance to do that, says Barberton football coach Tim Flossie.

"Dave was a volunteer assistant with me when I coached at Buchtel in the late 1980s," says Flossie. "The kids liked him. He knew the game. But he had the drug habit. For the first few years, I didn't notice it. Then he really started going downhill."

One day, another Buchtel coach was giving Young a ride to his mother's house. Young asked the coach to stop on a corner, went into a crack house and made a buy.

"That was when I had to let him go," says Flossie. "But if Dave really has been straight for 17 months and can stay straight, I'd let him work with our kids here for a while and see how he does."

Rev. Curtis Thomas also might hire Young full time. "David has come a long way," says Thomas. "He relates well with men who were in his position. And it doesn't hurt to have a big guy around here. On Christmas, we had a problem with a man, and David just picked the man up and carried him out of the building."

End of problem. But only the beginning for Young.

"People ask me if Dave will be a success," says Thomas. "What is a success? To me, he already is a success. He hasn't done any drugs, he hasn't committed any crimes, he has been a productive member of society for the last 17 months. He has saved enough money for a deposit and a few months' rent on an apartment when he leaves here. He is enrolled in school."

Thomas paused.

"Two years ago, I saw Dave sitting alone on a picnic table in a park," he says. "He was staring at nothing, a picture of total despair. Now, he has hope. Don't you think that is a success?"

5/9/1999

Laying the past to rest

DON'T LEAVE THINGS UNSAID.

That's what Luke Witte thought when he heard that Bill Musselman had been buried in Wooster yesterday.

Witte didn't rehash the infamous fight of 28 years ago. Neither did he blame Musselman's coaching tactics for leading to that brawl that short-circuited his basketball career.

Words such as anger, bitterness and revenge no longer are part of his vocabulary when he speaks about Musselman.

"But I just wish we could have sat down and really talked it out," he said. "Just the two of us in a room somewhere. I would have liked to have had a chance to let Bill know that I forgave him. And I know Bill would have listened, that I'd have had his ear."

While the two men had spoken a few times over the past 28 years, they never really talked. They never said what was on their minds.

"I'd get these calls from Bill late at night, maybe 2 A.M.," Witte said. "The first one came at 5:30 in the morning."

What did Musselman want?

"He was usually coaching somewhere like Reno or Rapid City, and he wanted me to come play for him," Witte said. "One time, he talked to my wife [Donita] and was telling her about how he could set us up in an apartment somewhere, and they had a great swimming pool. Bill really knew how to recruit, and a good place to start was the wife, because the husband would follow."

A few minutes later, the Wittes realized, "Who needs a swimming pool during basketball season in South Dakota?"

He declined that offer, and the others that came from Musselman over the years.

"Usually, I said something like, 'You've got to be kidding,'" Witte said. "Now, I can see that was probably Bill's way of reconciliation. He wanted to do something for me, maybe get me next to him."

Musselman never apologized to Witte. He never mentioned Jan. 25, 1972.

Witte, who had been the *Beacon Journal*'s Player of the Year at Marlington, was Ohio State's starting center when the Buckeyes faced a Minnesota team coached by a 31-year-old Musselman. Ohio State was ranked third in the nation, Minnesota was No. 4.

Witte tried to make a layup and was knocked down. Minnesota's Corky Taylor offered him a hand up. Witte took it. Taylor then kneed him in the groin.

While he was down on the court, several Minnesota players stomped Witte. He was carried from Williams Arena on a stretcher, and needed 27 stitches to close the cuts, mostly to his head and jaw.

To this day, Witte remembers very few details of the attack and never has watched a tape of it.

Those who watched Witte say he never was the same player, and the statistics prove it. He averaged 19 points and 12 rebounds before the fight, but 14 points and 8.3 rebounds after the fight during his senior year.

"I was supposed to be a first-round NBA draft choice," he said. "I ended up going in the fourth round [to the Cleveland Cavaliers in 1973]."

The two men lived with the day for the next 28 years.

Musselman's reputation changed, from a bright young coach to someone so obsessed with winning that he drove his team into a blood-thirsty frenzy by hanging signs in the dressing room that read: DEFEAT IS WORSE THAN DEATH, BECAUSE YOU HAVE TO LIVE WITH DEFEAT.

"Bill fell into the same trap as many coaches," Witte said. "He was so intense, so driven and he lived in a society where winning at all costs is pretty much accepted. Listen, this is in any of us."

Witte now is pastor at Forest Hill Presbyterian Church in Charlotte. He also is team chaplain for the Charlotte Hornets.

"A coach starts to think he can never watch enough film, he can never do enough preparation, he can never have enough success," Witte said. "It can play with your head, and I know that Bill was frustrated by a lot of things in his life."

So was Witte, at least for a while.

At 7 feet and 230 pounds, the kid from Alliance was a first team All-Big Ten selection as a sophomore. His senior year, he didn't even make the second team.

"Toward the end, I was getting booed by my own fans," he said.

"For a few games, I lost my starting position. I remember coming off the bench in a game at St. John Arena, and the fans were all over me. I'm just 21 years old, and I didn't want to deal with it. I told [Coach] Fred Taylor that I didn't want to go into the game. He said, 'If you quit now, you'll quit everything in life.' I'll never forget those words."

Witte played. It was one of his better games that season.

"I still worked hard, but in a game, I'd flinch," he said. "Under the boards, you need to put your elbows out and stick your nose in there to get rebounds."

Witte was a bench-warmer for the Cavs for three years. He played a couple of seasons in Europe. He tried business, before pursuing the ministry.

Musselman's coaching career also was checkered. His Minnesota team had a 69-32 record in his four years, then the program was flattened by the NCAA, which charged it with more than 100 recruiting violations.

Musselman spent the rest of his life as a basketball vagabond, never spending more than two years in any one place. He coached in four different pro leagues, and won four titles in the Continental Basketball Association, accomplishing that in Tampa, Rapid City and Albany.

He coached the Cavs in the early 1980s during the stormy Ted Stepien era. His final tour of duty was as an assistant with the Portland Trail Blazers. The Wooster native, who began his coaching career at Ashland University, was 59 when he died last week from cancer.

"I went through a lot of stages in dealing with this," Witte said. "At first, I had people telling me to sue Musselman, sue the University of Minnesota, sue somebody."

He refused. Not because there was forgiveness in his heart, but because he didn't want to relive the incident.

But it wouldn't go away.

For years, he'd run into people who'd say: "Luke Witte? You were the guy who got beat up in that fight. What was all that about?"

"I developed a pat answer I'd give in about 30 seconds," he said.

But the questioned lingered inside him for years: What was all that about? What did it mean to him?

"I'd meet someone from Minnesota, and say something sarcastic," Witte said. "Finally, it hit me. I was blaming an entire state for what happened; that was ridiculous."

When Musselman's name was mentioned, Witte seethed.

"I remember seeing a picture of Bill smiling where someone wrote, 'Would you buy a used car from that man?' And I sort of reveled in that," he said. "I said and thought a lot of things about him for which I'm ashamed."

Witte called himself "a one-hour-a-week Christian—maybe," while he was in college. About 15 years ago, when he found himself being drawn closer to the Lord, he discovered something else.

He had to forgive Musselman, forgive the players who had attacked him, forgive all the people who ever had said stupid things about the fight.

"If you're going to be serious [about Christianity], you have to do all that," he said. "It wasn't easy, but one day God put it on my heart to start praying for Bill Musselman."

Witte also grew close to Taylor, who kneed him in the groin. Taylor also came to a faith in Jesus Christ, and sent Witte a letter of apology. The two men now correspond regularly.

Witte will tell you that only faith and the power of forgiveness can heal wounds this deep—can bring together two men such as Taylor and himself.

As Witte found himself back in the world of high-pressure basketball as the Hornets' chaplain and having to deal with the death of Charlotte guard Bobby Phills in an auto crash, he came to an even a greater understanding of Musselman.

"The win-at-all-costs mentality, the desire to achieve—it overrides everything else," Witte said.

Until something like death puts up the ultimate STOP sign.

Witte knows other people such as Musselman—"of incredible desire and passion. But you just wish those passions and desires were channeled in a different direction, because think of all they could accomplish."

Witte took the final step in the process on March 19, when he spoke at his church on the subject, "Loving Your Enemy." It came at the urging of David Chadwick, a former North Carolina basketball player and now pastor of a Presbyterian church.

About 1,800 people sat in silence as huge photos of a bloodied and battered Witte appeared on the screens and Witte talked about the brawl.

"I can choose to live in anger and hurt and bitterness, or I can choose to live in the freedom of knowing that Christ is in charge," he told the congregation.

Two months after Witte's first public speech about the incident, Musselman died.

"My prayer for Bill is that in coping with his illness, he became a different person," Witte said. "I grieve for him, I really do. I just pray that he's in a better place."

5/10/2000

If you're 8 or 88, it's mystifying

THIS E-MAIL CAME from 8-year-old Matt Ridinger of Medina:

"I just want to know why baseball players are going on strike. I mean, if you have over 1 million dollars, you're rich and should be happy with what you have. I love baseball, Mr. Pluto. Go Tribe, go-go-go."

Matt's father, Mike, asked me to write about the baseball labor situation in "terms an 8-year-old can understand."

I wish I could. I wish I had something new to say.

I wish that anything Mike and Matt Ridinger and all the other fans had to say actually mattered. But it doesn't.

If you'd like to tell your children that, so be it.

You can tell them they don't matter to baseball. At least, not to millionaires who have been fighting for nearly 30 years and shut down the game nine times.

You can tell them about greed; that's a good lesson.

You can tell them that not much has changed over the years on the baseball labor front, other than that salaries go up, ticket prices skyrocket and teams are continually sold for far more than they were purchased.

You can tell them that a lot of money changes hands. A lot of people get rich. A lot is said about trying to take care of the fans, but how much is really done? How much of this an 8-year-old fan will understand (or even an 88-year-old) is beyond me.

I just know that there is not a single thing I can say that matters.

Nor is there one name I can call them that they haven't been called before.

New ideas? Fans send in thousands. The media suggest hundreds. All of them are ignored. I'm down to this: If they want to shut down the game and blow up their mega-billion dollar industry, so be it.

I refuse to let these millionaires ruin my day, and I suggest you do the same. I'm more concerned about my friends in the airline industry keeping their jobs and their companies in business, because many of them have made major financial sacrifices for the good of their businesses, and still thousands have been laid off.

Just about everybody knows somebody who is worried about their job, which is why it's hard for me to shed tears for the players and owners.

Mike Ridinger also wrote that he started to tell his son about "the salary cap, the luxury tax, and I found out that I don't really know about that myself."

Dear Mike: Don't sweat it.

No fan should be required to have CPA or MBA written next to his or her name to follow baseball. I'm not going to even bother to attempt to explain it. The question is whether these guys truly want to create a system where the toys are shared, or do they want to continue to act like a bunch of petulant 2-year-olds?

There, I verbally spanked them.

They don't care. They've heard it a million times before. Just like they've read zillions of letters from fans such as Mike and Matt, and nothing has changed.

How to explain?

What do you tell the kids?

You can tell them about the people who sell the hot dogs and the tickets, about the people who serve as ushers, secretaries, elevator operators and the stadium cleanup crew. Talk about how they are the ones hurt the most by a strike.

You can tell the kids that these people have kids just like you—and they don't have guaranteed million-dollar contracts; they don't own companies.

They make the food, pick up the trash, answer the phone, clean the toilets and handle the tickets. They work in baseball and they love baseball, but baseball doesn't care about them, either.

They're the ones you should care about, the ones who deserve your prayers.

6/22/2002

You want to play

YOU HOLD THE WATER BOTTLES.

You are 6 feet tall and 275 pounds. Some people see you and wonder why you are not wearing shoulder pads and a helmet like the other players.

You'd love to tell them. You want them to know what it means to be you. You want to explain, to answer, to just say *something*!

You hear the words in your head. You know what you want to say. But the best you can do is make sounds: moans, screeches, laughs, grunts.

And no one understands.

They say you are autistic, something like Dustin Hoffman in the movie *Rain Man*. Only you can't talk at all, while Hoffman spoke in a distracted monotone. They say there are a lot of people like you, about 15 of every 10,000 births, and it's four times more likely to happen to males.

They can say all they want, but they just don't know.

They don't know how your brain works.

They don't know that when Hudson High football coach Tom Narducci said you could come to practice, you thought it was to play, that you crashed into the tackling dummy like a charging bull.

But they led you to the water and the bottles, saying you're a team manager. You're one of several "special needs" students who help the team, but none of the others is battling the obstacles you face.

Your name is Mark Mesko.

Your father and mother are John and Phyllis Mesko. They love Narducci for doing what no coach was willing to try before. He let you be a part of the team.

You're 18 years old. Your favorite color is red. You love football teams that wear red, especially Ohio State and Nebraska. You like firetrucks. You sometimes carry a red book bag with your pictures of firetrucks. You have a firetruck as a screen saver on your computer. You have a framed picture of you in a firetruck. Your older sister, Heather, drives around with a camera, and when she sees a neat firetruck, she takes a picture for you.

You'd like to be a firefighter, or a football player.

But it probably won't happen.

If only you could talk. If only you could be like the other kids. As your oldest sister, Jennifer, said, "If only I could know if he's happy."

You are happy. And you're frustrated. And you're lonely. And you feel loved. And sometimes you don't know how you feel.

That's how it is for many teen-agers.

You get mad at your parents, you glare at them, you stalk off, you slam the door and hide in your room. You're likely to put on a videotape of Scooby Doo or the Care Bears. But Heather has seen you with a Victoria's Secret catalog. You seem to have one foot in a child's world, another leg in the life of any teen-age boy.

Heather understands this. She bought you a poster of Pamela Sue Anderson. She says, "I wish Mark could go on a date, just do the things everyone does in high school."

Sometimes, Heather takes you to the Stow Cafe, where you get hamburgers together. You love hamburgers. You love your 23-year-old sister. Sometimes, she holds your hand. Sometimes, people think you're her boyfriend. She doesn't care. She loves you.

You're her brother, you're special, and you know that.

One day, your mom found her eyes tearing up, her throat going dry as she sat next to you by the computer. She told you how much she loved you. She so wanted to hear that voice from your soul, to know what thoughts are in your heart.

Phyllis Mesko whispered, "Mark Mesko, why can't you talk?"

You typed: TOO HARD.

They say that for the first two years of your life, you were like most infants. Your mother insists that you said "Mama daddy cookie" and about 30 other words.

Then something happened. Those words are gone. Except you do hear them in your head. Sometimes, you can even type them on the computer. Sometimes, you can't.

You don't know why that happens; it just does.

Just like you don't know why the words fail to come out. They just don't.

They say it's a neurological problem; the brain didn't develop in the usual way. They took you to doctors in Cleveland, Baltimore and North Carolina. By the time you were 7, they finally put a label on you.

Autistic.

How much of this you comprehend, it's hard to know. You're just aware that you're different, that you really don't have friends like most of the kids at Hudson High. Sometimes, you feel walled in. The walls are glass. You see them. They see you. But communication is lost.

You give water to football players such as Toney Morton and Tyson Meikle. They say thank you. Once in a while, they pat you on the back. You whack their shoulder pads, as you've seen the other coaches and players do.

Meikle says the team respects you, that you're at practice every day, and at every game. Morton wishes he could talk to you, that you could "play football like the other guys."

They don't know that one day you brought your mother into your room, pointed at a football player on TV who looked like you, and then pointed at yourself. Yes, you wanted to play, and you knew you had the right size.

Your coach, Tom Narducci, says, "Mark is so big, sometimes I think I should put him in pads and a helmet and let him stand on the sidelines just to scare the other team."

But he can't do that. Just like you want to play, but you can't.

Your mom recalls meeting Narducci at Holy Family Church in Stow, how Coach Narducci shook your hand, stared you in the eye and introduced himself. Talked to you like you were a regular person, which is how he sees you. A regular person with unique circumstances, but a person who needs football.

At Hudson, football is about kids being involved. It's about 78 players on the varsity and junior varsity. It about another 35 on the freshman team. And about 300 marching band members.

And some special needs kids on the sidelines.

Narducci says you're "the most severe" of the challenged managers he has had in his 20 years of coaching. But he believes in giving people chances.

It goes back to 1972, when he was a young coach at Padua Franciscan High School in Parma. He was asked to teach a Wednesday night religion class for special needs kids at St. Anthony of Padua Catholic

Church. It hurt to see them dealing with their disabilities, yet it raised his spirits to watch them battle, to feel their love.

He never forgot that.

Narducci is impressed by your progress. He says he barely notices you, which is a compliment, because it means you're doing your job well.

"The other day, Mark really became a member of the team," says your coach. "He was a little late getting into the dressing room at halftime, and I screamed at whoever was at the door. It was Mark and his dad."

Narducci laughs.

"I tell everyone that they really know they're with us when I yell at them," he says. "That goes for Mark, too."

At games and practices, you need help.

Often, it comes from Charly Murphy, a health aide who has his own photography business and is studying to be a minister. He was hired last fall to be with you at practice.

He wasn't sure it would work. You seemed to take an eternity, just finding a way to turn the knob on those huge orange igloos that hold the water, and then correctly lining up the plastic bottles so the water flowed inside.

"At first, Mark couldn't even fill a single bottle by himself," says Murphy in front of you. "Now, look at him. He does about all the work; I just make sure he's concentrating."

You had to learn every step. It wasn't easy to unscrew the plastic caps, then screw them back on. It took practice to get all the bottles in the carry-case, so you could then take them to the players.

Then there's walking.

You move slowly, sort of dragging your feet. At least most of the time. Once in a while, you sprint for 15 to 20 yards. Then stop. No one is sure why.

Mostly, you seem to plod, plod, plod. One foot in front of another.

In the past, people with your disabilities were dismissed. Locked away and forgotten. Some people still think like that.

They don't know that when you want pizza, you cut a coupon out of the newspaper and give it to your parents. Or that you load the dishwasher. You make your bed. You've done some woodworking. You've had part-time jobs stocking shelves at a grocery store.

You need supervision, but you can do it.

You just have to practice, over and over. People don't know what you can do.

There's something else they don't know.

The noise. The lights. The crowds.

It's called "overstimulation."

When all that hits you, it scares you. It pushes your nerves to the limit. You take six pills a day for problems such as anxiety and attention deficit disorder. When you were small, you'd get upset and bite your sister's shoulder as she held you, trying to calm you.

You're much better now.

But the games are hard because there is just so much of everything.

You began by barely tolerating it for one quarter, and finished last year being able to stay until the fourth period. The goal for this season is to make it through an entire game.

Your coach says, "I just want Mark to show up and do his best for as long as he can. It's not like he has to punch in and punch out."

Sometimes, you don't feel like going to practice. You hide your Hudson cap in the cupboard right before Charly arrives to pick you up. Other times, you are dressed and ready, waiting outside for him, rushing to his truck when he pulls into the driveway.

At the end of last season, you were awarded a varsity letter.

How could they know what it means to you? You used to wear your oldest sister Jennifer's cheerleading jacket. A few years later, it was Heather's softball letter jacket from Hudson. Your mother said, "Mark Mesko, one day you will get your own letter jacket," but she had no idea how that would ever happen.

Only, it did.

You're like many teen-agers. Right before dinner, you wander into the kitchen and sneak doughnut holes for snacks. You get on the computer and order things, surprising your parents.

Once, there was gutbuster-type exercise equipment that arrived at the door. You pointed to the TV and then your abdomen, telling your mother you wanted to lose weight and saw something on the screen that would help.

Another time, you locked your father out of the house because you wanted some ice cream and he had a different plan. He was furious. You thought it was hilarious.

One of your favorite places is the beach, where you ride the waves, build sand castles, chase the seagulls. You also like the beach because you don't have to wear shoes, and you sometimes get tired of shoes.

But other times, you don't make eye contact. You seem somewhere else, distracted, depressed. You have routines, always wearing a golf shirt and khaki pants to school.

Your family worries that someone will hurt you but you won't be able to tell them. When you were 5, you asked for a Popsicle. You put it on your arm. Turns out, the arm had been fractured at least three days earlier.

No one knew.

You couldn't say.

Heather is still embarrassed about the time many years ago when she threw a ball through a window, but blamed you. It took three months for her to finally confess.

One day, a stranger sits next to you by your computer.

He has given you an Ohio State football guide. You type: THANKS.

Awhile later, the two of you are the only ones in the kitchen.

The stranger asks, "Mark, how does it feel not to be able to talk?"

In your left hand, your roll a rubber band, over and over.

With your right hand, you type: PIG, BLUE, GREEN, NEWS-PAPER.

You know the stranger is from a newspaper. You don't know what he really wants. He tells you about his father, who couldn't talk, either.

You roll that rubber band some more.

You type: PIG, BLUE, GREEN, NEWSPAPER.

Over and over: PIG, BLUE, GREEN, NEWSPAPER.

And roll the rubber band, over and over.

That's how you feel when you're anxious. You fall into a routine. You try to get some control of your life. You long for a comfort zone, where you could be like everyone else, and everyone could understand you.

You're Mark Mesko.

Your sister, Jennifer, was just married to Chris Kimmick. He had to first pass "The Mark Test." He didn't know it, but he had to show he liked you.

"When Chris spent 30 minutes on the floor watching a football game with Mark, just the two of them in Mark's room, I knew our relationship had a chance," says Jennifer. "I'm a package deal."

Your family is like that. They don't know what the future is for you. Maybe a group home setting. Maybe something else. But they vow to be there for you, just as they have been for 18 years.

Your dad is a postal worker, your mom a nurse. They combine with your two older sisters to form a special family, one they say God set aside for you.

Down deep, you know that.

You hug them. You hug them a lot.

And there's no need for anyone to say a word about love.

9/29/02

Players Part II

At the end, she couldn't take his pain

HEIDI DAUGHERTY just couldn't watch it anymore.

Her husband is 7 feet tall, 260 pounds and 29 years old—but he couldn't bend over to pick up their 3-year-old son.

She saw him wince when he tried to walk up a few stairs.

"Here is how bad it got," Heidi Daugherty said. "When Brad sneezed, it hurt his back. There were days when he was in absolute agony."

Daugherty injured his back in February. He has endured several rehabilitation programs. Some were better than others, but none worked.

For the longest time, Heidi Daugherty had one of the worst feelings in the world. She felt helpless. Hugs and understanding weren't enough. Rather than just cry when she was alone, Heidi Daugherty decided to do something.

"I started going to the library and making calls, doing research on backs," she said.

She visited specialists at Case Western Reserve. She contacted more specialists at Cornell and Georgetown. She learned about the spine, vertebrae and discs. She began to get familiar with the lingo, talking the medical talk with the specialists.

Then she told her husband what she had learned. They went to four back specialists across the country. They wanted answers, but learned that a spine with two herniated discs often looks like a huge question mark in medical journals.

Meanwhile, Daugherty's legs sometimes felt numb. They were getting weaker. How could this be happening to someone who isn't even 30?

Try to imagine being Heidi Daugherty for a moment. You were a waitress at a Friendly's in Florida when you met Daugherty. You knew nothing about basketball and never heard of him. All you knew was that he was this nice guy—a very big, very nice guy.

You date and eventually are married. He is the strongest man you've ever known. Then you see him hurting. You see tears in his eyes from the frustration and the pain as he holds 18-month-old Brianna in his enormous lap.

You are scared and so is he. Who ever imagined it would be like this?

"It was Heidi who encouraged me to look around, to study all the options," Daugherty said. "If it wasn't for her, I don't know if we'd have reached this stage."

Daugherty had considered surgery before, but no one could make any promises. In some cases, back surgery made it worse. There was even a slight chance of waking up in a hospital bed to learn that he'd never walk again.

"I heard horror stories about other teams pressuring players to have surgery, and then the guy finds out that all the operation did was wreck his back for the rest of his life," Daugherty said. "The Cavs were never like that. They told me to take my time, to do what I thought was best for me. Even now, they aren't forcing me to have this operation."

That tells you a lot about Cavs owner Gordon Gund and General Manager Wayne Embry. They have $32 million tied up in this guy over the next six years. The easy thing would be to say: "For that kind of money, you'll have the surgery and have it now."

As Heidi researched, Daugherty joined in the quest. They kept hearing a name—Dr. Henry Bohlman at University Hospitals.

"I felt like I was spinning my wheels," Daugherty said. "I don't know if this surgery will work. There seems to be a good chance that it will, but it is different than the other back surgeries that athletes have had."

Once they were convinced that the odds of paralysis were minuscule, Daugherty and his wife made a decision.

"We are going for it, because at least we are doing something," he said. "This will become a defining moment for my back. After the surgery, it will either heal enough for me to play or it won't."

If nothing else, the surgery should at least relieve the pain in his back and legs so that he can lift his son and give him a kiss. It should make him feel normal again.

"That is really what I wanted to do," Heidi Daugherty said. "I wanted to just find something so his back wouldn't hurt him anymore."

12/3/1994

Martinez revived a career

THE ACE OF THE INDIANS pitching staff has a secret.

"Don't tell anybody, but I'm a grandfather," he whispered.

Then Dennis Martinez laughed. His hair is streaked with gray and he will be 40 years old on May 14.

At a recent spring-training game, Martinez's 20-year-old daughter, Erica, was there with a bundle in her arms—her 7-month-old daughter.

Martinez has a son, too, 21-year-old Dennis Martinez, Jr.

"He's a closer for St. Thomas University in Miami . . . throws 88 mph," Martinez said. "'I hear that he has a good chance to be picked in the [free-agent] draft. I'd love that. I'd love to play on the same team with my son."

A man with adult children and a grandchild.

A man who nearly lost his life to alcoholism, but also managed to keep his 22-year marriage intact.

A man who has won at least 14 games in 11 different seasons.

A man who spent a year in the bullpen and racked up 40 saves.

"You gotta admit, I have a lot of experience," Martinez said with a laugh.

No denying that.

And last year was more of the same, as Martinez led the Tribe with 11 victories and 176 innings pitched in a strike-marred season.

"But I know what people say. They talk about you getting to be 40 years old," he said. "Even if you have a good year, they think that you're old. They say you did it last year, but you won't do it again."

OK, will he do it again?

"I think so," he said, suddenly turning very serious. "When I was young, I had a great arm. I don't have that anymore.

"But when I was young, they always said how I should win 20 games every year, but I didn't work hard or I was too dumb.

"Now most people would say that I am a smart pitcher. I don't throw as hard as I did, but I pitch better."

Martinez then made it clear that he expects to pitch the same way again this season.

Catcher Sandy Alomar agreed. "Dennis has one of those loose, free arms. He just seems like he is always ready to pitch."

The Indians hope they're right. If the team is to make its first postseason appearance in 41 years, the grandfather has to give Cleveland close to 15 victories and more than 200 innings.

Think about the starting rotation for a moment. Charles Nagy has a history of shoulder problems. Mark Clark is coming off a broken wrist. Orel Hershiser should be better than Jack Morris, but his arm isn't strong enough to anchor the staff.

If you had one game to win for the Tribe, who would you pick? It has to be Granddad Dennis.

Think about the four-hitter he threw at Comiskey Park against the White Sox last July 13, beating Chicago 2-0.

Think about his final start of the season, a two-hit, 7-0 victory over Boston at Fenway Park.

Think about the fact that this guy averaged seven innings per start.

At the age of 39, he wasn't just the Tribe's premier pitcher last year, he was one of the best in baseball.

"I take pride in that," he said. "I want the ball. I can pitch the innings. I learned pitching the right way with Earl Weaver in Baltimore.

"On that staff, we had Jim Palmer, Scotty McGregor, Mike Flanagan and myself. We had a lot of competition. If McGregor threw a complete game one day, then I wanted to do the same the next—maybe even pitch a shutout.

"We need to get that kind of attitude here—the starters all pulling for each other, but also trying to out-do each other. That is what makes a great pitching staff."

Martinez came to the big leagues with the Orioles in 1977. As a 21-year-old rookie, he won 14 games and saved 40 more—all out of the bullpen.

That is why many in Baltimore assumed he'd be the next Palmer. He could start. He could relieve. He had a 93 mph fastball and an 87 mph slider.

"My arm is a gift from God," Martinez said.

But he nearly was lost in the hell of alcoholism during the first half of the 1980s. At 31, he was in a rehabilitation center and, many assumed, had wasted his career.

"It is like I had two careers," he said. "I don't dwell on it, but I remember all the bad things people said about me and who said them back when I was having my problems. I know they never thought I'd come back, and they sure never thought I'd be pitching at 40.

"Sometimes I see those people and I want to tell them to kiss my butt, but I just let it go. Why go back into the past again?"

While Martinez often was hurt and insulted by the gruff discipline imposed by Weaver and the Orioles, he has become a walking textbook on the old Baltimore approach to pitching.

He throws strikes. He fields his position well. He likes to surprise you with a breaking pitch early in the count.

"But a couple of times a game, I can still throw the fastball that really makes the glove pop," he said. "I can usually get that pitch when I really need it."

Most of his fastballs are in the 87 mph range, but he'll reach back for a 92 mph lightning bolt in stormy situations.

"Sometimes I think [about] what I might have accomplished if I didn't have the drinking problem," he said. "Would I have won 20 games in a season? Would I have 300 wins by now?

"But I've still made three All-Star teams. I've pitched a perfect game. Maybe I needed to go through all that to be a better person and pitcher now."

Martinez enters this season with 219 victories. He won 108 before he swore off the booze—109 since.

"What I want to do is become the winningest Latin pitcher ever," he said. "I need 24 wins to catch Juan Marichal. I figure I can do that over the next two years."

So he plans to pitch for two more years?

"At least," he said.

"They are going to have to tear the uniform off my back. This game is too good and you can make too much money here to quit."

4/25/1995

It's goodbye for Price

AT 4:30 YESTERDAY AFTERNOON, Mark Price gathered his family around the radio. With his wife, Laura, and two daughters, Brittany Ann and Caroline Elizabeth, Price listened to the news like the rest of the Cavs' fans.

"It was real strange, hearing the press conference on the radio when you've been traded," Price said. "I'm still in shock. It was like they were talking about me, but it wasn't me. I heard my name, but it was like they were talking about someone else.

"All I know is that leaving here is going to be tough—real tough."

What the Price family of Hudson heard was that the Cavs had just traded the best player in the history of their franchise to Washington for a No. 1 draft pick in 1996. They also learned that five-time All-Star Brad Daugherty will be out at least until midseason—assuming he ever recovers from that major back surgery of 10 months ago.

"[General Manager] Wayne Embry called me a few days ago to see how I felt about maybe getting traded," Price said. "He told me that Brad wasn't ready to play, and that they were going with young players. I told them that trading was his department and that I'd like to stay. If he did trade me, I hoped to go to a contender."

Instead, Washington—perennially near the back of the pack—was the highest bidder for Price. Maybe Price will join Juwan Howard and Chris Webber and spark the Bullets into the playoffs, hurting the Cavs' draft position.

"I'm not thinking about that [revenge]," he said. "That's not me. I am a professional. I'm looking at Washington as an opportunity. They do have some good young players. I consider myself a good leader, and maybe my leadership is what they need to get over the hump and become a quality team."

Price is 31, a four-time All-Star and a member of the 1994 Dream Team II. But a case can be made that all the injuries he's sustained— knees, hands, wrists and ankles—have taken their toll. The Cavs also have 25-year-old Terrell Brandon recovered from his broken leg and ready to take over at point guard.

"As a business decision, I understand it," Price said. "It is time to rebuild the team here, and I guess I'm one of the guys who has to go to make it happen. But I have very mixed emotions.

"I played here for nine years. In my nine years, we had some very good teams. We've always had teams that played hard, teams the community could be proud of because of how we conducted ourselves off the court. I'm trying not to take this personally, but I loved playing for Cleveland."

The era of the Cavs as most fans knew them—the teams of Price, Daugherty, John Williams, Larry Nance and Lenny Wilkens—is over. Don't be surprised if veteran Hot Rod Williams is traded somewhere soon, as the Cavs take a dive out of the playoffs and into the lottery for the No. 1 draft choice.

"There was one year [1992] where we seemed to have a window of opportunity," Price said. "But I don't know if losing to Chicago [in the Eastern Conference Finals] was because of too many injuries or just too much Michael Jordan. But I do think we gave the fans something to cheer about."

By the time Price turned on the radio, he knew the deal was done. "[WWWE's] Mike Snyder called me first to ask if I had heard the rumor about the trade," Price said. "That was a little after noon, and it was news to me. Then Richard [agent Richard Howell] called with the news. Then Wayne Embry and Gordon Gund called about an hour before the press conference. They told me how much they appreciated what I did for the Cavs, and I thanked them for their support."

As Price listened to the conference and all the nice things said about him, he did find himself thinking about coming to the Cavs as a second-round pick in 1986 out of Georgia Tech.

"Never in my wildest dreams did I expect to have a career like this," he said. "I thought I might be able to play two or three years in the NBA, maybe come off the bench and enjoy myself. Then I thought I'd get on with the rest of my life. I am so grateful that God allowed all these things to happen to me."

As a rookie, Price played behind John Bagley.

The Cavs were so underwhelmed by the 6-footer Price, they immediately drafted another point guard in 1987, another future All-Star by the name of Kevin Johnson. It was in the training camp of 1987 that Price and the Cavs learned so much about each other.

"I'm sure they wanted Kevin to win the job," he said.

Price had other ideas. He destroyed Johnson day after day (sometimes even twice a day during double sessions) in the upstairs practice gym at the old Coliseum. Price came into the NBA labeled as a slow, short, white guard who had one pro skill—a jump shot. He is always the first to admit, "I'm not the most athletic guy in the world."

But he surprised everyone.

Former Cavs Coach Lenny Wilkens said, "Price is quicker than most people realize." Detroit's Isiah Thomas said, "Mark came into this league like a lamb, and he's turned out to be a lion."

In February 1988, Johnson was traded to Phoenix in the Larry Nance deal—and the Cavs were Price's team.

He made four All-Star teams.

He won two NBA 3-point shooting contests.

He came back from reconstructive knee surgery and countless other injuries, and yet he kept improving as a player.

He is the NBA's all-time leading free-throw shooter, making 90 percent.

From 1988 through 1993, the Cavs would win 2-of-3 games when

Price played, only 1-of-3 when he was hurt. That is why the case can be made that he is the most valuable player in the history of the franchise.

"I'm very proud of what I did on the court," Price said. "But I hope that people view me as a person. For nine years, we lived here and became a part of the community. I've tried to represent the team well, off the court."

Price is active in The Chapel in downtown Akron and in other local and charitable organizations. He is quiet and classy, a family man who grew up in Enid, Oklahoma, singing in the church choir.

Cavs fans were familiar with his life story. Those in Summit County often saw him in church, at a mall or a restaurant. Even if they never did more than cheer for Price at the old Coliseum or perhaps say hello to him somewhere—they felt they knew him.

Now that he is leaving, Price wants to go out with grace.

"I am grateful for all the kindness the fans have given me and my family," he said. "I'm still trying to sort all these things out, but one thing I do know is that down deep, I'll always be a Cavalier."

9/28/1995

Thome caught eye of the beholder

YOU PROBABLY have never heard of Tom Couston, but you should.

"If it weren't for Tom, I wouldn't be with the Indians," said Jim Thome.

That's an understatement. Thome would probably still be home in Peoria, playing some softball at night and coaching Little Leaguers on the weekends. He certainly would not be on the verge of becoming an All-Star third baseman.

That's because Tom Couston was the only baseball scout who thought Thome was worth a second look.

"I first saw Jimmy play in high school," Couston said. "He was tall [6-foot-4], but pretty thin. He was a shortstop, and that wasn't his position. But he had a quick bat. I wrote that down. I remembered it. But I heard that he was headed to a junior college, and I thought that was a good idea."

Couston is the Tribe's Midwestern scout based in Chicago. He knew that Thome was more than four long arms and legs. Thome's family is populated with great softball players. He was the leading scorer on his high school basketball team, and threw in 36 points when Limestone

High won its league title.

But there are thousands of kids like Jim Thome on dusty diamonds across America . . . kids with some promise and a lot of question marks . . . kids most scouts figure aren't worth the time.

"In this job, it is easy to become negative," Couston said. "You can talk yourself out of liking a kid. A scout has to remember that every player has a weakness, even All-Stars in the big leagues."

After that high school game, Couston promised himself that he'd check up on Thome, maybe in a year or two. He had to see Thome swing the bat again.

"The next time I saw Jimmy play was when he was with Illinois Central [Junior] College," Couston said. "I wasn't even there to see him. There was a shortstop on the other team that was considered a prospect, and a lot of scouts were there to see him."

The moment he spotted Thome, Couston remembered him as the high school kid from Peoria with the strong wrists and quick bat.

"In that game, Jimmy came to the plate four times and hit four rockets," Couston said. "He still was pretty thin, but he was only 18 years old. He hadn't grown into his body."

At least five other scouts watched that game, and while a few of them thought Thome could hit a bit, they saw an awkward kid at shortstop. He didn't run well. He didn't have much range. His arm was decent, but erratic. He wouldn't even be able to play shortstop at a major college.

Instead, they concentrated on the other team's shortstop, the designated prospect.

Couston knew that scouts watch and listen to each other, so he pulled out one of his favorite tricks.

"After the game, Tom came up to me and said something strange," Thome said.

"I told him to keep his back to me and I'll keep my back to him," Couston said.

This confused Thome.

"I thought I had done something wrong," Thome said.

Couston told him, "I want to talk to you, but I don't want you to look at me."

Thome said, "OK, I guess."

Thome stared at the baseball field. Facing the opposite direction, Couston seemed to be watching a bird flying above.

Couston said, "I'm Tom Couston, a scout from the Indians. If we draft you, will you sign?"

Thome was thunderstruck. He couldn't believe it. Those were the words he prayed he would hear and he could barely talk.

"I always wanted to play pro baseball," he finally told the scout.

Thome started to turn around, but stopped when Couston said, "Don't move! I don't want the other scouts to know I'm talking to you." Thome stopped.

"OK, you'll be hearing from me," Couston said.

By the time Thome did turn around, the scout was gone.

Couston then had to convince the Indians to draft this kid, whose name was on none of the master scouting lists. Thome's abilities were so raw and his junior college team was so bad, he was on no other scouting lists—none but Couston's.

"Donny Mitchell was my scouting supervisor," Couston said. "I told him that once we get to the 10th round, they should take this kid Thome. Donny never heard of him. No one had. None of the scouts from other teams who did see Jimmy thought he could play. But Donny went to bat for the kid."

In the 13th round of the 1989 June draft, the Indians called the name of Jim Thome. Other teams sat in their draft headquarters, flipping through their computer printouts and asking themselves, "Who did Cleveland pick?"

Couston's next job was to sign his diamond in the Peoria rough.

"His parents are great people," Couston said. "But Peoria is really middle America, very small town. They were worried about Jimmy signing a contract, going away from home. They wanted to make sure someone would watch over their son."

A scout is part sleuth, part salesman.

Couston had sniffed out Thome because he loved the kid's bat speed. He also was convinced that once his 6-foot-4, lanky frame filled out, Thome would become a very strong young man. He was no shortstop, but Couston projected Thome at third base . . . first base . . . just somewhere to keep that bat in the lineup.

But Thome had the option of returning for his sophomore year at college—and going back into the draft. Couston couldn't lose this kid now. He knew Thome would not stay a secret forever. If he played one more year, Couston was sure some scout would find him.

He tried to sign Thome for $10,000, but Thome's parents thought that was low. Couston had to go back to the front office for authorization to offer more money.

To the credit of the Indians' farm department, they invested $15,000 worth of faith in this one scout who was putting himself and his reputation out on a limb. It is easier to convince the front office to spend a million bucks on a first-round pick than it is for them to part with another five grand for a kid who was drafted seemingly as an afterthought.

Couston came back with the $15,000—and Thome signed.

Couston told this story last week as he watched Thome take batting practice at the Tribe's spring headquarters in Winter Haven.

After he signed with the Tribe, Thome was moved to third base and has put on 30 pounds of muscle.

But he wasn't an instant hit.

In fact, Couston warned the front office that they'd need patience. Thome was only 18 when he reported to the Indians' rookie league team in Florida's Gulf Coast League. Sarasota was a long way from Peoria, and Thome was more than a little homesick.

He batted only .237 that first pro summer of 1989. The man who hammered 45 homers the last two years didn't hit one ball out of the park back in 1989.

But the Tribe stuck with Thome, who added strength and confidence. The bat speed that so enamored Couston began to carry Thome through the Tribe's farm system. He banged out one .300 season after another, gaining more power by the year.

Last season, he hit .314 with 25 homers for the pennant-winning Tribe, good enough to be named the best third baseman in the American League by *The Sporting News*.

Not bad for a kid no one wanted—no one but one scout.

Last week, Thome and Couston headed off to dinner. Thome paid. It was the least he could do.

2/26/1996

Spielman? He's old school

FOOTBALL OR FAMILY?

For Chris Spielman, there was no choice.

"I'm a husband and a father—first," he said.

You hear that a lot from men in all walks of life, often as they are finishing a 60-hour week at the office.

Or returning from a 10-day business trip.

How many of us say family is our top priority, then head off to work.

Not Spielman, who joined the Browns yesterday in a trade for "past considerations" with the Buffalo Bills. A little more than a year ago his wife, Stefanie, was diagnosed with breast cancer.

It changed his life.

"I thought I knew about pressure from football," Spielman said. "That was nothing compared to waiting for test results from a biopsy when you know that it doesn't look good."

There was more.

"I watched my wife and I learned about real mental toughness, real courage—the kind that goes beyond football," he said.

And even more.

"Some people asked me how I could take last year off to take care of my wife," he said. "What kind of a man would I be if I didn't?"

Spielman gave more than a press conference yesterday, he gave a lesson in morality. It was an echo from another era, when a man's word and a man's family were bonds that could not be broken.

Many of us would have found a way around this. Sure, we would have worried about our wife and supported her. But would we have sacrificed our career?

Spielman talked about having the financial means to sit out a season and be a husband, a companion, a strong shoulder and a pair of comforting arms.

He shrugs as if it's no big deal.

Understand that Spielman suffered a major back injury nine games into the 1997 season. He then had neck-fusion surgery—a major, career-threatening operation.

In 1998, he needed to prove he still could play.

Instead, he determined that the words "for better or worse, in sickness and health," mean something.

So at the age of 33 and coming off a serious injury, he put football on hold—and did so without hesitation.

He learned about chemotherapy and radiation. He saw treatments that are supposed to make you well, yet make you so sick, you swear you're going to die.

He watched his wife vomit until it seemed nothing could come up. He watched her lose her hair. He watched her endure chills one minute, then cold sweats the next. What he watched reduced the NFL linebacker to tears.

He felt so helpless, yet so needed—all at the same time.

"For 10 years, my wife was by my side," he said. "I'm talking about unconditional love, unconditional support...."

His voice trailed off.

For 10 years, a woman supports you, the least you can do is to be there for her.

During his wife's death-defying duel with cancer, Spielman took refuge in the weight room at Ohio State, where he was an All-American linebacker.

"Everything I did was pointed toward making me a better football player," he said. "All the drills, all the workouts, all the sweat—it was aimed toward this day."

It was a day of answered prayers, the day that Chris could be a football player again because Stefanie was free of cancer.

"If she weren't cancer-free, I doubt I'd be here," he said. "But we got the news on January 3. She officially went into remission. And now she just goes back every three months for tests."

Then he smiled.

"Her hair is growing back, her genuine smile is back," he said. "And when I got traded to the Browns, I ran into the room and told her, 'Honey, I got a job again.' It was a great day for both of us."

Spielman made four All-Pro teams with Detroit before going to Buffalo as a free agent in 1996. He was known for his dedication, his preparation—and for turning up the air conditioning full-blast in his hotel room the night before he played a game in frigid weather.

"I know some people think it's a gamble for the Browns to trade for me," he said. "Anyone who has ever bet against me on the football field has lost. On the field, I have a certain standard to live up to. I will represent the Browns well. If not, I expect to be criticized."

He paused.

"To me, it's a privilege to play in the NFL, not a privilege for the NFL to have me in it," he said. "I will not become the kind of player I despise. I will go full-bore. If I can't play [up to his standards], I will give my money back. I will play without hesitation."

Spielman was a star at Massillon. He talks like a man who has something to prove, especially after Buffalo simply turned his contract over to the Browns.

"I was traded for a box of tape," he said. "But that doesn't bother me. I want to play for the Browns. I'm a Northeast Ohio guy, as Northeast Ohio as you can get."

Then Spielman gave his philosophy of life.

"I always wear my old cleats," he said.

And he hangs on to his old values.

2/17/1999

Just spell Manny M-o-n-e-y

HOW CAN Manny Ramirez turn down $75 million from the Indians?

Try ego.

Try agents.

Try a twisted culture in which too many athletes ultimately measure their worth by the $$$ next to their names.

Ramirez's agent rejected the Indians' five-year, $75 million offer because it's not "market value."

Agents are obsessive about "market value." Sometimes, they don't even know what "market value" is, they just want it. Or, as in the case of Ramirez, are out "to set the market."

Albert Belle and his agents had much the same goal after the 1996 season. Belle wouldn't be satisfied until he was "the highest-paid player in the game."

Which he became, signing with the Chicago White Sox for $55 million over five years. It seemed to last for only five minutes, but for those five minutes, Belle could stand on his pile of money and stare down on everyone else in caps and spikes.

Belle never was happier than when he played for the Indians and hasn't even come close to the playoffs since leaving. He now plays for the sagging Baltimore Orioles, but Belle doesn't seem especially concerned.

In pro sports, respect is shown in cold, hard cash.

Never forget that, especially every time you hear one of these gladiators proclaim, "It's not about money."

They actually say this with a straight face after they've signed a contract that would enable them to buy Norway.

Of course it's about money.

Ramirez is about money. Belle is about money. It's all about money.

Countless players have tied their self-esteem to their paychecks. Sure, the other guy might play on a better team—or even have superior statistics—but I make more money.

So there!

And if they aren't hung up on money when they first play the game, just give them time. The friends, the wives, the girlfriends, the agents and the teammates all get into the act.

Over and over, they talk about money: "Hey, Manny, did you see what Shawn Green got? Fourteen million, man! Can you believe that? Man, you're twice as good as that guy!"

Who makes what becomes far more important than *Who wins what.*

If Ramirez didn't consider himself "underpaid" for the past few years, when he's had to scrape by on a mere $4.5 million annually, he's had plenty of people tell him so. They probably have reminded him that he signed "a bad deal"—that he looks like a sap because he makes "only" $4.5 million.

Now, it's payback time.

"They owe me," is the rallying cry. "Look at all I've done for the team and the city," they say, as if they just cured cancer.

Agents use this line of argument to harden their players against management, especially when the agent did not negotiate the old contract. He tells the player, "Look, you stick with me, and they won't stick it to you again."

The player begins to believe he was "cheated" on his last long-term contract, forgetting how "happy" he was when he signed it only a few years earlier.

The agent also has a financial interest in grabbing every dollar. Most make at least 4 percent of the total contract.

So 4 percent of $75 million is $3 million.

Compare that with 4 percent of $100 million—where the agent's fee is $4 million.

If you're an agent, which sounds better to you?

Then, add in the other millions that the agent can make using the huge contract he negotiated for one player to entice another to hire him. Agents compare themselves by the $$$, just as players—and often, their egos are even more bloated.

This is not meant to vilify Ramirez, or even his agent.

But it's to show what this world has become, how both players and management love to tell us how "this is a game," except it's really a business.

A greedy, heartless business.

6/30/2000

Regrets will hang heavy for Kemp

AN HOUR BEFORE THE GAME, Larry Nance was on the court, shooting around with the Cavs players.

Nance is a lean 41, still looks like he could block a few shots—and, no doubt, swish a few of those line-drive jumpers—as he did last night.

You know Nance would love to wear his old No. 22 for the Cavs. Instead, he is a special assistant for the Cavs, doing a little coaching, a little scouting, a lot of retirement.

It has been seven years since Nance retired, his career cut short by major knee and ankle injuries at the age of 34. Given how big guys seem to play forever, the 6-foot-10 Nance could have been in uniform on his 40th birthday, if only those knees hadn't crumpled.

Then there's Brad Daugherty, looking in great shape while sitting in the ESPN studios. Daugherty is only 35, and it has been seven years since he was the man in the middle for the Cavs.

Daugherty still should be the Cavs center and probably still would be an All-Star. But he had serious back surgery that banished him to the sidelines at the age of 28.

What's the point of all this?

So many guys wish they could be Shawn Kemp today, a member of perhaps the most talented team in the league as the Portland Trail Blazers came to the Gund Arena last night.

Kemp has what Nance and Daugherty would love—a career and decent health. But there is Kemp at 31 looking all of 51. They say he's 280, but he appears to be the same 300 pounds that he was during most of his three years with the Cavs.

Kemp has been exiled to the Portland bench. He was on the court for only six scoreless minutes against Sacramento on Saturday. He's playing 17 minutes a game, averaging about seven points, four rebounds and shooting 40 percent.

It's easy to reduce Kemp to one big joke, but he is a far more pathetic case than that.

He was supposed to be the savior of the Cavs when he was acquired from Seattle before the 1997–98 season. He was out of shape when the Cavs brought him to town, then they gave him a hefty contract, which didn't exactly inspire him to lose any weight.

Kemp was never the player in Cleveland who was the Reign Man in

Seattle. He wasn't even 30, yet he was playing like a guy closing in on 40, his game below the rim as he lowers his shoulder, grunts, then bulls his way to the basket with all the grace of a moose falling down a flight of stairs.

You have to wonder what Kemp really thought when he watched films of himself. Couldn't he see how his skills had diminished? Didn't he know his ever expanding waistline was the reason? Wasn't he embarrassed by his declining production, by the fans and media turning him into a symbol of what's wrong with the modern NBA?

Kemp refuses to answer, or even confront, those questions.

Not long before the Cavs tipped off against Portland, Clarence Weatherspoon left the court. He had just put himself through a demanding warmup session. He was soaked in sweat, yet the veteran forward stopped to sign autographs with several fans.

Weatherspoon is listed at 6-7, but can't be much more than 6-5. Yet, he leads the Cavs by averaging close to 10 rebounds per game, a marvel given his lack of size. His vertical leap would barely clear a phonebook—of Mogadore.

But he rebounds with a vengeance. He defends his territory like a pit bull. He has a surprisingly soft and accurate mid-range jumper.

Someone once said, "If Weatherspoon had a body like Kemp . . ."

Actually, Weatherspoon wouldn't have Kemp's body, he'd have one that's like the chiseled Karl Malone.

Weatherspoon is one of the players the Cavs received in the Kemp trade. He's a guy who "respects the game and himself," in the words of former Cavs player-turned-broadcaster Austin Carr.

Carr is now 52 and is probably very near his playing weight of 200. It has been 20 years since Carr played for the Cavs, forced to quit at 32 because of aching knees.

But for Carr, Nance, Daugherty and Weatherspoon, there will be no regrets about their careers, something Kemp never will be able to say.

1/23/2001

Youth

The few, the proud, the Vikings

In the North High dressing room is this sign: CAN'T IS THE WORST WORD THAT IS WRITTEN.

Every time a North football player or coach passes that sign, he kneels down and touches it.

That's because everybody tells the North players and coaches what they can't do. Or as assistant coach Fred Sellers said, "They say we are on a sinking ship."

Fred Sellers is an Akron policeman. He works the midnight shift, then volunteers to help with the North football team, a team that has lost every game this season.

He also comes to the school a few days each week, just to walk the halls in the afternoon and help with security.

Is he a loser?

Or how about Steve Cross? Works nights at Giant Eagle. Spends his days helping with the North football team. Doesn't get paid a penny.

Or James Sharpe? Runs a floral business. Helps coach the North track team in the spring and is the receivers coach in the fall. Doing it all for free.

Or how about Tom O'Neil? He is North's head coach. He played at North in the 1980s, along with six of his assistants. Understand that O'Neil makes $4,600 for being the head coach. Three of the assistants make $2,300. It breaks down to about a nickel an hour.

As for the other six assistant coaches . . . they are here because they love these small, overmatched kids . . . kids most football coaches wouldn't give a second thought.

At North, the players receive hundreds of hours of coaching from guys who could be sitting in front of the TV set or at their favorite sports bar, throwing down a few beers and talking about the Good Old Days.

Instead, they stand tall with their small team. They take the beatings with the kids, yelling at them one moment, hugging them the next.

Seven of these coaches played together at North. It's a case of a bunch of guys who are being true to their school when most graduates have forgotten it.

There is Tom O'Neil, Sellers, Joe Lattarulo, Larry (brother of Tom) O'Neil, Ralph Petrucelli, Chris Fassnacht and Tom Lambert. They are white guys, black guys, Irish guys and Italian guys. All together.

Why go to football practice every day? Why stand in the mud? The rain? The sleet of October? The sweltering sun of August?

Especially when you know most of the time, you'll lose.

But they keep coming back. They buy T-shirts for their players and coaches: THE FEW, THE PROUD, NORTH FOOTBALL.

They believe it.

Two weeks ago, North played powerful Buchtel High.

"I saw those 24 kids get off the bus, and some of them were kind of scrawny," Buchtel coach Tim Flossie said. "They have no numbers, no size. I tried not to run the score up on them. Their coaches, Tom O'Neil and those guys, are doing it the right way, working hard. I feel for them."

Buchtel beat North 65-6.

At the end of the game, only 19 of the 24 North players were left standing.

Five were helped off the field. Three went to the hospital.

"By the second half, we were running around trying to find guys to put on the field," offensive coordinator Larry O'Neil said. "It was like, 'Who do we have left?' Some of their kids were 260 pounds. Our biggest kid [James Patonai] is only 220. Our line probably averages 180."

Why don't more kids play football?

It's not just at North. Numbers are down at Kenmore, East and Central-Hower, too—although North is the most extreme case.

"It's a sign of the times," said Mike Buckner, athletic director for the Akron Public Schools and former head football coach at Buchtel High. "With open enrollment, some good athletes transfer to schools with winning records. I know that North has lost five or six kids from last year that way. Others don't like the discipline."

Tom O'Neil believes in discipline. Miss a practice without an excuse, you run five miles.

"He is a young coach from the old school," said assistant James Sharpe.

O'Neil called off his freshman football season with one game to go.

"We had four kids throwing helmets and shoulder pads, cussing and refusing to shake hands after a game," he said. "We won't tolerate that."

There were about 20 players on the freshman team. He told the four offenders that their season was finished. He invited the rest to join the varsity at practice the next day.

The following day, he saw five freshmen players lingering by the dressing room.

"Want to come in and play with the varsity?" O'Neil asked.

The kids looked at each other. One kid said, "Coach, I don't think so." He left, the other four followed.

When North did take the field, two freshmen were in uniform—Dominic Donatelli and Richard Bolds.

"Let's give these two freshmen a real hand," O'Neill said. "They had the heart to join us."

Players applauded and patted the kids on the back. The coaches were pleased with the two kids, but wondered what happened to the rest.

When they were freshmen and someone had invited them to play with the varsity, a ball-and-chain could not have held them back.

North High is in a working-class neighborhood known as North Hill. Many of the families are Catholic and send their children to schools such as Hoban, Walsh and St. Vincent-St. Mary.

"That's one factor," said Larry O'Neil. "Most of these kids don't have money. I taught in Medina for a year. Those parents buy their kids cars, clothes and pay for the insurance. Here, if kids want that, most of them have to go to work—and that means no sports."

North has more than 800 students. When most of the North coaches played at the school in the middle 1980s, there were about 40 kids on the team.

North has one senior, Chad Leib. He is 5-foot-9, 155 pounds—and he's a defensive end. That's like being a 6-foot center in the NBA.

Leib was a punter on the freshman team. Didn't play as a sophomore or junior. He worked at Friendly's instead. He decided to answer O'Neil's plea for players and went out for the team as a senior.

"I wanted just to kick," he said. "But they let me play both offense and defense."

And?

"A lot of kids crack jokes about us losing all the time," he said. "Sometimes the teams we play are so big, we worry a little bit about getting hurt. But our coaches tell us if we stay aggressive, we'll be all right. Football is hard, but being on this team makes me feel so good."

There is sophomore Jimmy Noussias. Last week, he was on crutches, recovering from a strained ligament in his knee. He is an honor student, and he was at practice . . . on those crutches . . . somehow slogging through the mud, cheering for his teammates.

"Some kids don't like the discipline," he said. "They don't like it because we lose some games really bad. But they don't understand how we play our hearts out. Our coaches are so great. They don't yell at us— well, they do yell, but then they teach us. They are good guys."

Just so they can have enough players to have a full-scale practice, some of the coaches put on helmets and pads. It's amazing none of them have ended up in the hospital.

The kids like it, especially when a coach falls down. They tell you that the coaches are big, like the players they face. It is a good idea to see size in practice, even if it comes from guys who haven't played football in 10 years.

As junior Mike Sezhue said, "I'd play football anywhere, anytime. The fact that we are strong enough to stick this out while other kids quit, even if we get killed sometimes, that shows we're not afraid of hard work."

Like their coaches, the players are true believers, even Randale Richmond, who is only 130 pounds.

Tom and Larry O'Neil are identical twins. They live five minutes from the high school. They both teach English and history. They both even have the same 1950s-style haircut. Tom teaches at North, Larry at Central-Hower.

They share an apartment with assistant coach Joe Lattarulo.

"I tell the kids that I walked the same streets, cut down the same alleys as they do," Tom O'Neil said. "I know life can be hard. When Larry and I were seniors at North, our father passed away. We both worked our way through Akron U. We were the last of eight kids. We can talk about sacrifice because we made sacrifices ourselves."

This is O'Neil's second year as North's head coach. He was North's freshman coach for five years. He also was an assistant at Firestone. He is only 27 years old.

Buckner tells you that O'Neil and his staff are doing a good job. So does Charlie Marquess, the former North coach from the 1980s. Marquess coached Mike Fox and Leonard Humphries, who went on to play in the NFL, along with O'Neil and most of the current North coaches.

"Tom has study halls for the players," Marquess said. "He has a good weight program. He about lives in the building. He lets the kids play other sports. He has rules, but he's fair."

Al Bell has two sons on the team, Alfred and Andre. Last week, he was the only parent watching Wednesday's practice.

"The coaching is good, the conditioning is good," Bell said. "The kids try so hard, but they just aren't very good right now."

That is apparent from the scores—losses by 45-6 to Medina, 53-0 to Hoban, 56-6 to Youngstown Cardinal Mooney, 44-6 to Firestone, 49-0 to Garfield, 68-8 to Ellet. The Vikings' only close game was a 15-14 loss to Central-Hower, and they end the season tonight against 2-7 Kenmore.

But each week, the kids and coaches are back out there. Running, sweating, sometimes crying.

After a recent practice, O'Neil talked to his players about pride. How proud he is of them and the dignity with which they play. He asked them to help recruit players from the halls for next year.

"Our weight program starts in two weeks," he said, "and we always have at least six coaches in the weight room to help you in the off-season."

When it was over, O'Neil led his players into the dressing room. He stopped in front of the CAN'T sign, kneeling down to touch it. The kids did the same.

11/1/1996

Kids, values, and sports

LAST WEEK, I SPOKE to Steve Culp's sixth-grade class at Rankin School.

Guess what is the kids' favorite television show?

Jerry Springer.

That's right, Jerry Springer. Sixth-graders watching Jerry Springer. Sixth-graders watching heaven knows what on Jerry Springer.

Twenty kids in the class.

Nineteen voted for Springer.

The other kid liked Spiderman, but he was hooted when he stood up for his favorite cartoon character.

Why Springer?

"Because it's wild," said one girl. "They have lesbians fighting. They got weird fat people."

When I was in the sixth grade, I never even heard of a lesbian, much less saw them wrestling on TV. Culp said his kids rush home to watch Springer after school—and some of the other sleazy afternoon talk shows.

This is not just at Rankin School.

"Jerry Springer?" asked Orrville basketball coach Steve Smith. "A lot of my kids watch it."

"Springer?" sighed East football coach Cornelius Parson. "I know kids who tape it. In my house, we have a rule that no one watches it. But my kids tell me everyone else watches it."

"They talk a lot about Jerry Springer," confirmed John Scott, an English teacher and track coach at Buchtel.

Here was my next question for the Rankin kids: How many of you have $100 tennis shoes?

Twenty kids in the class; 10 said they had $100 shoes.

Five of them were wearing Michael Jordan's, which are $150.

"I'm not surprised," said East's Parson. "Shoes are status. But want to hear something crazy? We have kids who wear Michael Jordan's around the hallways, but not to basketball practice."

This is not just happening in the city.

Randy Montgomery is the basketball coach at Triway in Wayne County. He cut a deal with Reebok to buy shoes for his team at $30 under what it would cost for them to wear Nikes.

"But my kids catch it from all the other teams because we're not wearing Nikes," he said. "A few of my kids even bought Nikes to wear in school. That's fine. But they are a member of our team, and we wear purple Reeboks because they are a good shoe and they are cheaper."

Our teachers and coaches are on the front line of the cultural revolution, and it's not just in the city. They know Nike is the king of shoes because of its association with Jordan and its attention-grabbing commercials.

"It's not just shoes," said Montgomery. "We're down in Wayne County and we have kids with red and green hair, kids with their tongues pierced. We've got kids with baggy jeans hanging down off their butts. It's a lifestyle."

And it's what they see on TV.

This is not meant to indict the youth of America. Teacher after teacher will tell you that most of their kids have a sense of what is right and what is wrong in a world of very muddled values.

"But it's so hard for them to apply it," said Buchtel's Scott. "The kids feel as if there are no absolutes. Everything is relative."

Or as Orrville's Smith said, "They know cheating on a test is wrong, but they tell themselves it's OK to cheat because everyone else is doing it. You catch them, and they act as if it's your problem. 'What's the big deal?' That's their attitude."

In his English class at Buchtel, Scott said the subject of ATM machines came up. He asked the kids what they'd do if they asked for $20 and received $200 instead.

"All of them said they'd keep the money," he said.

Scott believes a few felt otherwise, but kept silent. It isn't cool to admit to being honest. But the majority believed it was their right to keep the money, even if they did nothing to earn it.

"I asked them what they'd do if the machine kept a record, and the bank might come back to them for the extra money," Scott said. "Most said they'd take their chances and still keep the money."

The kids know it's wrong, but their world is situational ethics. "Can I get over?" is their question.

That means, "Will I get away with it?"

East's Parson said there was a fight in the stands at a high school game a few months ago.

"Not one kid stepped in to stop it," he said. "They waited for the teachers to do it."

Barberton football coach Tim Flossie knows why.

"The things these kids see every day, both in their lives and on TV—it has desensitized them," he said. "When I was at Buchtel, my kids saw their friends and relatives doing drugs, getting shot—so doggone much sad stuff."

A fight in the stands during a basketball game? It's like battling lesbians on the Springer show, just another form of entertainment.

"For the most part, kids just react," said Flossie. "They don't think real far ahead. They have values, but the values aren't real strong because they don't have someone pushing them to do the right thing."

Parson added, "If a kid breaks up a fight or shows compassion to someone else, it often is taken as a sign of weakness."

Most of all, kids don't want to look like a wimp in front of their friends.

In the schools, you hear a lot about respect.

The teachers believe kids don't respect them.

The kids are sure teachers don't give them proper respect.

Sometimes fierce, even deadly, fights erupt because one kid believes another kid has no respect for him. The street talk is, "He dissed me."

"A lot of the problems come from the language they use," said Parson. "The profanity. We'd never swear around an adult. These kids don't care, and they see nothing wrong with it when you do correct them."

Part of the reason is TV and movies.

"On Springer, about every third word is bleeped out," said Smith.

In school hallways, a censor would wear out his fingers trying to press the button on the offending language.

"Some of it is good-natured," said Scott. "But other times, kids just rip into each other in very violent, foul language."

To many kids, respect is a one-way street.

"They just live for the moment," said Scott. "What feels good now overtakes their sense of right and wrong. I know kids who skip out when the proficiency tests are given, figuring they'll take it later. We are in a society where we hope someone will cover for us."

Much is made of the message kids supposedly receive from pro athletes.

But listening to the voices of the men on the front lines, you realize there is no message.

That's right, no message from pro sports.

There are so many messages that collide. Dennis Rodman, Latrell Sprewell, Michael Jordan, Albert Belle, Orel Hershiser. All different men with different values.

But in the end, it's just a lot of noise.

"I was just watching an interview with Latrell Sprewell on '60 Minutes,'" said Garfield football coach Bill McGee. "It was everyone else's fault that he attacked his coach. Things like that are why I rarely watch pro sports anymore."

Flossie said, "My kids tell me that Sprewell really didn't intend to kill [Coach] P.J. Carlesimo, he was just talking. If Sprewell wanted to kill him, he'd have gotten a gun and wasted him."

That's how it's done on TV, or even in some of their neighborhoods.

"Like it or not, these players are role models," McGee said. "In the pro games, I see all this taunting, trash talking and celebrating—things that are wrong and will get a team penalized in a high school game."

Or as Parson said, "The big thing now in basketball is the Allen Iverson crossover dribble. I see games where kids do the crossover, then blow an easy shot—but the kids in the stands still think it's a great play anyway."

Triway's Montgomery is heartsick by the Sprewell episode: "What does the guy need to do to lose his job, murder the coach? I wrote [Cavs General Manager] Wayne Embry. I respect Wayne and his team. But I will never go to another NBA game again because of Sprewell."

Given the number of divorces, the bizarre television, the obsession with shoes, it is amazing that there are a remarkable number of good kids.

"It's just so much harder for them now," said Smith.

There remains some light.

"I'm convinced sports is good for most kids," said Smith. "Too bad a teacher can't run his classroom like a coach. A kid steps out of line in practice, you can make him do 100 push-ups or run a couple of miles."

Not so in school.

"I make my players sign a code of conduct," said Montgomery. "They will act like gentlemen. They will tuck in their shirts. They will wear a tie on game day. They won't drink. They won't have hair over their collars.

"But if I tried that in a classroom, I'd have five parents telling me that I can't enforce my values on the kids."

But in sports, there can be values.

"Most kids want to play," said Flossie. "You can get them to be on time and do the right things. You can have discipline on your team."

These are lessons that can serve them later in life.

"We are in a Me-Society," said Scott. "But sports does stress team-work, looking out for the other guy. It can bring order to some kids who really need it in their lives."

A lot of the pressure is on the coach. He has to set the standard. He has to enforce the rules. He also has to win, and he has to answer to his bosses and the parents.

"I really believe we are in a cultural war," said Montgomery. "I don't want to see us go the way of the Roman Empire. That is why we in education have to stand up for the right things whenever we get the chance."

3/10/1998

Sport—as it was meant to be

THE PLACE OOZES OF HIGH SCHOOL FOOTBALL.

The wooden, ramshackle bleachers. The old light poles with wires and four beams on top. The quaint scoreboard with a black panther looming.

This is Manchester's Jim France Stadium.

This is high school football, the way it ought to be.

It's the kind of place that reminds us why this night is important—this, the first Friday night of the 1998 high school football season.

It reminds us that for most kids, high school football is not a ticket to college. It's not played in a super stadium on artificial turf in front of 15,000 maniacs who want to fire the coach because he lost to the wrong local rival.

It reminds us that high school football is for the kids. The players. The band. The cheerleaders. The dance team.

It reminds us there are coaches like Jim France, men who don't have to swear and scream to squeeze the most out of their team.

"You guys, you're like a bunch of cows out there," grumbles France during practice.

That's about as blue as it gets from this man who took Manchester to the Division IV state finals last year.

France will turn 55 in two weeks. This is his 27th year as Manchester's coach, his 15th year as school principal. His school is a small one, but it's a school where one of every three boys is involved in the football program at some level.

It's where football is important, but it's not everything. France doesn't demand that his kids play only football or that they spend every free moment in the weight room.

"I believe in kids' playing as many sports as they'd like," he said. "Just as I believe in little kids' playing in sandboxes and riding bikes. I believe in kids' being allowed to be kids, not forced to specialize in one sport when they're 12 years old."

This was one of France's final practices before tonight's opener against rival Northwest High School in nearby Canal Fulton. The Manchester stadium is named after the coach, and he stands at midfield on this quiet afternoon.

You hear birds chirping. You see huge trees looming over those wooden bleachers, and you hear the leaves rustling in the wind.

You hear shoulder pads clinking as the players run to the line of scrimmage, and you hear kids grunting as the ball is snapped and bodies slam into each other.

France watches it all and grumbles. He has a middle-aged paunch and a leathery face that's in a perpetual squint from all those football practices under the unrelenting sun.

"You can't lope like that," he said. "You have to run that pattern hard, right through the end zone to Fay's house."

Fay's house?

France means the yellow house located behind the end zone, past the fence and the trees. Fay's house. Even though Fay doesn't live there anymore.

"Hey, Joe," mumbles the coach. "See that guy who went past you? The guy who just sent our quarterback to the hospital?"

Actually, no one even touched the quarterback on the play, but it could have happened because the kid missed a blocking assignment.

"Why did you do that?" France grumbles.

Here is where it becomes interesting. Here is Jim France in his 27th season as a coach, a man who has won virtually every coaching award worth winning, and he's asking a 16-year-old, "Why?"

And he really does want to hear the answer.

The kid explains. France nods his head. The kid begins to smile because he realizes the coach actually listened. The coach is thinking about it.

In the end, this Summit County Hall of Fame coach accepts the answer from a 16-year-old. It doesn't happen often, but when it does, it's something a high school kid will never forget.

This is happening all over our area tonight, veteran coaches like Jim France working with 16-year-olds—and still caring, still relishing it.

It can be Joe Pappano at Revere, Tim Flossie at Barberton, Bill McGee at Garfield, Joe Yost at Ellet, John Nemec at Kent Roosevelt, Don Ross at Cuyahoga Falls, Bill McMillan at Orrville, Keith Wakefield at Perry or Jeff Durbin at Lake—men who are institutions.

OK, sometimes they tell you that they feel like they belong in an institution after a rough practice, but there's nothing they'd rather do.

Know why?

Watch France.

Watch France look at his fullback, a kid named Rodney Salter. His father, Nate Salter, also played for France at Manchester in the 1970s.

"Both wear No. 40," says the coach.

He thinks of Cliff Bond, who played on his first Manchester team in 1971. And he thinks of Matt Bond, the son who played on last year's team.

He thinks of all the kids who have passed through, maybe a thousand by now. They are not kids who played in the NFL, kids who played for Ohio State.

They are doctors, lawyers, teachers, truck drivers, plumbers, computer programmers—and more than a few are his assistant coaches.

You walk across the grass field with France and listen to him talk about these kids—kids who are adults in the community.

Kids who have become fathers, and who send their sons to France.

You look at his team. Most of his linemen are 180 pounds. One running back is a kid named Joe Veitko—he's 5-foot-8, 155 pounds. The other back is Rick Sponseller, who is all of 5-foot-6 and 135 pounds.

At schools like Manchester, you don't have to be a genetic superman to play football. You have normal kids doing extraordinary things on the field, kids who want to wear their school colors, kids who believe in their coaches and their schools.

Yes, even in the 1990s, you can find this.

Just go to a high school football game tonight. Go to a place like Manchester.

9/4/1998

Weighty issue? You bet

I REMEMBER TRYING to be a high school athlete. I had twigs for hands, broom sticks for legs.

I went out for the freshman football team.

I was the bug. The kid who hit me was the freight train. And just one hit, that's all it took.

My football career was over.

I played basketball at 5-feet-10, 125 pounds. Actually, I sat basketball during the games. In practice, I was tossed about like a paper airplane in a hurricane.

And I played baseball. The bat in my hands was a fly swatter. The pitch was a cannon ball. It wasn't pretty. I really did have the bat knocked out of my hands by a fastball—more than once.

Almost 30 years later, the laughter still burns in my ears.

Coach after coach told me that I had to get stronger. Eat more. Lift weights. Take vitamins.

When I was 18, I was 5-feet-11. I played college baseball (actually, sat) at 135 pounds.

Nothing worked.

I can tell you right now, if creatine had been around when I was an athlete—I'd have taken it, especially if my teammates believed it made them bigger and stronger.

All I knew was that milkshakes didn't work. Meat, potatoes and other foods that supposedly put on weight didn't work. The primitive weight training that existed in the early 1970s had virtually no impact.

Nothing worked.

No matter what sport I played, I stunk. I wasn't a teenager, I was a scarecrow shuddering in the slightest breeze.

I remember my strapping father looking at me, shaking his head. How could a son of his be so skinny? And why couldn't I do something about it? He never said those exact words, but I knew what was on his mind.

So I understand the kids who take creatine.

One of my relatives played college baseball. He was stuck with the same miserable build. His coach told him to get stronger so he could hit the ball farther. He was on a partial scholarship, so the pressure really was on.

He bought a big can of creatine for $50, then someone climbed through the window and stole it from his dorm room. He thought it was a football player, another kid desperate to add weight and strength.

I'm not saying any of this is right, I'm just saying it's reality.

Athletes will look for an edge, and they don't look very far down the road.

Remember how you were as a teenager. Did you think about what you'd be like in 25 years? When someone talked to you about being in your 40s, did you actually listen?

Come on.

Being a teenager is desperation. It's the most self-absorbed time of your life. The "future" is next weekend. Anything after that, who cares?

That is why the argument about creatine—"it might work, but we don't know the long-term effects" has absolutely no credibility with most kids.

They don't care. Their minds don't work that way. They simply are sick of being skinny and weak and want something to make them feel better.

This year, it's creatine, which is legal.

Young athletes have coaches telling them, "If you want to start next year, you have to get a lot stronger and add 20 pounds."

The kid doesn't hear the warnings about the uncertain long-term prognosis of creatine. All the kid thinks is, "Coach says I gotta gain weight if I wanna play, and I wanna play."

So the kid tries creatine. He tries androstenedione. If they were to tell the truth, most parents and coaches are happy if the kids just don't take anything that's illegal.

Here's the other problem.

The experts keep changing their minds.

It used to be that milkshakes, ice cream and other sweets were a great way to gain weight and get an instant energy boost. Now, it turns out that all these sweets send your system into chaos, with possible major health consequences.

Forty years ago, basketball players were told not to lift weights, because they'd become too musclebound and it would mess up their outside shots.

Baseball players were told to be careful with weights, because if their chests became too big, it would wreck their swings.

Now, weight training is good for everyone from linebackers to Ping-Pong players to senior citizens.

Remember when most athletes wore canvas tennis shoes, and nearly all of them were low-tops signed by a guy named Chuck Taylor?

Now, it's leather. Now, everything looks like a ski boot. Now, you need to take out a second mortgage to buy most shoes.

As we head into the next century, who knows what kids will be wearing on their feet? Who knows what they'll be ingesting to gain weight and strength?

But this much you can be sure of—the skinny kids will be ready to try almost anything.

1/24/1999

Where they just let 'em play ball

IMAGINE YOUTH BASEBALL with no crazed parents allowed.

No second-guessing the manager.

No screaming at the umpires.

No berating the kids.

Just let 'em play ball, and play their own way. Let the parents from both teams sit next to each other and talk like . . . well, parents, as they cheer for both teams.

"These kids have made us better people," Keith Samples said.

He was looking at his son Joey, who is 16 years old and has had 20 operations on everything from his eyes to his legs. He is one of 45 kids on four teams in Barberton's Challenger Baseball League for physically and mentally challenged children.

"Don't say Joey suffers from cerebral palsy. He just has it," said Christine Samples, seeing her son at second base—in a wheelchair.

There are eight Challenger Leagues in Ohio, and three are in Summit County. The parents love this kind of baseball as much as the kids, because it gives them a place to go. They talk to people who are facing the same sometimes overwhelming problems that they do.

The kids feel comfortable in this setting. So do the parents; it's as much a support group as it is baseball.

"It's a place where none of the children are 'the slow kid,'" said Sue Burdicko, mother of 15-year-old Christy. And none of the parents have to go into great detail about their children's conditions with people who are clueless about the consequences.

These parents know. They live with it every day. They call each other. They cry on the phone. They tell the kinds of jokes that only they understand, and laugh as only those in the same foxhole can.

Christy Burdicko's cerebral palsy is so severe, she can't move her arms or legs. She can't even feel them, much less do something such as feed or dress herself.

"She also has a form of blindness where she'll see an image of me, but not recognize me," Sue Burdicko said.

It's like pictures without captions. Of course, Christy knows Sue is her mother. That's clear the moment she hears Sue's voice.

"But until then, I'm some nice stranger smiling at her," Sue Burdicko said.

Christy's coach is Kevin Shaffer. Her helper is Sarah Roehrick. When Christy is wheeled down to first base, Shaffer beams.

"I see her smiling," he said. "That alone makes it worth coming out here."

The games are unlike anything you've seen. Everyone bats, no one is out. Coaches do the pitching—and try to hit the bat with the ball. If that doesn't work, a tee is brought out and kids can whack away.

You see kids motoring around the bases in wheelchairs, kids limping, kids running the bases in directions and ways you've never seen elsewhere.

Most players are assigned a "buddy," a sort of helper to aid in everything from directions on where to throw the ball, to putting a glove on the correct hand.

For Jordan Muwalla, the buddy is his older sister, Laureen.

She's 11, Jordan is 7.

She can run and yell and play and do everything most kids do.

Jordan is in a wheelchair, paralyzed from the chest down. He can move his head and his arms—a bit.

"The doctors told me that Jordan wouldn't make it past his first birthday because of his spina bifida," said his mother, Sally Muwalla. "Then, they told me that I better keep him in the house all the time."

But sometimes, moms know more than doctors. Sometimes, moms have to take control, and that might mean taking some chances.

"I wanted Jordan to have a life, so I enrolled him in school," she said. "Now, we're playing baseball. They told me that he'd never say a word. Now, there are times when I can't shut him up."

And she laughs.

So often, that's what you hear from parents as they talk about their kids—the laughter. At home, in those bleak moments when nothing seems to go right, when they are pushed beyond exhaustion, when every ounce of patience has been squeezed out, you know it's different.

You know that unless you have been through the waiting rooms and operations and therapists and tears, you can't begin to comprehend what they feel.

But on Wednesdays and Sundays, when these kids and parents come together, it's smiles and compassion and togetherness.

"It's what youth baseball is supposed to be about," said Mark Matthews, who, with wife Michelle, helped to bring the league to Barberton.

"If a kid wants to pick flowers in the outfield, he picks flowers," Michelle Matthews said. "If he wants to wander off second base, he can wander off."

The league is perfect for Brian Salyer, who is in the seventh grade and suffers from autism. Sometimes, he's completely connected to his surroundings. Other times, he's somewhere else.

His nickname is "Bring 'em Home Brian," because he's hit a couple of balls to the 200-foot fence.

During the game, he rhythmically chants: "Who's up next? Who's up next?"

Or he chants: "Good swing. Good swing. Good swing."

His parents are Darlene and Walter Saylor, and they say this is the first league in which their son has been accepted.

"He had been asked to leave a lot of other activities before this," Darlene Saylor said. "He just finished eight months in Cleveland Clinic. Just being outside is great for all of us."

You listen to these stories, and marvel at the parents and the children.

Twenty operations . . . eight months in the Cleveland Clinic . . . a child who sees you, but doesn't recognize you . . . a teenage girl who can't move her hands or feet.

Then, Michelle Matthews tells you about her son, Michael. He's 9 years old, "But emotionally, he's about 4. He has white brain matter disease."

And that means?

"Sometimes he just stares off into space and you can't get his attention," she said.

"Sometimes, he shakes. Sometimes, it seems like he's going to throw up. There are times when you wake up in the morning and ask yourself, 'Can I go through this again?' But you do. You have to."

And if you're Mark and Michelle Matthews, you want something special—not just for your child, but also for all the children who find themselves on the inside, pressing their noses against the window as they stare out at a world that seems to have no place for them.

"For so many years, these kids have had to stay home when their brothers and sisters went out to play their games," Michelle Matthews said. "Now, they have their own games, their own league."

And that's important.

"When Michael starts to throw a fit and won't stop, I found one way to get his attention," she said.

"I tell him, 'Cut it out, or there's no baseball.' That usually works."

And that tells you what you need to know about this league.

6/16/2000

A kid too good to be true

HERE IS WHY so many people love Chuck Moore:

Good Kid. Good Player. Good Student.

But there's more.

He's also a Good Son.

His parents divorced during his junior year at Mogadore High.

"I had worked for 26 years at a grocery store," Cathy Moore said. "All that standing when I managed the deli department, it started to get to me."

Moore encouraged his mother to try college.

"He kept telling me that it wasn't that hard," she said. "I was 42 years old and afraid to go back to school. Chuck said he did well, so I could."

Moore, the star running back on Mount Union's undefeated football team, has a 3.7 grade-point average. His major is finance; his minor is accounting. He would read his mother's papers, especially those for her English courses, checking grammar. They talked about her business courses.

"One of the great things for me was when my mom got an [associate's] degree in business," Moore said. "She just started a job at East Ohio Gas. I'm proud of her."

"You know what was one of my best days?" Cathy Moore asked. "It was when Chuck asked me to help with one of his accounting problems. That's when I knew I arrived."

This is the story of a young man who does the right thing. Is there anything wrong with that? But in our society, young people who play by the rules, study hard, mind their manners, respect others. . . .

Well, that doesn't exactly land you a spot on MTV, or even in most newspapers.

Too many times, news is defined as Bad News.

This is a Good News story.

It's about a former High School Hero who overcame adversity, went to a small college where he's destined to be a Division III All-American. It's about an athlete aiming for the "next level," but in this case, the next level is the real world of work.

For several years, Moore has been a caddie at Congress Lake, where the money was good, the contacts even better.

He turned that into an internship with Capital Investments in Hartville last summer, a job he'll have again this summer.

He is preparing himself not for the NFL, but possibly an MBA degree and a chance to carry the ball in the investment world.

Chuck Moore's story is that of many small-college athletes, a story worth hearing.

There was a time when Chuck Moore was grounded.

He stayed out way past dark. His mother was ready to start calling local hospitals. She frantically searched their Mogadore neighborhood and eventually found him, sled-riding.

"He was only 5 years old," Cathy Moore said. "That was the last time he missed a curfew."

Then she laughed, talking about her son, on his way to becoming the greatest running back in the history of Mount Union's small-college powerhouse.

"He is as close to a perfect kid as you'll find; he even keeps his room really neat," she said. "One of his teammates told me that they never could get Chuck to go out with them."

Or as Mount Union coach Larry Kehres said, "I've never heard Chuck swear. I've never even seen him really angry. He's just what he seems, a good, hard-working kid. He's not a phony; he's genuine."

Come on, there must be something.

"OK, he's a really picky eater," Cathy Moore said.

How picky?

"He won't eat casseroles," she said. "I don't think he's ever eaten a potato in his life. He hates vegetables. His idea of a salad is shredded lettuce, no dressing. He likes steak."

What does he eat at college?

"Taco Bell," she said. "I know he eats there all the time. I have no idea how he stays so strong eating all that Taco Bell."

For Moore, the honors keep piling up.

As a junior, he's already Mount Union's all-time leading scorer. He gained 1,115 yards rushing last year and has 752 yards this season after gaining 152 in yesterday's 42-7 victory over Wilmington. He's set an

NCAA Division III record by scoring a touchdown in 21 consecutive games.

"I've been watching Mount Union football for more than 20 years, and they've never had a back like Chuck Moore," said Joe Tait, the Cavaliers broadcaster who also calls a few Purple Raiders games each fall. "They had a great back named Russ Kring, but Chuck is special. He's fast, but he can gain those tough yards inside. He catches passes. He returns kicks. He's an exceptional person."

And he can't even make Larry Kehres frown.

Kehres is known for his attention to detail to the point of obsession. Mount hasn't won four Division III national titles since 1993 by accident. Yes, the Raiders have terrific players, but they also have a great coach pushing them, demanding excellence.

"Chuck Moore may be the first player who has never been in Coach's doghouse for at least five minutes," said a Mount insider.

Kehres thought about that for a moment.

"I don't think I've ever yelled at Chuck, not even once," he said, sounding amazed as those words were leaving his lips.

Moore is a legend in Mogadore, a small town east of Akron on the Summit/Portage County line. It's a place that loves its high school team, which plays in Division VI, the smallest division.

The Moore legend goes back to the state title game in 1996, when Mogadore was behind by 32 points to St. Henry in the second quarter. Moore had set countless school rushing records, but he was playing on a bad knee.

Later, they would find out it was a shredded knee, a knee that needed reconstructive surgery.

On that cold, chilly afternoon, Moore limped back to the huddle after each carry. But he gained 100 yards. He scored three touchdowns. His team came back to win 61-58 in triple overtime.

It remains one of the greatest high school football games played in Ohio, ever.

"When Chuck goes back to watch Mogadore games, he usually sits on the visitors' side of the field," Cathy Moore said. "A lot of people want to talk to him. He's very friendly, but he also likes to watch the game."

But after that seemingly mythical game came reality.

The knee was a mess. The colleges from the Mid-American Conference ceased recruiting him. He had close to straight A's in school, a high score on the standardized tests. He was the *Beacon Journal* Player of the Year.

He did everything right, everything by the rules.

But the big schools backed away because he was known more for his desire and character than his speed, and the fear was if he lost even a half step, he never could play major college football.

It also counted against him that he was from such a tiny high school, where the competition was supposed to be suspect.

"That was the first time I've ever had to deal with rejection," Moore said. "I remember when Kent and Akron started recruiting me, and I figured more would come."

Instead, the phone barely rang.

One coach who kept calling was Kehres, who said he'd be glad to take Moore at Mount, no matter what the outcome of the knee surgery. But Mount is a Division III program, meaning no athletic scholarships.

"I just didn't know how it would work out," he said. "This wasn't what I figured would happen."

Especially not after the reconstructive knee surgery.

"It's done out-patient," Cathy Moore said. "He had to be helped into and out of bed. He had to be helped to go to the bathroom, to even turn over. Those first few days, it was agony."

Then came therapy.

"After a while, I couldn't even watch it," Cathy Moore said. "He'd be doing those exercises, and his body would shake. I'd start to cry and leave the room."

The reason it's important to know what Moore endured to play college football is that this didn't just happen to one knee, it happened again.

He enrolled at Mount Union, made the team, then blew out the other knee.

"When you see that, you ask yourself if the kid would ever be able to play football," Kehres said. "I thought Chuck is a good baseball player, too. Maybe he'll just forget football and stay with baseball. It will be easier on his knees."

Cathy Moore wondered if her son should even try football, if it was worth it.

"I just had to give it another shot," Moore said. "I heard of a couple of athletes who came back from ACL surgeries on each knee, and I figured if they could do, I'd do it."

So there was another operation, another period where his mother had to almost carry him around the house for a few days. There was more therapy, more tears, more shaking, more pain.

And all to play football at a school where he didn't have a scholarship, where the goal wasn't to make the NFL.

All to play football simply because he loved it.

That's the essence of Division III football, Mount Union football.

Yes, it's about winning. There are four national titles since 1993, the No. 1 ranking in Division III and a 54-game winning streak in the late 1990s that remains the longest in the history of all college football.

But Division III also means that players such as Moore join receiver Adam Marino, quarterback Gary Smeck and defensive back Brook Greenleaf after a game and wash the team's uniforms as part of their job to help pay their tuition.

"I'm just glad to be playing," Moore said. "My knees have held up. I feel like right now, I'm good enough to play at a school such as Akron or Kent. But I wouldn't trade this for anything."

Moore is eligible to graduate in June, but he's decided to take a few more courses so he can play again next fall.

His father (Don), grandfather (Florian Buda) and mother all said they'd support him if he wanted one last season of fall Saturdays at old Mount Union Stadium, which is packed with at least 5,000 fans for every game, standing room only when rivals such as John Carroll or Baldwin-Wallace are in Alliance.

Moore's parents and grandfather come to every game. The team plays each season with the very realistic goal of winning a national title.

"People all over town wear purple Mount Union clothes," Moore said. "This is a lot of fun. That's why I decided to play next year. I'll only have one more shot at this."

Something else Moore can do at Mount is play baseball, where he batted .355 as a center fielder. Most Division I football coaches don't permit their athletes to play other sports.

"I look at this as a real college experience," he said.

It's the kind you seldom see on TV, but that's fine with Chuck Moore.

"To me, playing for a good team, getting a good education and being close to my family, that's what counts the most," he said.

10/15/2000

The game goes on at Norwayne

THE NAMES WERE READ over the public-address system:
  Bruce Camp Bell.
  Jennifer Elliston.
  Christine Elliston.
  Jeff Kaufmann.
  Paul Marshall.
  Cory Pelfrey.
  Six names.
  Six kids between the ages of 13 and 18.
  Six dead in a December 27th car crash in little Canaan Township. Six deaths that rocked Norwayne High. Six names that caused Brad Hilson to shudder.
  "I almost lost it, right there before the game," said the 5-foot-10 senior forward for Norwayne High, talking about the names echoing in his ears.
  Through it all, Cory Pelfrey's brother, Kyle, was in the stands.
  "How can any of us know what that poor kid is going through?" asked Doug Hanzie, the veteran Norwayne basketball coach.
  Norwayne was scheduled to play at Doylestown last night. While none of the six who died in the wreck were basketball players, most of them were friends with at least someone in school.
  "Jeff Kaufmann sat next to me in math," said Norwayne forward Josh Saefkow.
  Now, he's gone.
  "When it comes to this stuff, I admit it, I'm a coward," said Hanzie. "I don't know what I'm supposed to say, so I don't say much of anything. I mostly listen."
  Hanzie is a bull of a man, 38 years old. He's the son of the owner of Hanzie's meats, which was operated for years by his family—almost directly across the street from Norwayne High on Route 3, outside of Creston.
  Hanzie played at Norwayne. Now, he's the school's athletic director and teaches Occupational Work Education, in addition to coaching basketball. In the summer, he cuts the grass around the school.
  His life is Norwayne.
  He's the kind of coach who tapes his players' ankles. He constantly tells them to drink more water. He screams at them when they are out

of position in their zone defense. His school is rural. His kids all wear shirts and ties before the game, and this year, he didn't cut a player.

In his eight years, he's never had a player taller than 6-foot-5. In the past, a few of his athletes might have had a chance to play small-college ball, but they decided to stay, help on the family farm.

"Our kids play for the right reasons, no hidden agenda," he said. "They aren't looking to play for Division I scholarships. They like the game. Their fathers or brothers played at Norwayne, and they want to play."

All so simple.

Small school. Good kids. Love of the game.

Then comes death.

"Most people don't know, but we had a player last spring named John Fleming who died in a drowning accident," said Hanzie. "The whole team went to the viewing. . . ."

Hanzie's voice dropped; the words stopped.

He didn't think they would be burying so many kids again, not so soon.

Hanzie didn't know what to do after the car wreck.

"I called the players together and said they should decide if they wanted to keep practicing and playing," he said. "Then, I left the room. I didn't want to pressure them."

Seniors Nick Slater and Hilson were in charge of the meeting.

"It didn't take long; we wanted to play," said Slater.

Then, he shrugged.

What else is there to do? Life does go on. Tears are shed, but eventually, they must stop, even if a hole in the heart remains forever.

"I thought of something Coach told us," said Saefkow. "He talks about how when you play basketball, nothing else matters for that time on the floor. You can put it all aside, just play the game."

He paused.

"After what happened, we needed to do that," he said.

So last night at Chippewa Gym, Norwayne played.

The cheerleaders did just that, cheering: "WE ARE THE CATS. MIGHTY, MIGHTY CATS. GO BOBCATS!"

"This game will be a real crapshoot; who knows how the kids will react?" Hanzie said, a few moments before tipoff.

You look at the faces, and you see hope. You see anxiety. You see acne. You see teenagers, who usually think they're bullet-proof, who believe they'll live forever.

But not these kids. Not after hearing the names read, the bodies buried, the tears shed.

"We put all that aside," said Saefkow. "We played our best game of the year."

Saefkow was the spark, scoring 11 points, anchoring the bottom of the team's 1-3-1 defense, running back and forth from one end of the court to another, as Norwayne raised its record to 3-4, 3-1 in the Wayne County League.

Slater threw in some key 3-point shots en route to a 13-point night.

Hilson had some nice drives to the basket.

A skinny kid named Steve Watkins floated in a pair of clutch, rainbow 3-pointers when his team needed them the most.

Hanzie bellowed at his players, at the refs, sweat beading up on his forehead. Players took bellyflops on the court after loose balls. Fans moaned when free throws were missed, and they cheered wildly when jumpers were swished.

Final score: Norwayne 52, Doylestown 44.

It seemed like just another night of high school basketball.

Only, it wasn't.

"After what happened, I think this team is closer than it ever was before," said Saefkow. "It's like, we really don't know when will be our last day."

And in this case, you know this high school junior really meant it.

1/6/2001

Varsity jacket

IT WAS A NAVY BLUE LEATHER JACKET. It had a little tiger on the sleeve and the word BENGALS across the chest.

My varsity jacket.

And I almost retched to death to get it.

The year was 1971, and I was a junior at Cleveland Benedictine High School.

Occasionally, I'll mention that I played baseball and basketball in school.

Truth is, I sat basketball. To be exact, I sat freshman and junior-varsity basketball. I was the kid at the end of the bench who prayed that every game would be a blowout, who would watch the scoreboard and say, "Let's see, it's 62-28, wonder if that spread is big enough for me to get in the game."

Usually, it wasn't.

Unfortunately for me, my coaches had seen me try to play in practice and immediately they knew I had a great career ahead of me as a sportswriter—the guy who thinks he knows everything about all sports but can't play any of them.

I looked sort of like I do now, only I was about 5-foot-10, 130 pounds. Sticks for arms. Geeky glasses. Bald.

I also sat baseball. Kept the scorebook most games.

More great training for a sportswriter.

Anyway, I wanted a varsity jacket from Benedictine. My father had one. My brother had one. About all my friends had one. I had a jump shot that dented the front of the rim, a bat with a hole in it and a body that made the other guys on the team keep asking me for a towel and a bottle of water.

In the fall of my junior year, a basketball coach suggested that I run cross country to get in shape.

I wondered, "In shape for what? To hold up the end of the bench? To pick up the sweaty towels?"

I told my friend about the cross country idea, and he said, "You'll hate it."

Reassuring words.

Then he said: "Father Dominic is the coach. Great guy."

I knew Father Dominic. He was and still is the ultimate priest/teacher. He loved kids. He was assistant principal, taught a couple of history classes, helped coach two sports.

My friend said: "Father Dominic doesn't cut anybody. If you stick with it, you'll get a letter."

A varsity letter.

A varsity jacket.

A little running was all it took? Sign me up.

First practice, we ran two miles.

And stopped for 15 minutes.

And ran two more miles.

And stopped for 20 minutes.

And ran two more miles.

I stopped running long before the third set. Probably between Miles 2 and 3. My lungs burned. My legs ached. My glasses kept steaming up, and I couldn't see where I was going. Even my shoulders were sore, because I didn't even know there was a certain way to move your arms as you run.

And I threw up everything that I ever thought of eating.

Father Dominic, the saint that he is, kept encouraging me. He said I had a "good stride." He said I could help the team. He said I should keep at it.

Lord love Father Dominic, but he lied.

My stride stunk, and any team that needed my help really required a miracle on the level of the loaves and fishes.

But I stayed with it, thinking about that jacket.

When I couldn't run, I walked. When my lungs were on fire, my guts gurgling and my feet turning to blisters, I sort of dragged myself over the course, visions of the BENGALS jacket dancing in my brain.

Father Dominic kept telling me that I was improving. The saintly man was delusional.

But I also discovered something else: I wasn't the only one who hated cross country. Lots of kids did, and they quit.

The one sport in my life that I wished I could sit instead of play was the one where everyone ran.

Just my luck.

But I survived the season. I got the jacket and wore it every day, even when it was 90 degrees.

I didn't care. I earned it.

Boy, did I ever earn it.

And when Father Dominic asked me to run cross country again as a senior, I said I'd pass. I had my jacket and my life's calling. I'd figured out that it was a lot easier to just sit sports rather than play them.

5/12/2002

It's Personal

Eyes on the game, but mind on dad

THERE ARE SOME THINGS we all wish we could do over.

This summer, my father spent six weeks visiting his sister in Broadview Heights. We saw a lot of each other, going bowling, to Browns practices and to dinner.

"I'd like to go to a ballgame," he said, knowing this was the last year that the Indians would play at the Stadium.

I said it was a good idea, but it never happened. It amounted to this—I could have fitted it into my schedule, but I didn't.

There were other things I thought were more important.

In early September, my father returned to his home in Florida and I went on with my life.

And I never gave it another thought—until Sunday.

That's because it was three weeks ago that my father had a stroke.

The man who first took me to a baseball game . . . the man who loved the Indians as if they were part of his family . . . the man who had the most to do with me being a sportswriter. . . .

Today, that man can only say a few words.

Today, the man who once spent a summer as a minor-league first baseman can't move his right arm, his right leg, or anything on his right side.

Today, that man is in a rehabilitation center showing more courage and dignity than anyone showed at the Stadium this weekend.

While the Indians finished the 1993 season, I hardly paid attention to Sunday's game. Instead, I thought of my father and wished he were there.

He deserved at least that much.

Tom Pluto is 73 years old, and he will be very embarrassed by this story. He is a man who never liked the light of attention to shine on himself, but reveled when his son was noticed by the public.

Tom Pluto was like a lot of men who came out of the Depression. His parents barely spoke English. He was the first in his family to graduate from high school.

He went into the Army in World War II, he went to work, raised his family, played with his kids, went to church and did what he thought was right.

To him, that was doing what was expected. In today's world of dysfunctional families, what he did would make him an exception.

Tom Pluto also loved baseball, and we probably went to 25 games a year during the 1960s—when it wasn't easy being an Indians fan.

We'd sit in the general admission seats for the first few innings, then sneak down into the boxes.

My dad's plan was to stop at the concession stand, load up with popcorn and Cokes, grab my hand and lead me right down to a pair of vacant seats behind the plate.

"Just follow me and look like you know what you're doing," he'd say. "It will look like we've been sitting here all night."

By the fourth inning, the bored ushers never cared. Besides, at the Stadium there were always empty box seats all over the place.

His strategy invariably worked, and we'd find ourselves 10 to 15 rows from the field.

From there, my father would tell me about how the game often was dictated by the count on the hitter—what a pitcher should throw and when . . . and what a hitter should be doing in a certain situation.

He was the best kind of fan—not a know-it-all, not a manager-basher, just a guy who was locked into the game.

Until today, I never told him that those lessons are ones I never forgot. That those lessons served me well when I covered Major League Baseball for six years.

My father knew the difference between good baseball and bad. He was raised watching Bob Feller. He saw a World Series game in 1948. He was heartbroken when Herb Score was injured, when Rocky Colavito was traded and when Tony Horton (one of his favorites) had a mental breakdown.

He watched the Indians self-destruct, and he wasn't conned when they told him that Eddie Leon and Jack Heidemann were supposed be another Lou Boudreau and Ray Mack.

But he kept coming to the games. He knew that baseball was bigger than the Indians.

"Just because they don't have a good team, they can still have some good players," he said.

Perhaps because my father did spend a year in the minors and because he played with big leaguers in the Army, he knew just how hard it was to be a major-leaguer.

Instead of his failure as a baseball player turning him bitter, it caused him to respect those who did make it.

How many of us could have done the same?

While my father works to regain his speech and his mobility, his mind is stronger than ever. He knows exactly what happened to him and what lies ahead. I was always proud that he was my father, but never more proud than I am watching him endure his stroke.

But that is something we don't talk much about. When we did, it brought tears to his eyes, and it felt like there was a fist around my throat.

The Indians are one of the things that have carried us through these frightening times.

Because he is limited to answering most questions with a yes or a no, I often fall into long monologues when I'm at his bedside.

I'll tell him about the team, about how Albert Belle may be the next Rocky Colavito, about how Kenny Lofton is the most exciting Indian I've ever seen and how they've just got to do something about the pitching.

This week, I'll tell him about the huge crowds at the Stadium, about how my friend Frank Sarmir flew in from San Francisco just to be here. I'll talk about how people came from all over the country just to be here one last time. Then I'll tell him about the new stadium, about how it really has a chance to be this team's field of dreams.

Finally, I'll tell him that when Gateway is open next summer, God willing, we will both be there.

That is a promise.

This time, I'll buy the tickets— box seats, right behind the plate

10/4/1993

The Stadium was our special place

A FEW WEEKS AGO, I told my father about Cleveland Stadium coming down.

He stared at me.

"They are going to build a new one," I said. "For the Browns."

He looked at me again.

"But . . . but . . . but," he said.

"I know, Art Modell moved the Browns to Baltimore," I said. "But there are going to be new Browns and a new stadium."

"But . . . but . . . Oh, man."

"It gets a little complicated," I said.

My father lets out a huge sigh.

My father had a stroke a little more than three years ago. He cannot move his right hand. The movement in his right leg is limited. But worst of all, his speech is limited to a few words.

His favorite is "Man."

When he disagrees, he'll utter "but . . . but . . . but" until he sounds like a machine gun . . . but no words follow.

My father is 77. He remembers going to baseball games at old League Park. He remembers when Cleveland Stadium opened in 1932. It was to be a sports palace. Now it will be a man-made reef.

Or at least parts of it are to be thrown into Lake Erie to create a reef for perch and walleye.

Even though my father was once an avid fisherman, I didn't try to explain this part to him. At this stage, why tell him that yet another part of his life is going to be reduced to rubble and tossed in the lake?

I can't help it. When I think of the Stadium, I think of my father. Then I think about what the stroke has done to him.

Not only can't he talk, but he can no longer read.

Worst of all, the stroke means he no longer feels like the big man who took me by the hand down to the old Stadium. And looking at him, I know things will never quite be the same for me, either.

I am now on the other side of 40.

My father is on the other side of his life.

My mother died of a heart attack in 1984.

My father has not had much luck lately. The last three years of his life have been lots of frustration and even more therapy.

When I sense that melancholy coming on, I tell him how proud he makes me, how he has fought the stroke with guts and dignity. I tell him how I can't imagine anyone handling it better than he has—and I mean it.

He grabs my hand and cries. That is something else about stroke victims. They cry. They cry when they are happy. They cry when something hurts. They cry because they can't really tell you what they think.

When he is in one of those moods, I sometimes remind him how the Stadium was a special place for us.

It was a place to see the Indians. That the Indians were a bunch of guys named Joe Azcue, Ted Abernathy and Larry Brown who lived in the American League basement didn't matter.

It still was a place we could see them in living color.

Today that is not a big deal. Today games are on TV all the time. If you subscribe to SportsChannel, you could watch the Indians nearly every night.

My generation grew up in a three-channel, black and white world. You were lucky if there were 20 games a year on TV, and you had to adjust the rabbit ears that served as the aerials.

To my father, even a snowy, black-and-white picture was a miracle. He grew up without TV. He grew up without a car. He grew up buying fruit and vegetables from a guy sitting on top of a wagon—a wagon pulled by a horse.

He grew up in a Cleveland where neighborhoods were defined by the ethnic group that lived there—and the churches they attended.

"I live by St. Benedict's," people would say, and you knew exactly where that was.

When my father was younger, he liked to tell me about those days.

I really didn't care to listen.

Now that I want to know more about that part of his life—he can't talk.

So I talk to him.

I tell him about us going to the Stadium, how the grass was so green, the Stadium so big.

Later, I'd realized the grass was the greenest I'd seen partly because I was used to seeing it on black-and-white TV—and partly because team president Gabe Paul would order the grounds crew to paint it green.

The Stadium was enormous, and usually empty.

"That's OK," he'd say. "More places for us to sit."

We'd watch a couple of innings from left field, a couple from behind the plate—then we'd head to the upper deck.

It was like the Stadium was our house and we could sit anywhere. My father often picked games in the middle of the week against lousy teams because he knew no one would be there—and we could buy tickets for less than face value from a scalper and wander about.

That is what I remember the most. Not the players. Certainly not the games themselves.

I remember my small hand in his enormous hand. I remember huge buckets of sometimes stale stadium popcorn. I remember the good hot dogs and the flat, fizzed-out Coke.

Most of all, I remember when my father was tall and strong.

12/1/1996

A good man is gone; we are lessened

WHEN PEOPLE such as my father die, you never read about it on the front page.

They never made a million dollars.

They never broke a contract or demanded to be traded.

They never embarrassed themselves or their families.

They never did anything that ends up in headlines.

That's the shame of it.

Being a good father is taken for granted. Being a loyal husband is shrugged off. Working at the same miserable job for too many years to support a family is considered rather antiquated.

People such as my father grew up during the Depression. They served their country in World War II. They sent their kids to college. They saved and bought houses and cars—and hated credit cards.

They believed in God and country.

They didn't rock the boat.

They made this country work.

For that, most of them have been ridiculed or even worse—ignored.

They lived, they raised families, they died. A couple of paragraphs on the obituary page serves as the final words.

Those words don't tell you that people like Tom Pluto are why so many of us are teachers, coaches, lawyers, doctors and writers. They don't show how these people paid a big part of the bill for us, how they demanded that our lives be better than theirs.

They just seem to die as they lived—quietly and with little fuss.

This story is about my father, who died of heart failure yesterday morning.

But it's about so many from his generation, those who never forgot "that anyone can end up in the poorhouse."

I heard a lot about the Depression and the poorhouse from my father.

I heard a lot about FDR and World War II and gas rations.

I heard a lot about a hard life I'll never know.

Then I saw what it meant to my father.

In September of 1993, he suffered a major stroke.

Couldn't move his right hand.

Couldn't walk.

Couldn't really talk.

Had to wear diapers.

This proud man, once a strapping minor-league first baseman, in diapers.

This was the man who took me to ballgames, my little hand disappearing in his huge paw as we walked down the West Third Street Bridge to watch yet another awful Indians team play.

This was the man who worked six days a week in a grocery warehouse, a man who put in at least 10 hours a day—yet had time for a game of catch with his son.

I'll always remember those games, his potbelly hanging low, a cigarette dangling from his mouth as we tossed the ball back and forth in the driveway.

I'll always remember him taking me to ballgames when he'd rather just take a nap. I'll always remember him telling me to get a job I enjoyed, so I wouldn't have to endure the same grind that he faced day after day—and decade after decade.

I also remember my father in his final years.

I'll remember how he struggled to take just a few steps with his walker. I'll remember how proud he was to be able to take off his own shirt.

I'll remember how he was a little like Rain Man.

He had to brush his dentures, comb his hair and use his electric razor in the same way—every day.

I'll remember how he loved to play the same card game he called Greek Rummy—and play it hour after hour.

I'll remember his final happy moments.

They came during October, when the Indians made their glorious run through the American League playoffs and came within a couple of pitches of winning the World Series.

I'll remember knowing he was sitting in his favorite reclining chair, feet up and eating popcorn while watching those games—the same games I was writing about from the press box.

I'll always be grateful that baseball could make him happy when he had little else to smile about, as the final year of my father's life was trip after trip to the hospital, gasp after gasp for breath.

I'll remember how he wanted to die at home, how he clutched my left hand, looked at me with wide, frightened blue eyes. I'll remember the bleeding ulcers, the blood clots that turned his leg black and the suffering that seemed like it would never end.

I'll remember how he died at home, in his sleep—quietly.

It happened on his 78th birthday.

I'll remember him as a wonderful man, just like so many others—men we never appreciate until they are gone.

2/12/1998

If only he could see it

I SIT IN YANKEE STADIUM, waiting for the Indians to face New York in the American League Championship Series, and I think about how my father never saw a game here.

Last week, it was Boston's Fenway Park, where the Tribe beat the Red Sox in the Division Series.

He never made it there, either.

My father died February 11 following a five-year battle with strokes and heart disease. The final six months of his life were six different trips to the hospital for six different health problems.

When he passed away, he was relieved. And so was I.

I have missed my father, but the ordeal of his final years never made me wish that he still were alive.

But today, I do.

Today, I know he'd have awakened with one thing in mind—the Indians play the Yankees tonight. He'd build his day around waiting for the game, watching ESPN and other all-sports stations for their reports from Yankee Stadium.

He was like a lot of shut-ins and elderly people who can't get out to the ballpark—even if they somehow found a way to buy a ticket.

These games make breakfast taste better. They make the sun shine brighter, the chair feel softer and the people who take care of them seem a little nicer.

For people such as my father, these games made life better. He was never happier than watching the Indians in the playoffs.

Yes, even after the stroke, even with a paralyzed right side that had sentenced him to a wheelchair. And yes, even with the loss of his speech that had reduced his communication to a single word—man.

Over and over and over he said that one word: Man, MAN, MAN!!!

His voice still echoes in my head. His bright blue eyes that tried to say what his mouth could not remain branded in my brain. His youthful zest come playoff time inspired me, made me remember how lucky I was to have the job I do today.

My father was like most men of his generation. The biggest trips they took were courtesy of the U.S. military during World War II.

As far as I know, my father never was in New York City, Boston, Seattle, Los Angeles or so many of the other places my job has taken me.

Heck, my father was the kind of guy who hated to make long-distance calls because of the cost—and was uncomfortable when I called him and talked for more than 10 minutes.

He worried what the call was costing me. In many ways, he never got over having grown up during the Depression.

For years, my father was dumbfounded that he'd turn on the TV and see the Indians playing in a place such as Boston or New York—and his son would be there in the press box.

"You're paid to go to ballgames," he'd say, shaking his head.

That was true, although I reminded him that I was actually paid to write about games.

But the point was clear.

My father was like most men of his generation. He was paid to work. He was paid to get his hands calloused and his back sore. He was paid to do a job he hated, but it was a job that needed to be done to support his family.

So he did the job and tried not to complain too much.

Then he came home, and turned on the Indians game.

Right now, I miss my father as much as any time since his death.

When I sit down to write stories, I think of men and women such as him reading them. I think about what they'd want to know. I try to talk to them as if they were sitting right next to me in the press box.

I know my father loved to see my stories, even after the stroke robbed him of his ability to read. During the playoffs, I'd mail the sports section to his Florida home.

He'd spend a long time staring at the big pictures of the players. He'd show my picture to anyone who happened to visit. I was told that sometimes, he'd just sit there and stare at one of my stories.

He could no longer read it, but just knowing I had written all those words made him smile.

I wish my father could have watched Charles Nagy pitch the game of his life last Friday at Fenway Park. I wish he could have seen David Justice's double rattle around the nooks and crannies of center field in Game 4 at Fenway.

I know he would have loved Manager Mike Hargrove going nose-to-nose with umpire Joe Brinkman. Watching the Indians come back to win Game 2 against the Red Sox would have made him absolutely joyful the next day.

Right now, I can see my father in his favorite chair. He's a symphony in Wahoo red—wearing his Tribe cap, Tribe jacket, Tribe sweat pants and waiting for the Indians to face the Yankees. There is a bowl of popcorn and a Diet Coke at the table next to him.

For my father and so many like him, this was his favorite time of year.

10/7/1998

Cheers for moms everywhere

IT WAS 15 YEARS AGO that my mother died.

I don't think about her as much as I should. I'm like most children; I just expected my mother to be . . . well, a mother.

You know how it works. Your clothes are dirty. You drop them in a basket. A few days later, they show up clean in your closet.

It's magic.

No, it was mom. Or now, it's my wife, Roberta.

It's people who do things men take for granted. We sit down, food appears in front of us. We get sick, they shove pills down our throats and make sure we wash it down with chicken soup and hot tea.

We moan and groan; they really do feel our pain.

Mothers drive us to practices. They fume when the coaches don't put us in the games. They try to say something nice when we played terrible—and all we do is glare at them.

But we all love our mothers, living or dead.

You can talk to the toughest convict in any prison, a guy who might like to put his iron fists around his father's throat and squeeze the life out of the guy. But this hard man with a steel heart will get tears in his eyes just saying the name of his mother.

We might not even know why, but something inside us screams that mothers are important, that they are the true saints. We don't know most of what they do for us, but we just know that no matter what— they love us.

That was so true of my mother, Mary Pluto.

Like many males, I felt I had to prove myself to my father. I had to accomplish things. I had to make him proud.

It's not a knock on fathers. It's just the way most fathers and sons are wired. Yes, we know that our fathers love us, but we also know they expect us to produce. It's the bottom-line, male-thing.

Mom loved us when we were little, our faces smeared with chocolate and our brand-new pants torn at the knees.

Mom loved us when we were teenagers and we dented the car. Meanwhile, we'd rather eat broken glass than admit the banged-up fender to our fathers.

Mom loved us when we went 0-for-3 with three strikeouts and left eight runners on base. I really did that in a high school baseball game. Didn't even hit a lame foul ball. When my dad innocently asked me how I played that day, I just broke into tears. My mother just hugged me, not waiting for an answer.

Mothers buy us baseball cards, even though they don't know the names of any of the players, or at least, that was true of my mother.

Mothers really are interested in what happened at school, what our friends are like, what we are feeling. That just comes natural to them, while fathers have to work at it.

Mothers worried when we came home too early from a date, "Something go wrong?" Or when we were late, "What was wrong, I was ready to start calling all the hospitals?"

Mothers are like no one else in our lives.

Both of my parents are now gone.

My father went through nearly five years of agony from his stroke. But it also changed both of our lives. His illness brought us closer to each other, and to God.

My mother didn't just die quickly, it was like she vanished. Kidnapped by aliens. One day, she was just gone.

It was 1984, and I was working in Savannah, Georgia. My father called to say that my mother had a heart attack. I left work and drove straight through the night and early morning hours, 750 miles back to Cleveland.

I saw my mother in the hospital.

She was fine. Talking. Her green eyes sparkling, insisting there was nothing to worry about.

I stayed three days. She seemed to be growing stronger, apparently out of danger. I drove those 750 miles back to Savannah, and I wasn't there for an hour when the phone rang.

My dad was in tears. Before he even spoke, I knew my mother was dead.

In a lot of ways, I never felt I had a chance to tell her goodbye, to tell her what she meant to me. At least, not until now.

5/14/2000

Let Dad know while you can

I REMEMBER VERY LITTLE of what my father ever said to me. OK, I do remember him calling me "Half-a-job Terry," which is something I'd like to forget.

And I remember threats that if we kept spending too much money, "We'll end up in the poorhouse." I remember some of his stories of playing baseball in the Army, his stories of bread lines during the Depression.

But I don't think I ever really got to know the man until he could no longer talk, until a stroke had robbed him of all words except one— *Man.*

That's because I knew that I had to be as much a father to him as he once was to me. And I knew that he needed me, that he respected me, that it made him happy just to see me walk in the room.

With that one word said over and over, with hugs with his one good arm, with his tears—he told me all that and more.

I just wish it hadn't taken 37 years of my life and his massive stroke to bring us to the point where we knew we had to express certain things to each other, before it was too late.

My father died two years ago. He took very little unfinished business to the grave. As awful as those nearly five years of his stroke were for us, it did give us a chance to really deal with each other.

That's my wish for each of you: Take today to try to talk to the old man.

Forget all the garbage, tell him from the heart about the good things.

The ballgames where he took you by the hand to the old Stadium to watch the Indians lose—as always. The days when he played catch with you in the back yard. The times he went to your recital, when he took his off day to drive you to practices and games.

Let him know that you appreciate the fact that he was there.

He might just look like you're from Mars and then grunt when you say these things.

That's all, just a grunt.

Or maybe a nod of the head. Don't expect him to say much.

Remember that fathers sometimes are that way. They have no clue how to deal with sincere gratitude. Just ask your mother, who has spent much of her life trying to talk to this guy.

But understand this: He loves to hear it.

Fathers long to know they matter, that what they did with their children counted for something. That they were noticed in a world where much of the culture tries to render them irrelevant, the butt of easy, lame-brained jokes.

I thought of this when I read Bob Greene's new remarkable book, *Duty*, which should be read by anyone who has a father/grandfather from the World War II generation.

Greene's father came of age in Akron. He was a salesman in Columbus when Greene grew up and later became a star columnist with the *Chicago Tribune*. The son spent much of his life trying to impress his father, to understand his father. But he never was able to really get to know the man, even in the final months of his father's long illness.

In frustration, Greene ended up talking to Paul Tibbets, who flew the Enola Gay, the plane that dropped the atomic bomb on Japan. My father and other World War II veterans would tell you The Bomb ended World War II, that Tibbets and his crew were heroes.

Tibbets lived near Greene's father. He was about the same age, had the same experiences. From Tibbets, an idea of what his father's life was like began to emerge. From Tibbets, Greene came to know his own father.

But it's a shame it came to that.

It's a shame it took my father's stroke to scale the walls that children and fathers often build around each other. It's a shame Greene never could quite make it over those walls, and that his father is no longer around for him to make one last attempt.

It's a shame that those of us who had fathers—yes, sometimes sullen, sometimes demanding fathers—can't talk to these men.

That's why today, when so many kids are growing up without fathers, those of us who have one should let them know how much they've meant to us.

6/18/2000

If no one else says it: Thank you

THIS IS JUST TO SAY THANKS.

Thank you for buying the paper.

Thank you for caring about the Indians, Browns and Cavs.

Thank you, because I don't have to get a real job.

As my father once said, "Let me get this straight, you get paid to go to ballgames?"

Yes.

Actually, I'm paid to write about the games and players.

And, thankfully, you pay to read it.

That can't always be easy.

What do you really think when Manny Ramirez turns down $119 million?

Or when you find out that the Indians could have signed him for considerably less in the spring of 1999, only Dick Jacobs didn't want to commit to any long-term deals because he had the team for sale and saw no reason to stick the next owner with a bill?

How do you still love the game when so much of it is business? How do you stick with teams when the players keep changing? When ticket prices keep rising?

Those in pro sports never will fully appreciate you.

Yes, they want to service the fans. And yes, they want to keep their stadiums clean and field a winning team.

But most have long forgotten what it's like to tell their kids: "Sorry, we'll just have to hope the game is on TV. We can't afford to go this week."

The NBA is a $50 a ticket, the Cavs are at $40. The Browns are in the same high-rent ticket ballpark, and the Indians no longer are the bargain they used to be.

Those in pro sports have no idea what it's like to explain to a child that their favorite player left town because millions upon millions wasn't enough, that there were even more millions to be had elsewhere.

What are you going to do with those Manny jerseys? Probably the same you did with the Carlos Baerga shirts. And the Albert Belle shirts. And the Earnest Byner shirts.

How do you make any sense out of the Browns moving to Baltimore?

Even more important, how do you tell children to study to be a teacher, a policeman, a nurse or a small business owner when a left-handed reliever who can't throw a strike in the clutch earns $1 million more than any of those professions?

Most athletes are amazed at the anger of fans. They see no connection between what they earn and ticket prices, or the expectations of the customers.

They are dumbfounded by what they consider to be your sense of entitlement, be it of a winning team or an excellent performance. Yet, they believe they are just as entitled to be paid like rock and movie stars, even though most of them don't sell a single ticket.

This is not to bash sports as much as it is to praise you.

For your loyalty.

Players and owners talk about loyalty, but players and owners come and go.

You stay.

You're the ones with a sense of history. You're the ones who really love your favorite team, even if that team is the Cavs, who have been around for 31 seasons and have yet to play in the NBA Finals.

Or the Browns, who were stolen from you and replaced with a gang of castoffs from an NFL rummage sale. Al Lerner, Chris Palmer & Co.

might build a winner, but you've already learned the hard lessons of expansion.

Or even the Indians, who have been the most successful team of late, yet continually have turned over their roster.

Assuming Sandy Alomar and Ramirez are, indeed, gone, the only players left from the 1995 World Series team are Jim Thome, Charles Nagy, Omar Vizquel and Kenny Lofton. Of course, Lofton missed the 1997 World Series because he was in Atlanta, spending a year with the Braves before returning to the Indians.

Sometimes, you must feel as if you're doing nothing but cheering for a uniform, because the faces change so fast.

Yet, you remain steadfast.

At the games.

In front of your TV sets.

And reading the paper.

For that, I say—thanks.

11/23/2000

Acknowledgments

Thanks to David Gray, who came up with the concept of this book and nursed it along as if it were his own. And to Phil Masturzo, for the great pictures. And to Faith Hamlin, who will always be more than just a great agent. Finally, to all the people at the *Akron Beacon Journal* who have helped over the years, especially Jan Leach, Larry Pantages, John Murphy, Tom Giffen, Ken Krause and Sheldon Ocker.

Index